"Mozambique has demonstrated both political maturity and economic progress over the past decade and a half. This is remarkable considering the bloody insurgency that dominated its history during much of the '70s and '80s. This war was responsible for the deaths of over a million of its citizens, displaced many more, and destroyed much of the infrastructure of the country. War weariness and good leadership have served the country well thus far in the 21st century. Dr Emerson has done a thoroughly remarkable job in researching and writing this book on the events of Mozambique's insurgency. Students of Africa and of military history will learn much about the causes, conduct, and completion of this conflict. Some lessons are unique to Mozambique, but some are applicable across the continent for other countries attempting to reconcile and restore governance to its people."

GENERAL CARLTON FULFORD, USMC (RET.)

Former Deputy Commander U.S. European Command, former Director of the African Center for Strategic Studies, and Desert Storm veteran

"Steve Emerson has written the most comprehensive account of the civil war in Mozambique that has yet been attempted. In particular, he has made extensive use of interviews with participants in trying to uncover the details of what happened in this savage and often secret conflict. The Mozambican civil war remains highly controversial with very differing interpretations which find its causes either in popular grievances against the Frelimo socialist reforms or in foreign intervention pure and simple. It is now widely accepted that the war changed character as it continued and that it has to be understood in the wider context of the closing phases of the Cold War and of the white supremacist regimes in Africa. However, it was also a very 'African' conflict, culturally rooted in the history of Mozambique and linked in many aspects to civil conflicts elsewhere in Africa in the 1980s and 1990s. Steve Emerson's account is largely a military history but as such is invaluable for any understanding of the post-colonial history of southern Africa."

DR MALYN NEWITT

Emeritus Professor of History at King's College London

Published in 2014 by:

Helion & Company Limited
26 Willow Road Solihull
West Midlands B91 1UE England
Tel. 0121 705 3393 Fax 0121 711 4075
email: info@helion.co.uk
website: www.helion.co.uk

and

30° South Publishers (Pty) Ltd.
16 Ivy Road
Pinetown 3610
South Africa
email: info@30degreessouth.co.za
website: www.30degreessouth.co.za

Designed & typeset by SA Publishing Services (kerrincocks@gmail.com)
Cover design by Kerrin Cocks
Printed in the UK by Henry Ling Ltd., Dorchester, Dorset
Printed in South Africa by Pinetown Printers (Pty) Ltd, KwaZulu-Natal

ISBN (UK) 978-1-909384-92-7
ISBN (RSA) 978-1-920143-91-6

British Library Cataloguing-in-Publication Data
A catalogue record for this book is available from the British Library

THE BATTLE FOR MOZAMBIQUE

The Frelimo–Renamo Struggle, 1977–1992

Stephen A. Emerson

Helion & Company Ltd

30° South Publishers

Stephen Emerson has spent more than 30 years of his life studying, researching and working on African political and security issues for the U.S. government and as an academic. He cut his teeth as a southern African regional specialist for the U.S. Department of Defense in the early 1980s, where he provided political and military analysis to senior American policymakers in Washington. Dr Emerson is the author of numerous classified and unclassified publications on African politics, terrorism, counter-insurgency, transnational security challenges, and the future of American security and foreign policy engagement in Africa. He has held numerous government and academic positions, including Security Studies Chair at National Defense University's Africa Center for Strategic Studies in Washington and more recently headed the Africa regional studies program at the U.S. Naval War College in Newport, Rhode Island. Among his degrees is a doctorate in International Relations/Comparative Politics from the University of Florida. He is married to a U.S. Foreign Service Officer and has accompanied her on multiple tours of duty with the Department of State in Africa and Latin America. They currently reside in Orlando, Florida, USA where Emerson continues to write, consult and lecture on African political and security issues.

CONTENTS

Acknowledgements		6
Preface		8
List of Illustrations		10
List of Maps		14
Glossary		16
Chapter 1:	Prelude to War	18
Chapter 2:	Birth of an Insurgency	25
Chapter 3:	Battleground Central Mozambique	41
Chapter 4:	Punch and Counterpunch	67
Chapter 5:	The South African Factor	96
Chapter 6:	Zimbabwe to the Rescue	125
Chapter 7:	The Slugfest Continues	153
Chapter 8:	The Hardest Battle of All	183
Notes		206
Selected Bibliography		231
Index		235

ACKNOWLEDGEMENTS

This story could not have been written without the extensive assistance and direct involvement of hundreds of individuals scattered across five continents. I am grateful to them all in helping make this an accurate as possible account of the war. I trust I have got it right, but where I have come up short I accept full responsibility and hopefully others will build on this book's foundation to expand and improve our understanding of the war.

In particular I would like to thank:

The dozens of former Frelimo and Renamo soldiers who shared their wartime experiences and their personal struggles with me. The Mozambican veterans' association and José Fuele for facilitating these meetings over the years. Former Frelimo and Renamo political officials, especially José Luis Cabaço and Raul Domingos who were willing to engage in candid discussions of the war.

Colonel Ricardo Timbe (FADM), Colonel Manuel Mazuze (FADM), and my former student, then Major John Roddy (USA), for making my research trips to Mozambique over the years successful and for all their assistance in facilitating contacts with veterans' groups.

João Cabrita for sharing his time, contacts, and research materials and in assisting me with my research while in Mozambique.

Thanks to Eddy Norris and the Old Rhodesian Air Force Sods, especially Prop Geldenhuys for his formidable knowledge of Rhodesian air operations and to John Reid-Rowland for sharing his photos. To the late John Fairey for his invaluable assistance in gaining access to, and help with deciphering, documents from the Rhodesian Army Association archives at the British Empire and Commonwealth Museum. Thanks to Dudley Cowderoy and Roy Nesbit, two exceptional Battle of Britain fighter pilot veterans, for their words of wisdom and friendship.

Danny Hartman, Des Robertson, and John Riddick for sharing their experiences and photographs from the early days of Renamo. Captain David Scott-Donelan and to the other former Rhodesian SAS personnel, as well as ex-SADF and SAAF members who asked to remain anonymous.

Colonel (retired) Lionel Dyck and the other former Zimbabwe National

Army (ZNA) officers for submitting with patience to my seemingly endless barrage of questions about Zimbabwe military operations in Mozambique.

Professor Mayln Newitt for his encouragement and friendship. Professor André Thomashausen for his hospitality and frank discussions and to Bill Minter for his willingness to share his raw research materials with me. Thanks also to Alex Vines, Paul Moorcraft, and Joe Hanlon in London. Professor Hussein Solomon for his hospitality during my visits to Pretoria.

Marlene Burger for her help with the Roland Hunter court documents and sharing her research.

My good friend, Guy Friedmann, and his staff at Bookdealers of Rosebank in Johannesburg for their assistance in finding scarce out-of-print books and Guy's hospitality, as well as his encouragement over the years to "just write the damn book."

The staff of the Hotel Rovuma for their hospitality during my visits to Maputo.

Chris Cocks and the staff at 30 Degrees South for all they have done to make this book's publication a reality.

PREFACE

The war that raged in Mozambique from 1977 to 1992 is one of the most overlooked and misunderstood of the conflicts engulfing the continent during the height of the Cold War. It was also the final act of the African independence struggle. For sixteen years government and rebel forces battered each other in what would become an increasingly violent and brutal confrontation for supremacy. The resulting path of devastation would leave an estimated one million dead, millions more displaced or made refugees, and a country in ruins. But out of the ashes of this bitter conflict arose a new and prosperous Mozambique in the two decades since the final shots of the war; a country born from the sacrifice and blood of those who fought for a better future.

So why write a book about a seemingly minor sideshow to larger, better-known conflicts in Angola, Ethiopia or South Africa? As a political-military analyst writing about the Mozambican war for senior American policymakers in Washington back in the mid-1980s, I thought I had a very clear and accurate understanding of events, personalities, and the ebb and flow of the fighting. I was mistaken. And the more I delved into the existing literature while living in southern Africa in the mid-1990s, the more I discovered that I was not alone. Many others—including some notable academics, regional scholars and journalists—had got it wrong too. Some had become caught up in embracing a cause and their writing was deliberately skewed to make 'their side' look better. Others, in a desperate search for any seemingly reliable information on an under-reported conflict, found themselves caught up in apartheid South Africa's sophisticated campaign of disinformation and unwittingly repeated stories hook, line and sinker. Thus, many of the so-called facts surrounding the war and the people in it are more myth than reality. Moreover, to this day controversy continues to surround many pivotal events and the real story has yet to be revealed.

This critique is not intended to downplay the hard work and cutting edge scholarship on the war or the insurgency that was undertaken in the past. Many of these groundbreaking accounts contain highly usefully and relevant information and, accordingly, are cited extensively within this work where appropriate. Nonetheless, many popular accounts of the war are fraught with major inaccuracies. Over time, unfortunately, these flawed works have come to be widely accepted as a true reflection of the historical record without critical examination by those seeking to better understand the conflict. The pages of this book hopefully provide a desperately needed reality check.

This book attempts to set the record straight and provide an accurate—as best one can—military history of the war. It builds on the work of others but is supplemented by dozens of face-to-face interviews with war veterans, extensive email correspondence, field notes, and government and rebel documents gathered over the past fifteen years. It is a story of soldiers and of military campaigns. A story of hardship and suffering, of triumph and tragedy, and of all those forever changed by the experience of war. Some of those involved were professional soldiers doing their best, often in very difficult circumstances, at the behest of their political leaders and for causes they believed in. Others were young (many not more than children) Mozambican men and women caught up in a conflict they neither understood nor wanted to be part of, but were forced to make the best of their situation simply to survive. As one former guerrilla fighter remarked when I complimented her on the very detailed accounting of her abduction some 25 years previously, "I remember it well, because it changed my life forever."

LIST OF ILLUSTRATIONS

Rhodesian Period

André Matsangaissa, Renamo's first military commander; killed in action in October 1979. *Photo courtesy of André Thomashausen*

A young Afonso Dhlakama, then Renamo's deputy commander, talking with CIO officer Danny Hartman in 1979 at Odzi. *Photo courtesy of Danny Hartman*

Orlando Cristina (center) would rise to become secretary-general and head Renamo's political wing from November 1980 until his assassination in April 1983. *Photo courtesy André Thomashausen*

Regarded as a brave and charismatic leader, 'Commander André' instilled great loyalty among Renamo cadres by personally leading troops in combat. *Photo courtesy of Danny Hartman*

Thanks to Rhodesian largess, the ranks of the Renamo guerrillas swelled from a few dozen men in 1977 to nearly 3,000 well-trained men by early 1980. *Photo courtesy of Danny Hartman*

Following Mozambican independence in June 1975, Frelimo sought to transform its guerrilla forces into a conventional army with Soviet and Eastern Bloc assistance to counter the Rhodesian and South African military threat. *Photo courtesy of Centro de Formação Fotográfica, Maputo, Mozambique*

An abandoned tobacco farm at Odzi served as Renamo's rear base and the CIO's training and support facility until Zimbabwean independence. *Photo courtesy of Danny Hartman*

Samora Machel, guerrilla fighter, leader of Frelimo and future president of Mozambique in the early 1970s. *Photo Times Media*

Machel's granting of safe haven to ZANLA guerrillas following Mozambican independence in 1975 brought the wrath of the Rhodesian military down on his country from 1976 to 1979. *File photo*

The challenging drop zone high atop Mt Gorongosa. *Photo courtesy of John Reid-Rowland*

Rhodesian Air Force Dakota transport conducting Operation Bumper resupply flight in October 1979. *Photo courtesy of John Reid-Rowland*

Samora Machel, president of Mozambique from independence until his death in a controversial plane crash in October 1986.

Rhodesian Air Force Dakota transports prepare to drop supplies to Renamo forces at Gorongosa as part of Operation Bumper, October 1979. *Photo courtesy of John Reid-Rowland*

Rhodesian Air Force Dakota transport conducting Operation Bumper resupply flight in October 1979. *Photo courtesy of John Reid-Rowland*

By 1979 Rhodesian security forces were conducting regular, large-scale cross-border raids into Mozambique to disrupt ZANLA forces and infrastructure.

A heavily-armed Selous Scouts flying column during a raid into Gaza Province in late 1979.

South African Period

Afonso Dhlakama assumed leadership of Renamo following the death of André Matsangaissa in October 1979 and oversaw the enormous expansion of the insurgency during the period of South African military assistance. *Photo Times Media*

Under the leadership of P. W. Botha, apartheid South Africa engaged in an aggressive campaign of regional destabilization in the early 1980s. This included military assistance to anti-government insurgencies in Angola and Mozambique.

Flying out of Waterkloof airbase outside Pretoria, C-130 transports from 28 Squadron carried the burden of supplying Renamo force from 1980 to 1984. *File photo*

General Magnus Malan commander of the SADF at the height of South African assistance to Renamo in the early 1980s. *File photo*

Machel had hoped the ending of the Rhodesian war with the Lancaster House agreement in December 1979 would spell the end of the Renamo insurgency, but it was not to be. *File photo*

Major Frelimo offensives often resulted in the overrunning of Renamo bases and the capture of large quantities of weaponry and ammunition, but these operations rarely inflicted significant casualties on the guerrillas. *Photo courtesy of Centro de Formação Fotográfica, Maputo, Mozambique*

Lieutenant Alan Gingles (back row, third from left) and two of his men of 5 Recce Commando along with new recruits at Renamo's Chirrare base in 1981. *Photo courtesy of David Scott-Donelan*

Frelimo rallying the population in 1985: "Let us make the year of the 10th anniversary a decisive occasion in the struggle for the total liquidation of the armed bandits!" *Photo Robert Botha / Times Media*

Major Frelimo offensives often resulted in the overrunning of Renamo bases and the capture of large quantities of weaponry and ammunition, but these operations rarely inflicted significant casualties on the guerrillas. *Photo courtesy of Centro de Formação Fotográfica, Maputo, Mozambique*

South African and Mozambican delegations negotiating the treaty of non-aggression on the banks of the Incomati River in March 1984. *Photo courtesy of Centro de Formação Fotográfica, Maputo, Mozambique*

Celebrating the signing of the "Agreement on Non-Aggression and Good Neighbourliess", better known as the Nkomati Accord, on 16 March 1984. *Photo courtesy of Centro de Formação Fotográfica, Maputo, Mozambique*

SAS *Protea*. *Photo Times Media*

Backed into a corner, Machel tried to put the best face on the Nkomati Accord. *Photo courtesy of Centro de Formação Fotográfica, Maputo, Mozambique*

President Machel awards gifts to Zimbabwean officers following the capture of Renamo's Casa Banana headquarters in August 1985. Operational commander, Lieutenant-Colonel Lionel Dyck (foreground right) looks on. *Domingo, 5 September 1985*

The Swiss army knife with the Frelimo crest awarded to Dyck by President Machel. *Photo Author*

SAS Emily *Hobhouse. Photo Times Media*

Beginning in August 1985 the ZNA began carrying an increasingly heavy burden of the fighting in central Mozambique. *Photo courtesy of Centro de Formação Fotográfica, Maputo, Mozambique*

Last Phase

Renamo guerrillas resting at a stream in Maputo Province, 1987. *Photo Cloete Breytenbach*

Renamo soldier equipped with an RPG-7 near Maringue, Sofala Province, 1988. *Photo Cloete Breytenbach*

As the war dragged on, the quality and training of troops began to noticeably decline. *Photo Cloete Breytenbach*

FAM troops prepare for operations in southern Mozambique, the scene of heavy fighting in 1987–89. *Photo courtesy of Centro de Formação Fotográfica, Maputo, Mozambique*

Toward the latter years of the war, Frelimo forces increasingly found themselves relegated to a passive defensive role and thereby ceded the strategic initiative to Renamo forces. *Photo courtesy of Centro de Formação Fotográfica, Maputo, Mozambique*

Frelimo forces entering a destroyed village following a Renamo attack. The civilian population increasingly found itself caught in the crossfire of the war. *Photo courtesy of Centro de Formação Fotográfica, Maputo, Mozambique*

Female Renamo soldier, central Mozambique, 1988. *Photo Cloete Breytenbach*

Wreckage from the crash of President Machel's aircraft is strewn across the South African countryside, October 1986. *Photo Times Media*

Renamo child soldier, central Mozambique, 1988. Child soldiers, some as young as 13, were dragooned into the ranks of both guerrilla and government forces, especially in the later years of the war. *Photo courtesy of Paul Moorcraft*

By the end of the war millions of Mozambicans had been made refugees in Malawi, Zimbabwe, and South Africa and millions more were internally displaced. *Photo Newscom.com*

President Chissano's diplomatic offensive: May 1987 meeting with Prime Minister Thatcher at No. 10 Downing Street. *Photo Newscom.com*

President Chissano's diplomatic offensive: October 1987 meeting with President Reagan at the White House. *Photo Reagan Library*

Peace

The Rome peace talks lasted from July 1990 to October 1992 and would ultimately require the active involvement of regional leaders to hammer out an acceptable agreement. *Photo courtesy of Centro de Formação Fotográfica, Maputo, Mozambique*

The Renamo delegation, October 1992: Afonso Dhlakama (second from left), Vicente Ululu, and Raul Domingos. *Photo courtesy of Centro de Formação Fotográfica, Maputo, Mozambique*

The Frelimo delegation: Alberto Chissano (second from right), Amando Guebuza, and Pascoal Mocumbi; Archbishop Jamie Goncalves is to Chissano's left. *Photo courtesy of Centro de Formação Fotográfica, Maputo, Mozambique*

Frelimo President Chissano signs the General Peace Agreement on 4 October 1992. *Photo courtesy of Centro de Formação Fotográfica, Maputo, Mozambique*

Renamo President Dhlakama signs the General Peace Agreement on 4 October 1992. *Photo courtesy of Centro de Formação Fotográfica, Maputo, Mozambique*

"The war is over. Peace at last." *Photo courtesy of Centro de Formação Fotográfica, Maputo, Mozambique*

War Damage

Derailed train near Lamego, Sofala Province. Attacking road and rail infrastructure was a central part of Renamo's strategy to sever Frelimo's lines of communication and to immobilize the country. *Photo Ersnt Schade, www.ernstschade.com*

Rural villages and their inhabitants were often targets of Renamo raids. *Photo courtesy of Centro de Formação Fotográfica, Maputo, Mozambique*

The heavily damaged Dona Ana railroad bridge at Sena on the Zambezi River. Strategic towns along the Zambezi River witnessed some of the most brutal fighting of the war. *Photo courtesy of USAID*

Derailed and looted train in Maputo Province. In an effort to isolate the capital, rail lines to and from South Africa and Swaziland came under constant attack by Renamo forces from 1987 onward. *Photo courtesy of Centro de Formação Fotográfica, Maputo, Mozambique*

Heavy fighting in and around Caia, Sofala Province betyween 1986 and 1990 destroyed nearly all the town and much of the surrounding infrastructure. *Photo courtesy of Centro de Formação Fotográfica, Maputo, Mozambique*

Vehicles traveling the main north–south highway were under constant threat of ambush and hundreds of civilians died in these attacks. *Photo courtesy of Centro de Formação Fotográfica, Maputo, Mozambique*

LIST OF MAPS

Map 1: Mozambique Regional and Provincial 15

Map 2: Eastern Border Region 26

Map 3: Central Region 40

Map 4: Southern Region 68

Map 5: Central Region 126

Map 6: Casa Banana Headquarters Complex, August 1985 127

Map 7: Southern Region 154

Map 8: Northern Region 184

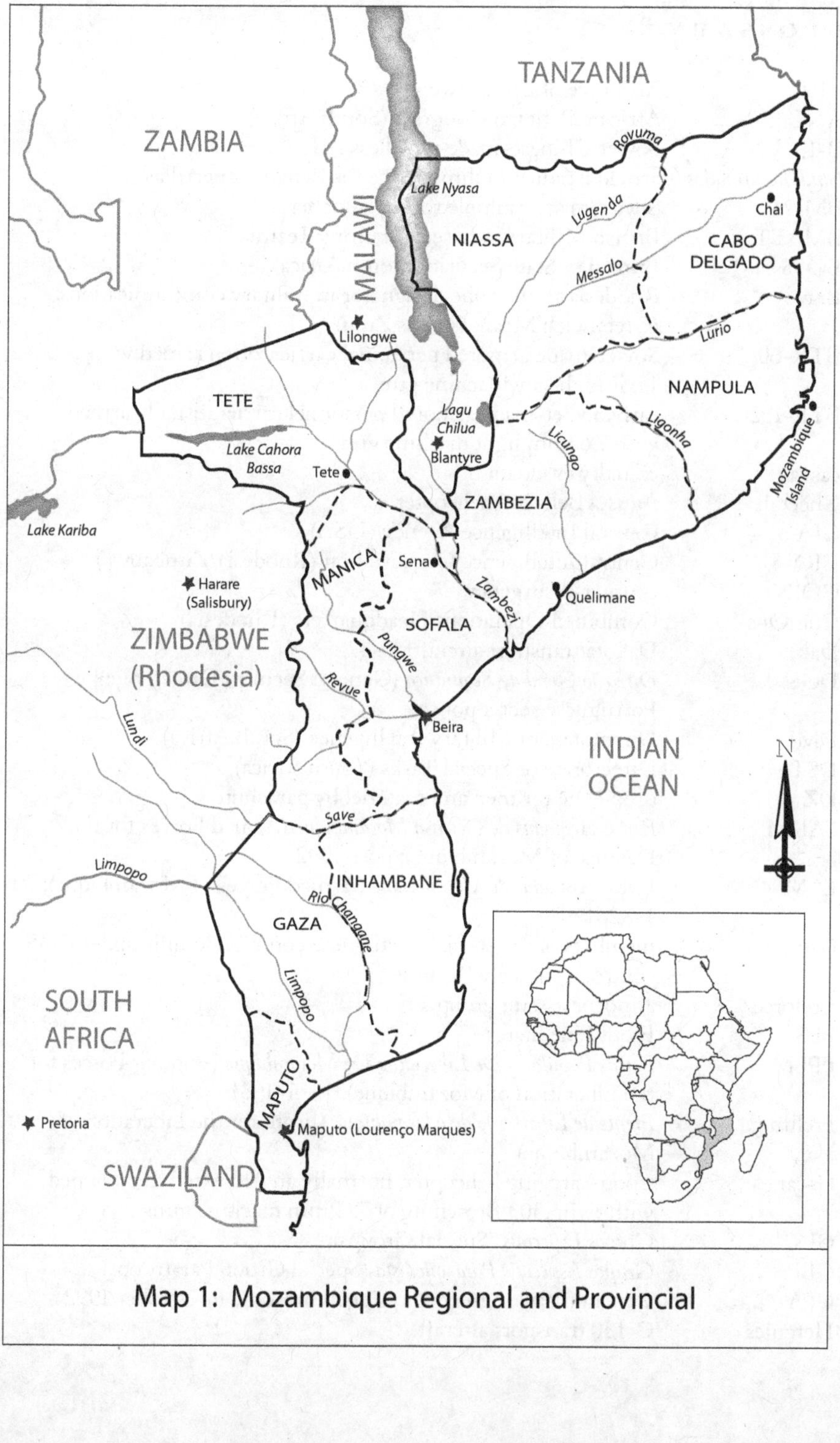

Map 1: Mozambique Regional and Provincial

GLOSSARY

AFZ	Air Force of Zimbabwe
ANC	African National Congress (South Africa)
B-10	Soviet/Chinese-made recoilless rifle
bandidos armados	armed bandits; Frelimo name for Renamo guerrillas
BM-21	Soviet-made multiple rocket launcher
BMATT	British Military Advisery Training Team
BOSS	Bureau of State Security (South Africa)
Bravo	Rhodesian time zone designator in military communications; (Greenwich Mean Time is Zulu)
BTR-60	Soviet-made armored personnel carrier, often armed with 14.5mm heavy machine gun
BTR-152	early Soviet-made armored personnel carrier, usually armed with 7.62mm light machine gun
casvac	casualty evacuation
Cheetah	Agusta Bell-205 helicopter
CIA	Central Intelligence Agency (USA)
CIO	Central Intelligence Organization (Rhodesia/Zimbabwe)
COIN	counter-insurgency
ComOps	Combined Operations Headquarters (Rhodesia)
Dak	Dakota transport aircraft; C-47
DGS	*Direcção Geral de Segurança* (General Security Directorate); Portuguese secret police
DMI	Directorate of Military Intelligence (South Africa)
DST	Directorate of Special Tasks (South Africa)
DZ	drop zone for men and matériel by parachute
FADM	*Forças Armadas de Defensa Moçambique* (Armed Forces for the Defence of Mozambique); post-1992
FAM	*Forças Armadas de Moçambique* (Armed Forces of Mozambique); 1982–1992
flechas	members of the special Portuguese commando unit under DGS control; primarily Bushmen
fireforce	airborne assault group
FLS	Front Line States
FPLM	*Forças Populares De Libertação De Moçambique* (Popular Forces for the Liberation of Mozambique); 1975–1981
Frelimo	*Frente de Libertação de Moçambique* (Front for the Liberation of Mozambique)
G-car	troop-carrying helicopter, normally an Alouette III, equipped with twin .303 Browning or 7.62mm machine guns
GEs	*Grupos Especiais* (Special Groups)
GEPs	*Grupos Especiais Pára-quedista* (Special Group Paratroops)
GPA	General Peace Agreement; signed in Rome in October 1992
Hercules	C-130 transport aircraft

intrep	intelligence report
JVC	Joint Verification Commission
K-car	command gunship, normally an Alouette III, equipped with 20mm cannon and often carrying Fireforce commander
Lynx	Reims-Cessna F-337 reconnaissance aircraft; often armed with rockets
LZ	landing zone for helicopters
MFA	*Movimento das Forças Armadas* (Armed Forces Movement); Portugal
MNR	Mozambique National Resistance
Ndau	one of the Shona-speaking subgroupings; historically found in eastern Zimbabwe and central Mozambique
NRZ	National Railways of Zimbabwe
recees	South African reconnaissance commandos
Red Berets	Mozambican commando unit
Renamo	*Resistência Nacional Moçambicana* (Mozambican National Resistance)
RF	Rhodesian Front; Ian Smith's party
RhAF	Rhodesian Air Force
RLI	Rhodesian Light Infantry
RPG-7	rocket-propelled grenade launcher
SAAF	South African Air Force
SACP	South African Communist Party
SADF	South African Defence Force
SAN	South African Navy
SAS	Special Air Service
sitrep	situation report
STF	Special Task Force (Zimbabwe)
stop line	pre-positioned troops placed in a blocking position
Sunray	Rhodesian military communications codename for local commander
SWAPO	South West Africa People's Organization
TGF	*Tropas de Guarda Fronteira* (Frelimo border guard brigades)
TPDF	Tanzania People's Defence Force
UANC	United African National Council; party of Bishop Abel Muzorewa
Voz da África Livre	Voice of Free Africa; Renamo radio station
ZANLA	Zimbabwe African National Liberation Army; armed wing of ZANU
ZANU	Zimbabwe African National Union; party of Robert Mugabe
ZANU-Ndonga	Zimbabwe African National Union-Ndonga; party of Ndabaningi Sithole
ZAPU	Zimbabwe African People's Union; party of Joshua Nkomo
ZIPRA	Zimbabwe People's Revolutionary Army; armed wing of ZAPU
ZNA	Zimbabwe National Army

CHAPTER 1
PRELUDE TO WAR

Mozambique is one of those flukes of history. Born of unbridled European imperialism and competitive Western nationalism, forged in conquest, and molded by factors largely outside its own control, the country and its people have rarely been able to determine their own fate. Across the latter half of the 20th century it would find itself caught up in the regional politics of the anti-apartheid struggle, wars of liberation—including the Mozambican people's own fight for independence from more than 450 years of Portuguese rule—and in the superpower competition of the Cold War. And it would become the venue for one of Africa's deadliest and most destructive conflicts from 1977 to 1992. Nonetheless, the Mozambican war clearly failed to attract the attention and the notoriety of other similar conflicts (such as Angola) although the stakes were just as high and the suffering just as profound.

Historical context[1]

As Vasco da Gama sailed north along the coast of what was to become Mozambique in early 1498, his historic first voyage to India, his mind was probably more focused on the riches that were awaiting him and the relief of having survived the ferocious seas that had battered his fleet as it rounded the tip of the continent, than on the distant African landscape. Except as a source of fresh water and provisions, this stretch of thinly inhabited coastline was probably of little concern to da Gama. After nearly a century of struggle and stubborn persistence, the Kingdom of Portugal was about to make its dream a reality—the establishment of a sea route around Africa to the treasures of the East. The land route monopoly was finally broken. No longer would Portugal be denied its share of the riches of India, China, and the Spice Islands. Although destined to play an important, albeit small, role in Portugal's maritime expansion this new place was merely another stepping stone on the path eastward. The future of Portugal, as the rulers in Lisbon were all too keenly aware, would be tied directly to its economic success in Asia, not Africa.

Just as in the case of Cape Verde, Portuguese Guinea, and Angola before it, Mozambique would become part of the chain of African supply stations for Portuguese shipping plying the lucrative Asian trade routes. To secure this route and wrest economic and political control from Muslim traders, who dominated Indian Ocean commerce, the Portuguese quickly established a permanent presence along the east coast of Africa at Kilwa (now in southern Tanzania), Mozambique Island and Sofala by 1507. Using overwhelming naval might Portugal expanded its influence along the Indian Ocean coastline from Delagoa Bay—future site of Lourenço Marques—at the southern end of Mozambique to Mombasa in present-day Kenya by the first half of the 16th century. Any opposition was ruthlessly crushed. Thriving Muslim towns were sacked and burnt to the ground and important trading settlements like Quelimane north of the Zambezi River delta were occupied. By the 1560s the Portuguese had pushed far up the Zambezi River installing themselves by force of arms in the river towns of Sena and Tete, gaining control over the main trade route from the coast to the African interior.

From its position along the Zambezi at Sena and Tete, the Portuguese Crown sought to gain control over the lucrative gold trade emanating from the highlands of what is now Zimbabwe and parts of central Mozambique. At the start of the 17th century, however, economic and military power would shift away from the official representatives of the Portuguese Crown to an emerging Afro-Portuguese community. These descendants of former Portuguese sailors, soldiers, and merchants who intermarried with local Africans would use their newfound power to circumvent the royal trade monopoly and developed their own largely autonomous socio-military structures. Increasingly it would be the independent-minded Afro-Portuguese community, and not Lisbon, that would dictate the course and direction of change within the African interior over the next two centuries.

The beginning of the 20th century and the onset of formal colonial rule ushered in a series of sweeping changes in Portugal and abroad that would have a major impact on the development of Lisbon's overseas empire. Nowhere else was this to become more readily apparent than in Portuguese Africa. Mozambique, along with Angola, would now become the jewels of

Portuguese colonialism in the new century, driving economic growth and lifting the motherland from the agrarian backwater of Europe.

Or so Lisbon hoped. But Portugal's African colonies would be both a blessing and a curse. A blessing in the sense that through the exploitation of Africa's human and natural resources, successive Portuguese governments were able to modernize the metropolitan economy, create protected markets for fledgling Portuguese businesses, generate badly needed hard currency, and provide a convenient safety valve for Portugal's increasingly marginalized agrarian populace. A curse in the latter part of the century, because they would draw a fragile Portugal into a series of long and devastating colonial wars that would drain its treasury, isolate Lisbon within the international community, and set the stage for Cold War-inspired conflicts that would produce decades of human suffering and misery for the people of Africa.

The pacification of Mozambique at the beginning of the 20th century signaled the formal end of African resistance to colonial rule. But Lisbon's idealist vision of assimilating millions of Mozambicans into a greater Lusophone empire quickly gave way to the harsh realities of colonialism. For all but a fortunate few, colonial rule brought few benefits and Mozambicans continued to keep the nascent flame of African nationalism alive.[2] Most often in the form of passive resistance, with the occasional outburst of violence, early protests tended to center on specific grievances against colonial policies and were inclined to be highly localized in nature. But as the winds of decolonization began to sweep across the continent in the late 1950s and early 1960s a growing sense of a broader Mozambican nationalism slowly began to emerge. Just as strong, however, was Lisbon's unwavering determination to cling firmly to its overseas empire.

Without a doubt the creation of the *Frente de Libertação de Moçambique* (Front for the Liberation of Mozambique) or Frelimo was a notable milestone in the independence struggle, because for the first time diverse nationalist groups were able to find common ground and put aside their own parochial interests. Nonetheless, divisions within Frelimo would continue to simmer below the surface, occasionally exploding from time to time and threatening to tear the organization apart. The party's early years were marred by expulsions, bitter personal infighting, ideological differences, and ethnic rivalries, according to the Isaacmans.[3] It would take a strong leader to hold such a fragile coalition together.

That man was Eduardo Mondlane, who was chosen as Frelimo's first president. A distinguished, U.S.-educated academic and expatriate nationalist from southern Mozambique, Mondlane brought immediate respectability to the new organization. Mondlane envisioned a democratic, non-discriminatory, and socialistic-type of society for the new Mozambique, but was not a committed ideologue and apparently seemed willing to allow the post-independent state to politically develop incrementally along its own lines—with the guidance of Frelimo. Viewed with suspicion by Marxist hardliners and other radicals within the party, because of his past connections to the West and the United States, Mondlane was a highly focused individual and became an extremely effective leader who, "turned Frelimo into what it became after his death [in February 1969], a remarkably cohesive and effective guerrilla movement."[4]

The launching of the armed struggle against Portugal began on 25 September 1964 with an attack by Frelimo forces on Chai, a government administrative post just south of the Messalo River in the Cabo Delgado District. This was the start of the liberation war. Portugal would desperately try to cling to Mozambique and its other African possessions, but fighting three major African insurgencies for well over a decade left some 10,000 Portuguese dead and another 30,000 wounded, Lisbon's treasury empty, and its economy and military in shambles. The writing was on the wall. On 25 April 1974 the government of Marcelo Caetano was overthrown by officers and men of the leftist *Movimento das Forças Armadas* (Armed Forces Movement) or MFA.[5] The Portuguese military had reached its breaking point and it was no longer willing to sacrifice itself for the greater glory of Portugal. As General Costa Gomes would later say bluntly, the military had "reached the limits of neuro-psychological exhaustion."[6]

Although the April coup signaled the acceptance of independence for all of Portuguese Africa, it did not bring an immediate end to the fighting in Mozambique. The MFA government, headed by General Spinola, sought ceasefire arrangements with Frelimo as it entered into negotiations to determine the political future of the country. Caught off guard by the sudden collapse of the Caetano regime, the insurgents quickly saw an opportunity to exploit Lisbon's weakness and improve its military position within Mozambique to gain the upper hand in future peace talks. To that end Frelimo poured troops into the central districts over the next several months with the guerrillas making impressive gains; expanding the war into Zambezia Province and capturing the town of Morrumbala on the Malawian border. Military order and discipline within the Portuguese forces rapidly broke down as units became demoralized and refused to fight. The coup also caused widespread panic among the Portuguese settler populace and the breakdown in law and order spurred an exodus to Portugal or South Africa at the rate of 1,000 per week in May.[7] Talks between Lisbon and Frelimo began in Zambia in early June. On 7 September 1974 the parties signed the Lusaka Accord ending the war, endorsing Frelimo's pre-eminence, and beginning a transition that would lead to independence from Portugal in June 1975.

The post-independence setting

The mid-1970s were a time of great change and turmoil in southern Africa and especially for Mozambique. The surging wave of African independence that began nearly two decades before was finally breaking on the shores of the white-minority ruled redoubt. Angola, Guinea-Bissau and Mozambique were now on the verge of independence. Meanwhile, newly energized African nationalist insurgencies in Rhodesia and South West Africa were escalating their attacks, forcing these regimes to fight for their very survival. Change was in the air, but how events would ultimately play out was far from certain.

Apartheid South Africa—the ideological and military center of resistance to majority rule—found itself under threat as never before. Pretoria's security buffer to the north was collapsing. Fueled by the 1976 Soweto student protests, a new wave of domestic violence spread across the country. A state of emergency came into effect. The wagons were drawn into a laager and the apartheid regime readied to battle to the end against all enemies, foreign and domestic.

The Cold War in Africa was also in full swing. With the rise of dozens of newly independent countries came a high stakes U.S.–Soviet geopolitical competition for allies and influence across the continent. Frequently this rivalry in Africa resulted in deadly proxy wars as Washington and Moscow backed competing sides. Newly independent and Marxist-led governments in Angola and Mozambique provided yet more fuel for fanning the flames of the superpower competition in southern Africa. Ultimately, these conflicts would become some of the most violent and longest running in Africa, and while certainly not the source of conflict in places like Angola and Mozambique, the superpower rivalry would play a critical role in sustaining them over the years. Likewise, the ending of the Cold War would create new opportunities for peace in these countries.

This complex environment greeted the victorious Frelimo as it formally took over the reins of power from the departing Portuguese in June 1975. Beyond pressing foreign policy challenges the new socialist government and its leaders were also facing monumental difficulties of uniting a highly diverse country, reforming a post-colonial economy and building the new society that they envisioned. Frelimo would make many mistakes along the way—serious mistakes born of ignorance and of arrogance. That Frelimo's ambitious efforts to recast Mozambique into a socialist state were met with political and social backlash was not entirely unexpected. The degree of this opposition and the readiness of anti-Frelimo groups to take up arms against their fellow countrymen, however, caught many by surprise. And it certainly caught the new government off guard. Moreover, the willingness of Mozambican opposition elements to actively work with pariah minority regimes in Rhodesia and later South Africa would cause Frelimo to fatally underestimate the nature of the threat posed to its survival by these 'armed bandits' (as the government called them). It would also make the coming conflict with the *Resistência Nacional Moçambicana* (Mozambican National Resistance) or Renamo nastier, longer lasting, and more difficult to resolve.

The ensuing war would grow increasingly bitter. It would expand from the limited confines of central Mozambique in the late 1970s to engulf not only the entire country and its citizens, but draw Mozambique's regional neighbors—from Zimbabwe, South Africa, Malawi and Tanzania—directly into the war's deadly web by the mid-1980s and become yet another African venue for the Cold War rivalry between the United States and the Soviet Union. At its height almost 100,000 men would be under arms.

The Frelimo–Renamo war would be a classic insurgency that pitted competing Mozambican ideologies, regions, and personalities against one another. That these and other factors in the post-independence period helped fuel the outbreak of conflict was probably a foregone conclusion in 1977 as the country and its people struggled to define the new Mozambique. It was, however, the entanglement of a wide variety of powerful external forces—often pursuing their own agendas—in this conflict that clearly escalated the level and scope of violence and would prolong the war and made peace so difficult to achieve. Ultimately, the disengagement of these international actors following the collapse of apartheid and the fall of the Berlin Wall created a changed environment by the start of the 1990s whereby Mozambicans could finally resolve their differences. And like the majority of insurgencies, the solution would be found in political accommodation rather than on the battlefield.

After 16 years of a terribly destructive war across the length and breadth of the country that left 800,000 to a million people dead, displaced some two million others and made refugees out of at least another million, peace would finally come to the divided nation with the signing of the General Peace Agreement on 4 October 1992. Just two years later on 27–29 October 1994 the Mozambican people would go to the polls for the country's first multi-party elections to elect a president and new parliament. The competition between Frelimo and Renamo would continue, albeit in the political arena now. And the guns would remain silent. More than 20 years after that historic October day in 1992 the country still remains at peace even as it continues to grapple with the difficult challenges of economic and social development.

CHAPTER TWO
BIRTH OF AN INSURGENCY

The mid-1970s were a time of extreme chaos and upheaval for the newly independent Mozambique. Uncertainty and fear of the unknown were the order of the day. In what seemed an instant, events over 5,000 miles away in Portugal upended more than four centuries of colonial rule and gave way to a completely new way of life on 25 June 1975. Under the leadership of a revolutionary Marxist movement, Frelimo, Mozambican society was being transformed. The old order was rapidly dissolving and the certainty of everyday life (harsh as it was for the average Mozambican) was being replaced with fresh ideas, new leaders, and untested institutions.

Although Frelimo now held the formal reins of power, its grip on the country itself was tenuous. An eclectic collection of demobilized colonial soldiers, disgruntled Portuguese settlers and business owners, regional political groupings, and nationalist politicians sought to contest Lisbon's unilateral handover of power to Frelimo. As the popular movement that won the war, Frelimo was finding it much harder to win the peace. Anti-government conspiracies, real and imagined, filled the air. Counter-revolutionaries, reactionaries, and foreign agents were seemingly everywhere just waiting to strike. They clearly posed a grave threat to the nation's hard won independence from the new government's perspective.

To make matters worse, Frelimo quickly embarked upon an ambitious effort to overhaul the entire political, social, and economic fabric of Mozambican society by implementing a radical socialist agenda throughout the country. All land was nationalized, abandoned private property and businesses were seized by the state, state farms and collectives were established, and power was increasingly centralized as Frelimo transformed itself from a mass nationalist movement into a restrictive party of the Marxist-Leninist elite. Political opposition to these measures was ruthlessly crushed, in the name of state security, and Frelimo purged of dissidents and those failing to adhere to the new ideological hard line. These actions, many party officials much later acknowledged, were ill-conceived, poorly timed, and badly handled, and they

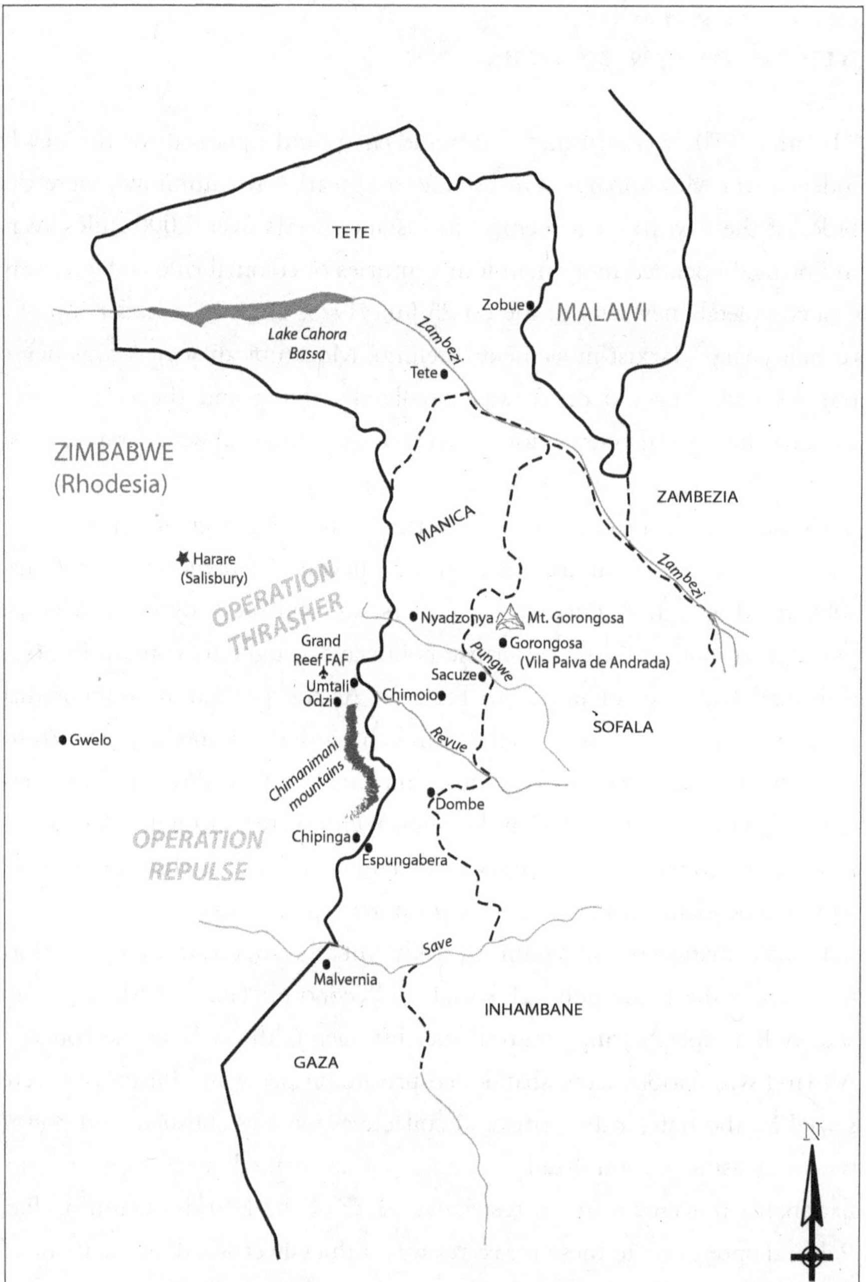

Map 2: Eastern Border Region

would fuel hostility to Frelimo in some parts of the country and swell the initial ranks of anti-government insurgents.

Disbelief, uncertainty and fear were rampant among the embattled white-minority regimes as the collapse of Portuguese rule set off alarm bells in both Pretoria and Salisbury. The unforeseen, swift collapse of the *cordon sanitaire*—the bulwark against 'the winds of change' that stretched from Angola across Rhodesia to Mozambique—had been breached decisively. The once powerful Lisbon–Pretoria–Salisbury military alliance against Communist-inspired African nationalism was now in shambles and nationalist guerrillas were on the doorstep of not only Rhodesia, but South Africa itself. The apartheid regime in Pretoria now faced the frightening prospect of having armed African nationalists from the African National Congress (ANC) and the South West Africa People's Organization (SWAPO) able to directly threaten both the South African homeland from Mozambique and South African-ruled South West Africa from Angola. A new aggressive strategy would have to be developed to counter these fresh security threats. In the nascent insurgencies in Angola and Mozambique the South Africans would find highly useful tools in the years ahead. For the embattled Rhodesian government, the loss of Portuguese Mozambique was a military disaster of strategic proportions. It exposed the entire 1,232 kilometer-long eastern flank of Rhodesia to infiltration by guerrilla forces of Robert Mugabe's Zimbabwe African National Liberation Army (ZANLA).[8] ZANLA guerrillas, with the active support and assistance of their long-standing Frelimo allies, could now operate from secure bases inside newly independent Mozambique. With their shortened lines of supplies and communication, thousands of Zimbabwean guerrillas could now maximize their operations in eastern Rhodesia. From Salisbury's perspective something had to be done and quickly.

Struggling against the winds of change

The evolving conflict in Mozambique, not surprisingly, would begin to mimic an all too familiar historical pattern, as domestic conflicts quickly became entangled in wider regional, and even global, confrontations. Political-military cooperation and coordination between Lisbon, Salisbury, and Pretoria was an extensive and indispensable feature of the national liberation wars of the 1960s and 1970s in both Mozambique and Rhodesia. Inter-service relationships between the three countries were strengthened, strategic planning put in place, and mutually supporting operations developed, to defeat the forces of African nationalism that all three governments viewed as a common threat.[9] Likewise, the liberation movements in Mozambique, Rhodesia, and South Africa formed their own symbiotic relationships as a counterweight to the Lisbon–Salisbury–Pretoria alliance. From their perspective a fight against any one of these repressive regimes was a fight against all; true liberation would be complete only when all these regimes were overthrown. Thus, the battlefields of southern Africa found South African guerrillas of the ANC fighting in Rhodesia alongside their Zimbabwean brethren. Frelimo guerrillas were actively assisting ZANLA fighters. Rhodesian security forces were coming to the aid of their Portuguese allies in Mozambique, while South African police and military forces were deployed to assist the Rhodesians.

The Rhodesian government of Ian Smith had been much more effective than its Portuguese colonial counterpart in containing its own insurgent threat and by 1970 the Rhodesian security situation was well in hand. Operating from bases in Zambia, nationalist guerrillas from ZANLA and Joshua Nkomo's competing Zimbabwe African People's Union (ZAPU) had repeatedly attempted to infiltrate bands of fighters into northern Rhodesia to attack white farms and government targets, but they were largely unsuccessful. A key reason for their lack of success was the arduous task of infiltrating across the forbidding Zambezi valley with its oppressive heat, lack of water, and sparse population. Groups of guerrillas were readily detected and either killed or captured by the awaiting Rhodesian security forces long before reaching farming or populated areas.

Frelimo's steady expansion of the war into Mozambique's Tete Province, however, caused growing concern in Salisbury about the vulnerability of its eastern flank. Despite a brief burst of anti-insurgent operations, Portuguese forces in the province soon adopted a defensive strategy, centering on protecting the massive Cahora Bassa Dam project, key installations, and lines of communications. The security situation continued to deteriorate in 1971.

As large swaths of the countryside, especially along the Rhodesian frontier, were abandoned to the insurgents, new ZANLA infiltration routes opened into northeastern Rhodesia and outflanked the Zambezi valley defensive line. Thus, Rhodesian ground forces began regularly crossing the border to attack both Zimbabwean and Mozambican guerrillas and on several occasions Rhodesian Air Force (RhAF) Canberra and Vampire bombers sortied against joint Frelimo–ZANLA encampments.[10] By 1973 elements of the Rhodesian Light Infantry (RLI) along with Special Air Service (SAS) reconnaissance teams were reportedly operating up to 100 kilometers inside the country, not only in Tete but also deep in central Mozambique for the first time. The 25 April 1974 coup in Lisbon by leftist Portuguese military officers put an abrupt end to this formal military cooperation, but Salisbury's forces continued to conduct hot-pursuit operations across the border well after the September 1974 ceasefire between Lisbon and Frelimo.

The collapse of Portuguese rule and the arrival of Mozambican independence in June 1975 put the Smith government in a quandary over how to deal with the newly installed Frelimo government of President Samora Machel in Maputo (formerly Lourenço Marques). Despite their past mutual hostility, Smith still held out hope of reaching a diplomatic rapprochement with Mozambique and sought to woo Machel away from supporting the Zimbabwean guerrillas through the use of political and economic enticements. The effort failed and Mozambique closed the border with Rhodesia in March 1976. Even more frightening for Salisbury, Frelimo's political-military alliance with ZANU and ZANLA blossomed. In early 1976 large arms shipments destined for Zimbabwean guerrilla forces in Mozambique were reportedly arriving from China and Eastern Europe. [11] Within a few months ZANLA was making extensive use of Mozambican territory to launch new offensives into Rhodesia and stepped up recruitment in the eastern highlands. A steady stream of Rhodesian intelligence reports also indicated the establishment of major guerrilla training camps and logistics bases across the border in Manica Province and by the end of the 1976, some press sources were reporting that some 5,000 to 8,000 Zimbabwean guerrillas were already in Mozambique.[12] The Rhodesian government's worse fears were fast becoming a reality.

The worsening security situation along its eastern border forced Salisbury to fall back on a military solution to its growing Mozambican problem. Where diplomacy and economic leverage had failed, perhaps the force of arms would prevail. New operational areas were created to counter rising Zimbabwean guerrilla infiltration along the Rhodesian frontier; Operation Thrasher in February 1976 along the eastern highland and Operation Repulse in May 1976 in the southeast.

Although fearful of the international political repercussions of widening its war against Zimbabwean nationalists and the ensuing strain on its limited military resources, the Smith government saw little choice but to expand its counter-insurgency operations inside Mozambique. These operations, built on the existing pattern of armed raids, ambushes, reconnaissance missions and intelligence collection by small teams of SAS and Selous Scouts operators, steadily evolved into larger full-scale assaults against ZANLA bases and infrastructure. The first major cross-border operation (Operation Eland) was launched 9 August 1976 against ZANLA's Nyadzonya base along the Pungwe River some 50 miles northeast of Umtali (now Mutare) by a flying column of heavily-armed Selous Scouts. The raid left more than 1,300 dead and was considered an overwhelming success by the Rhodesians.[13] Direct confrontations with Frelimo forces were generally avoided during these operations, although some clashes were inevitable.

The security situation within Rhodesia, however, continued to decline. According to a July 1977 Rhodesian Central Intelligence Organization (CIO) security assessment, "ZANLA's numerical potential will enable it to intensify and expand operations, specifically in the Hurricane, Thrasher and Repulse operational areas" (opposite the Rhodesian–Mozambican border) and that the Frelimo government was determined to support the Zimbabwean guerrillas "regardless of the consequences."[14] Under extreme pressure to do something to reverse the tide, the Rhodesian military ramped up external military operations in Mozambique (as well as in Zambia and Botswana) and by 1978 Rhodesian security forces were conducting full-scale conventional forays deep into Mozambique to break the bones of the country and force Machel into abandoning his support of Mugabe's forces. Heavily-armed columns of

Rhodesian soldiers with air support, working in conjunction with helicopter-borne troops repeatedly struck at ZANLA training camps, supply depots, and even Frelimo positions. They destroyed key bridges and communications links and "turned large swatches into a devastated no man's land" and frontier "towns such as Espungabera and Malvernia became heaps of rubble."[15]

The war was escalating out of control. Frelimo found itself facing the wrath of the Rhodesian security forces and a budding domestic insurgency—what was to become Renamo. From August 1976 to November 1979, the Rhodesians undertook at least a dozen major cross-border operations resulting in the deaths of thousands and costing the Mozambican economy hundreds of millions of dollars.[16] The resulting destruction of the Mozambican economy and infrastructure, which was already decimated by years of war against the Portuguese and the ensuing turmoil of independence, sent Mozambique into a downward spiral. By late 1979 the pressure from unrelenting Rhodesian and Mozambican anti-government insurgent attacks proved too much. Machel buckled. He reluctantly pressed Mugabe to seek a negotiated settlement with Smith, whose government too was reeling under some 20,000 armed guerrillas operating inside Rhodesia. Furthermore, despite all their cross-border successes, Rhodesian security forces were now finding the going increasingly difficult as they began to encounter better-defended positions and more heavily-armed Zimbabwean and Mozambican forces. For example, in early September 1979 during Operation Uric—a major three-day assault on a key ZANLA–Frelimo base in southern Mozambique—Salisbury's forces suffered their heaviest casualties of the war and failed to take the objective; "the most foreboding factor was that ZANLA and Frelimo had succeeded in repelling the Rhodesian army for the first time."[17] Both sides were clearly ready for peace. A settlement of the Rhodesian war would, Machel hoped, bring an end not only to the fighting with the Rhodesians, but also to the expanding anti-Frelimo insurgency within his own country. It was, however, not to be.

It has often been said that the origins of the *Resistência Nacional Moçambicana*, better known by its Portuguese acronym Renamo, are well known. But like many aspects surrounding Renamo—and even the war itself—the facts have become obscured by myths, half-truths, and outright distortions of the actual historical events. Both Renamo's supporters and its detractors each sought to craft an image of the insurgent movement that reflected their own specific agendas. Furthermore, much of the confusion surrounding the birth of Renamo and the resulting insurgency also reflects the chaotic times immediately before and just after Mozambican independence that gave rise to multiple anti-Frelimo groups and Rhodesia's role in prompting many of these competing interests. Thus, the challenge of separating fact from fiction is often a daunting task. Memories have faded, many of the original participants have died, and records have been lost or were never committed to writing in the first place. Nonetheless, a number of new studies of war veterans, personal accounts, and official documents have come to light since the war's end that create the opportunity to construct a more accurate and valid historical record.[18]

In the aftermath of the April 1974 Lisbon coup, Rhodesian military and intelligence officers sought to exploit anti-Frelimo sentiment within the thousands of Mozambican refugees flooding into Rhodesia. High on the Rhodesians' list were ex-colonial soldiers, white settlers, paramilitary militia members, and former Portuguese intelligence agents. Many of these people were extremely bitter and vitriolic in their hatred for the new Marxist government and their loss of position, property, and livelihood. It was hoped that at least some of these people would jump at the opportunity to get their revenge. While this picture contains elements of truth to varying degrees, it is a distorted one that relies too heavily on outdated, and often self-serving and unsubstantiated information from the early and mid-1980s created at the height of the Mozambican war and the highly politicized anti-apartheid struggle.

Thus, the most widespread—and misleading—accounts of Renamo's formation paint the guerrilla movement as an unseemly collection of "Portuguese settlers and mercenaries," "anti-Frelimo groups," "members of the elite special forces of the colonial army," "Portuguese secret police," and "some intellectuals, middle-class businessmen, and *regulos* (traditional chiefs)." To which were added "deserters from the Frelimo army" and "people convicted of corruption, thievery, and other crimes" who had been freed from reeducation camps and prisons.[19] This haphazard collection of black and white Mozambicans was then sown together by Rhodesian (and later South African) intelligence and tossed back across the Mozambican frontier to wreak havoc on the Frelimo government, its Zimbabwean guerrilla allies, and the Mozambican people, according to this popular and widely repeated version of the war.

In these accounts, the individuals most commonly claimed to have formed the core of Renamo were drawn from the *flechas* and other specialized Portuguese counter-insurgency units, such as the *Grupos Especiais* (GEs) and the *Grupos Especiais Pára-quedista* (GEPs). The *flechas* (meaning arrows in Portuguese), were created by the *Direcção Geral de Segurança* (DGS) or Portuguese secret police to conduct special military operations and gather intelligence in enemy-occupied territory in both Angola and Mozambique. They operated in small squad-size units of predominately Bushman troops and although their officers tended to be Portuguese, they functioned independently of the Portuguese army. The *flechas* in Mozambique, particularly a group operating in Tete Province under the command of Alvaro Manuel Alves Cardoso[20] were greatly admired by the Rhodesians for their effectiveness at infiltrating and killing Frelimo guerrilla groups.[21] The GEs and GEPs however were paramilitary formations that were drawn from the local African population and used as regional self-defense units. They were the creation of a prominent Portuguese businessman from Beira, Jorge Jardim, who would be repeatedly and inaccurately cited by outside observers as one of the driving forces behind the creation of Renamo. (Their formation and Jardim's role will be discussed later on.)

The *flecha* myth was given further credence in Ken Flower's widely quoted, but revisionist 1987 autobiography, *Serving Secretly: Rhodesia's CIO Chief on the Record*, where he claims using the Portuguese *flecha* concept to create Renamo in the *early 1970s* [emphasis added]. According to his 26 March 1974 notes, "I've been to Lourenço Marques and managed to get agreement from the DGS [Portuguese secret police] to form 'Flechas' for trans-border operations in

Mozambique."[22] Flower's goal as outlined in what he cites as an April 1974 top secret memo, *'Flechas' and the Formation of the 'Mozambique National Resistance'*, however, was to use flechas in "a pseudo-terrorist operation directed from Rhodesia into Mozambique."[23] In this version of Renamo's creation Flower claims that the CIO proceeded in early 1974, before the Lisbon coup, with the recruitment of Mozambicans who were encouraged to do their own thing with Rhodesian support. And Flower was surprised "at the ease with which the Mozambique Resistance Movement developed" indicating that the CIO "was proceeding along the right lines" and the success of the movement also signified that Frelimo lacked that essential popular support.[24] While the CIO was clearly behind the formation of Renamo (as we will later see), it was not formed as a *flecha*-type organization of pseudo-terrorists nor did it come into existence before Mozambican independence, and wasn't known as "Renamo" or the English equivalent "Mozambique National Resistance" (MNR) until at least late 1976.

The other element of the alleged *flecha* connection involves the arrival in Rhodesia of the Mozambican *flecha* commander Cardoso and some 40 of his men in April 1974 following the Lisbon coup. According to the Selous Scouts commander, Lieutenant-Colonel Ron Reid-Daly, this group forced its way across the border and it was hoped that the remainder of Cardoso's men would join him to form a company of *flecha* commandos within the Selous Scouts.[25] This never happened. Nonetheless, many Renamo histories continued to link the formation of Renamo to the Selous Scouts-*flecha* connection. "Some role in the creation of the MNR seems to have been played by the most notorious commando unit [sic] in the Rhodesian armed forces, the Selous Scouts," according to Paul Fauvet's often-cited 1984 article.[26] In the article he also gives credence to the claim that most Renamo guerrillas in 1980 "were [former] members of the crack *Flecha* unit established by Portugal to fight Frelimo."[27] The Selous Scouts were never involved in the creation or running of Renamo. As we shall see later, this responsibility would fall directly to the CIO and its personnel; some of these CIO officers had actively served in the SAS. Later on, small SAS calls signs would provide training and support to Renamo forces inside Mozambique.

The CIO did try to make use of former Mozambican *flechas* in late 1974, according to a former CIO officer. The goal was "to infiltrate them back into Mozambique with a view toward mobilizing the masses and carrying out a counter-coup," said the officer.[28] The effort, however, was stillborn. On their very first mission into Mozambique the group of mainly white soldiers was compromised by the local population and several were captured by Frelimo. "It became quite clear that we had been compromised because of the use of white soldiers," recalled the CIO officer coordinating the effort.[29] The project was then abandoned by the CIO and the unit demobilized; many of the men apparently departed for Angola to join Holden Roberto's CIA-supported Front for the National Liberation of Angola.[30] A very small handful of black *flechas* would continue to work with the CIO and be used to recruit anti-Frelimo dissents over the next year.[31] They, and those they recruited, would later be integrated into the yet-to-be created Renamo.

The CIO did flirt with supporting several black anti-Frelimo opposition groups also, who claimed to be militarily active in central Mozambique in the mid-1970s, but none of these would play a role in the formation of Renamo despite Frelimo claims. Only one of these groups (what was to become Gimo Phiri's *África Livre*) would play any future military role in the Renamo insurgency when it was absorbed in 1982.[32] And while some individuals from these early opposition groups would later join Renamo, none of them would rise to any prominence or assume leadership positions.

Somewhat surprisingly, Renamo's birth begins not on the battlefields of Mozambique, but in the offices of the Rhodesian CIO and the broadcasting studios of the Rhodesian Broadcasting Corporation (RBC). And while it is true that significant indigenous anti-Frelimo sentiment pre-dated this action, Salisbury's involvement clearly proved to be the essential catalyst in transforming latent anti-government opposition in central Mozambique into a serious military challenge to Frelimo rule. Without critical Rhodesian training, supplies and support, and safe haven in its first years of existence, it is unlikely that Renamo would have evolved into such an effective military organization or grown so rapidly. Moreover, Salisbury's immediate security needs drove it to create a military tool to threaten Frelimo rather than groom an indigenous political opposition. This as we shall see would have serious consequences that would haunt the Renamo insurgency throughout the conflict.

By mid-1976 it was apparent that the Rhodesian government needed to do something more to undercut President Machel's support to the ZANLA forces flowing into Mozambique and the growing operational threat that ZANLA presented to eastern Rhodesia. The only question was how best to do this. Like a number of similar debates concerning Rhodesian counter-insurgency strategy, there was a clear division between the military's direct action approach and the CIO's more subtle covert support for Mozambican dissidents. In the end, Flower and the CIO position won out, in no small part because of the scarcity of military resources that would be required to form, train, and equip an insurgent force on the size and scale that the Rhodesian military envisioned.

In keeping with this approach the CIO's initial effort was quite limited and focused on psychologically undermining the Machel government and encouraging anti-Frelimo dissidence. Through the use of daily radio broadcasts via the CIO-funded *Voz da África Livre* (Voice of Free Africa), which began transmitting on 5 July 1976, the Rhodesians sought to highlight the new Mozambican government's shortcomings and foment unrest. Utilizing a powerful transmitter, known as "Big Bertha" that was located in Gwelo, Rhodesia, the station's signal could be picked up throughout Mozambique. From its downtown Salisbury office the *Voz da África Livre*'s small staff of Mozambican exiles churned out anti-Frelimo and anti-Communist diatribes in daily broadcasts.[33]

At the center of this effort was a 49-year-old, white Mozambican exile named Orlando Cristina, who would play a key role in the future political evolution of Renamo. Although born in Portugal, he spent most of his adult life working as a big game hunter with his Portuguese father in the wilds of Niassa Province. According to João Cabrita, Cristina viewed himself as a true Mozambican nationalist who embraced African traditional culture and even married an Islamized Yao woman from Niassa. He apparently had a brief flirtation with Frelimo in the early 1960s, but quickly became disillusioned with the party's internal racial and ethnic fissures.[34] Following a short stint in jail in 1964 for his Frelimo dalliances, he was released at the behest of the influential Beira businessman, Jorge Jardim.[35] Jardim reportedly told Cristina that "he understood his motives in searching for Frelimo, but that there were other ways of resolving the Mozambican problem."[36] Thus began a close working relationship between the two men that would last until Jardim's death in 1982.

It appears that Cristina was seen as a kindred spirit by Jardim and one that could help him create a nationalist alternative to Frelimo in a future post-colonial Mozambique. Thus, with Jardim's money and Cristina's supervision, the *Grupos Especiais* were formed in 1971. Ostensibly local self-defense African units to assist the Portuguese war effort against Frelimo in northern Mozambique, Cristina saw them (and later the *Grupos Especiais Pára-quedista*) as the foundation of a truly Mozambican military force. Moreover they could serve as a potential counterweight to Frelimo in the newly-independent Mozambique. In short order, however, Cristina had a falling out with GE commander, Colonel Costa Campos, and cut his ties. Although some 5,000 villagers were recruited, Jardim's grand vision was never realized and both the GEs and GEPs were disbanded following the Portuguese collapse. Subsequently, Cristina traveled to Malawi where he helped train President Hasting Banda's Young Pioneers, but left the country for Rhodesia in the weeks following the 1974 Lisbon coup.[37]

It was in Salisbury that Cristina encountered the CIO's Peter Burt, who was serving on the Mozambique Desk in late 1975. From Burt, Cristina was able to obtain financial support for his anti-Frelimo propaganda efforts. Cristina used this relationship to convince Burt that the RBC's newly-established Portuguese broadcasts into Mozambique were completely misguided and ineffective. To Cristina's thinking the broadcasts failed to recognize the changed post-independence political and social landscape and their pro-colonial and reactionary tone would not resonant with, nor more importantly rally, anti-Frelimo elements. In short order he was able to convince the CIO to let him and his colleagues exercise editorial control over the Rhodesian broadcasts with the launching of the *Voz da África Livre* in July 1976. The new content struck an immediate nerve with the Machel regime, which labeled the station "the voice of the hyena." More importantly, it gained a wide following among many disgruntled and anti-Frelimo Mozambicans.

As with a number of events surrounding the formation of Renamo, there are differing accounts as to how the name "*Resistência Nacional Moçambicana*" or Renamo came to be. Cabrita in his book claims the name came from a listener in Maputo "whose brief missives to the station invariably ended with '*Viva a Resistancia*!'" and the *Voz da África Livre* simply adopted the slogan in its programing.[38] Others, however, claim the name came about in May 1977 after a meeting of Mozambican exiles and Portuguese nationals in Cristina's house in Salisbury.[39] To add to the confusion, up until the early 1980s the English-language press and most academics referred to the group by its English acronym, MNR. MNR was also common usage in Rhodesian military and intelligence reporting from 1977 onward. Whatever the case, a ghost military organization had been created in the minds of Mozambicans and to the CIO would fall the enormous task of turning it into a reality.

Despite the rising reservoir of anti-Frelimo sentiment, the Rhodesians were having a difficult time channeling this opposition into any effective form of organized armed resistance. All this began to change with the arrival in October 1976 of André Matsangaissa. And this is when the real story of Renamo begins to unfold.

André Matade Matsangaissa joined Frelimo in 1972 and rose to platoon commander while operating in the Gorongosa area of central Mozambique.[40] After independence he was assigned to the Engineering Corps near Beira, where he ran afoul of the government's corruption purges in 1975 for allegedly stealing a Mercedes Benz car for his personal use. He was convicted by a military tribunal and sent to Sacuze (also spelled Sacudza or Sacudzo) re-education camp.[41] The camp, located north of the Pungwe River and some 25 kilometers west of Gorongosa town (formerly Vila Paiva de Andrada), was one of dozens of camps established by Frelimo in the center and north of the country to imprison political opponents. Matsangaissa's brother, however, maintains that the imprisonment was actually the result of André's vocal opposition to Frelimo policies and specifically to the government's confiscation of some of his family's property.[42] Matsangaissa escaped from Sacuze in October 1976 and made his way to Rhodesia where he sought out the *Voz da África Livre*'s Orlando Cristina. According to Cabrita's account, Matsangaissa told Cristina that the only effective way to change the political situation in Mozambique was "by force of arms" and "that is what I intend to do."[43]

Convincing Burt and the CIO, however, proved to be an entirely different matter for this 26 year-old former Frelimo fighter. When challenged by Burt to return to Mozambique and begin raising an army of recruits, Matsangaissa did just that in December 1976. His plan was to raid the Sacuze re-education camp on Christmas day and free the inmates, who then would join him in forming the core of the new anti-Frelimo guerrilla army supported by Salisbury. The daring raid failed and Matsangaissa was rearrested and imprisoned at the camp. Never one to quit easily, he escaped Sacuze once again and returned to Rhodesia in March 1977 where he quickly began organizing another raid on the camp. On 6 May 1977 Matsangaissa and two other ex-Frelimo soldiers successfully raided the camp and freed more than 50 prisoners, telling them that 'if you want to join … the struggle against Frelimo, you should be prepared to walk from here on foot for the next two days until we reach our base.'[44]

After several difficult days of trekking through the bush and clashes with Frelimo patrols the group crossed the Rhodesian frontier. Some took refuge in Rhodesia while others sought asylum in other countries, but 28 opted to join with Commander André, as he was now known, in forming the nucleus of the future Renamo insurgency. Ken Flower and the CIO at last had found their charismatic and audacious leader, but never in the Rhodesians' wildest dreams did they foresee what was about to unfold. From this time on the anti-Frelimo opposition would do more than just talk about bringing change to Mozambique; this marked the start of what Renamo later labeled the "Second War of Liberation." The Machel, government for its part, dismissed this new threat as little more than Rhodesian-supported banditry. Unfortunately, it would end up paying a steep price for that miscalculation.

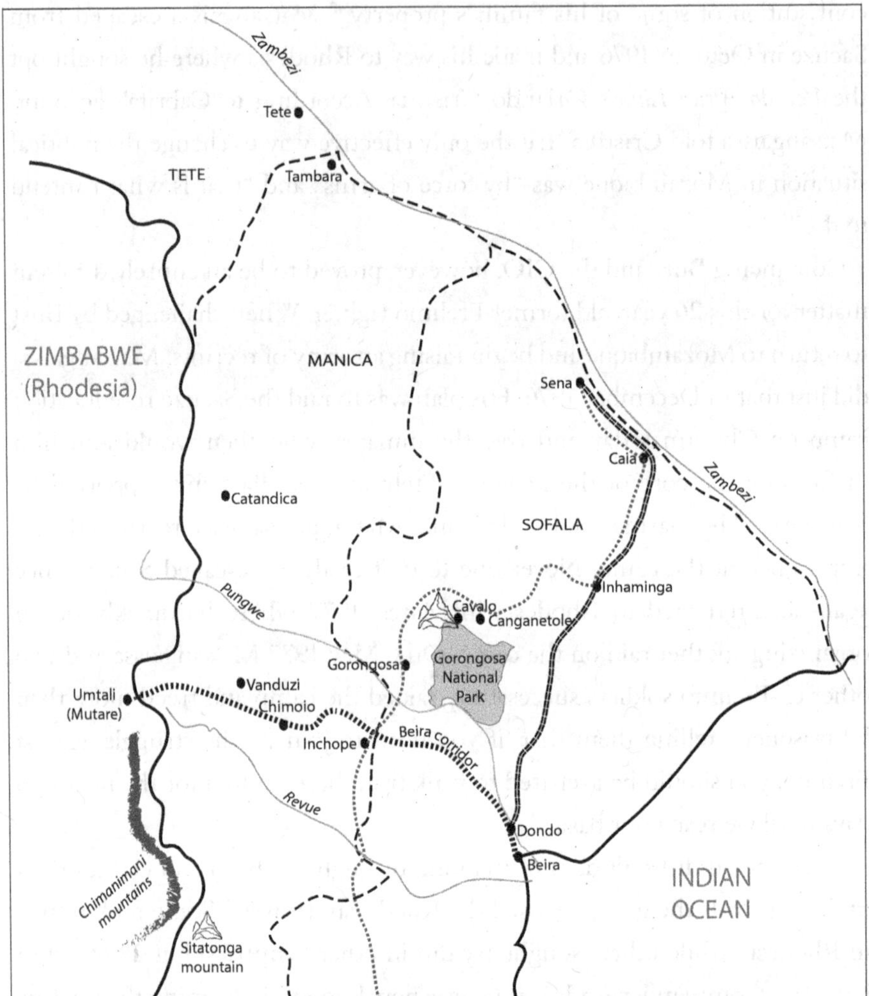

Map 3: Central Region

CHAPTER THREE
BATTLEGROUND CENTRAL MOZAMBIQUE

By the time of the May 1977 raid on Sacuze, relations between Mozambique and its neighbors were rapidly spiraling downward. Any past optimism about reaching an accommodation between the embattled white-minority governments in Salisbury and Pretoria and the self-proclaimed Marxist-Leninist rulers in Maputo had long since evaporated. The past year had seen the closing of the Rhodesian–Mozambican border and with it a key economic lifeline to the sea; a steady increase in the size and scope of Rhodesian cross-border operations against ZANLA guerrillas, including major operations deep inside Tete, Manica, and Gaza provinces; President Machel's unwavering public commitment to the liberation struggles in Rhodesia and South Africa; and a massive influx of Soviet military hardware and East Bloc advisers into Mozambique to meet the ever-looming conventional invasion threat posed by the Salisbury–Pretoria security axis. For all, it was now becoming a question of national survival.

Up until 1976 the Smith government had been fighting a defensive war of reacting to nationalist incursions inside the country, but a deteriorating strategic and operational picture forced a shift in Rhodesian military thinking. By tacitly ceding the initiative to the guerrillas, Rhodesian security forces and equipment were being stretched to the limit. Moreover, for every guerrilla killed, another two were waiting to take his or her place. It was a war of attrition that the Smith government could not hope to win by remaining on the defensive and something had to be done. A solution was to strike at safe havens of ZANLA and Zimbabwe People's Revolution Army (ZIPRA), the armed wing of Joshua Nkomo's ZAPU, in Mozambique and Zambia before the fighters had a chance to infiltrate into Rhodesia. But political considerations—including pressure from South Africa and the United States—had in the past limited these types of external operations to small-scale raids or selective intelligence activities. With the August 1976 Nyadzonya raid the Rhodesians seized the strategic initiative, signaling a new-found willingness to take the war to the enemy and ratchet up the pressure on its neighbors harboring the Zimbabwean guerrillas. The gloves were coming off. From 1977 to the end of 1979, Mozambique and its Zimbabwean nationalist allies would bear the full force of Salisbury's wrath. Over this three-year period, Rhodesian security forces launched some two dozen major cross-border operations and numerous other small raids and air attacks on both ZANLA and Frelimo forces and installations. Mozambique paid a heavy economic price for its support, estimated at some $556 million, according to official Mozambican government figures.[45]

The Rhodesian lifeline

Thanks to Matsangaissa's bold actions and *Voz da África Livre* broadcasts the ranks of the nascent Renamo began to grow steadily from mid-1977 onward, even as the Rhodesians themselves were grappling with how best to utilize this new force. Once again divisions among Salisbury's top security officials proved contentious, but Flower and the CIO got its way in the end. Flower envisioned the new organization as one that would serve as the "eyes and ears" of Rhodesian intelligence, with its primary focus on gathering information about ZANLA bases and guerrilla movements inside Mozambique. It would also be used to assess the level of Frelimo support to ZANLA, able to act as local guides or reconnaissance for Rhodesian army cross-border raids, and provide cover for sabotage operations. On a limited scale, Renamo would have the capability to strike at Mozambican economic and political targets to increase the costs to Frelimo of harboring ZANLA cadres. As such, Renamo would be molded into a small, but well-trained commando unit groomed to play a very limited and tightly-controlled part of the Rhodesian war effort. There was no question as to who was in charge and that the CIO was calling the shots; Matsangaissa was frequently overruled by his Rhodesian minders.[46] At no time, however, did the CIO seek to create Renamo as a political and military counterweight to the Frelimo government with its own political agenda and independent leadership. Certainly Flower and his CIO team never imagined that Renamo would morph into the serious military and political challenger that it was to become in less than a decade.

The CIO based its Renamo operations out of an old abandon tobacco farm at

Odzi, about 32 kilometers west of the border town of Umtali (now Mutare).[47] The base, which was established in late 1976, consisted of the main house that was used as the headquarters, stores building and instructors' housing, while the old tobacco barns were used to billet and feed the Renamo soldiers, according to a former Rhodesian instructor.[48] The camp was encircled by a 20 foot high earth embankment and security fencing. Although officially a 'secret base,' it was commonly known by locals and the police as "the funny farm," because of the secrecy surrounding the activities going on there. Eric "Ricky" May, who had replaced Peter Burt on the CIO's Mozambique Desk, was responsible for providing funding and coordinating activities with security officials in Salisbury. The CIO paid Matsangaissa 75 Rhodesian dollars a month, his deputy $65, and recruits received $20, as well as covering all the cost of billeting and equipping the new force.[49] Renamo thus was entirely dependent on Rhodesian government funds, despite the best efforts of Cristina to secure independent financing; for example from the expatriate Portuguese community in South Africa.[50]

Initially, all the Renamo training officers were Portuguese-speaking instructors, including some who undoubtedly fought with the Portuguese army in Mozambique but, because of opposition by Matsangaissa and his followers to working under these former colonial masters, they were quickly replaced with a group of handpicked CIO instructors. This small team of four to five CIO officers (most of whom were former SAS operators) was headed by Major Dudley Coventry, who was himself a former commander of the SAS.[51] In addition, the former Rhodesian instructor says that this core training team was supplemented at times with four to six specialists drawn from local territorial soldiers and Portuguese-speaking members of the Rhodesian army.[52]

In keeping with Flower's vision of a small and controllable force, a typical training class consisted of 25–30 recruits. They were required to complete a program of extensive physical fitness training, marksmanship, guerrilla tactics, and field craft. The Renamo training manual not only provided detailed instruction on how best to lay ambushes, assault enemy bases, and conduct sabotage operations, but also emphasized the operational advantages of using "surprise, mobility, and speed" in guerrilla warfare.[53] This program of instruction normally took about three months, but "training lasted as long as it took to build a core of [platoon] leaders and [until] the troops could fire with some accuracy."[54] Overall the Rhodesians were pleased with the motivation of the Renamo recruits, who appeared quite eager to learn and quickly became quite skilled. Weapons and ammunition were provided by the police armory in Salisbury through Special Branch, but recruits were given their own distinctive uniform to make them uniquely recognizable and to build self-esteem and morale.[55] By September 1977 Renamo was able to put 76 fighters in the field, rising to 288 at the beginning of the new year and ultimately reaching 914 by the end of 1978.[56]

Once Renamo established its own bases inside Mozambique starting with the Gorongosa camp in September 1979, the Rhodesian military assumed a larger and more direct role in supporting the insurgents. Known as Operation Bumper, which last from September to December 1979, both the SAS and the air force provided critical support that allowed Renamo to move toward the path of self-sufficiency inside Mozambique. Using three to four-man SAS call signs that were rotated in and out of the country by air on a six week basis, the SAS helped the insurgents site their defenses, provided on-site training to new locally recruited men, served in an advisery role to the local Renamo commander (known as "Sunray" in Rhodesian military communications) and passed time-sensitive intelligence reports back to Odzi. (Joint operational aspects of this relationship will be discussed later on.)

The RhAF air component of Operation Bumper consisted of aging, but amazingly reliable, Dakota C-47 transport aircraft from No. 3 Squadron as well as helicopters from No. 7 (Alouette III) and No. 8 (Agusta Bell-205) Squadrons providing an air bridge between Rhodesia and Renamo bases inside Mozambique. The primary destination for most of these missions was the Gorongosa plateau, which rose conspicuously some 1,200 meters above the flat countryside and was located 180 kilometers from Umtali. Other occasional supply drops were made to Renamo's southern base in the Gogoi area, which lies opposite the Chipinga border district of Rhodesia. Despite having men and equipment stretched to the breaking point in the latter half of 1979, the men of the RhAF were able to mount an impressive logistics effort over the three-and-a-half-month life of the operation that delivered more than 50 metric tons of weapons, ammunition, food and other supplies to Renamo forces in Mozambique.[57] In an eight-day period alone (28 September to 5 October 1979) at the beginning of Bumper, Dakota pilots airdropped 13.7 metric tons of supplies to the Gorongosa base, according to Rhodesian Air Force documents.[58]

Standard operating procedure required one to three Dakotas or "Daks" as they were called, carrying up to 1,900 kilograms of cargo, flying the two hour and 40 minute round trip from Salisbury's New Sarum airbase to Gorongosa every seven to 15 days and about once a month to the smaller southern base near Gogoi. Helicopters, mostly operating out of the forward airfield at Grand Reef near Umtali, were used mainly to uplift the departing SAS call signs and collect the used cargo parachutes, as well as conduct the occasional emergency supply run or provide casualty evacuation. The drop zone at Gorongosa, known as Bumper North, was a small clearing on the plateau. It "was covered with woods and little streams; it reminded [one] of the description of the plateau in Conan Doyle's *The Lost World*."[59] It was flying that often challenged the skill and nerves of the Dak pilots, as John Fairey relates in his flight journal:

> We took off at 4.00 pm [on 12 October 1979] and had an uneventful flight to the Gorgongosa Plateau although the visibility was pretty poor. Unfortunately, to our dismay, we found that the top of the plateau was covered with a cap of cloud. I flew twice round the plateau and decided that, although I could see the occasional gap between the base of the cloud and the top of the plateau, it would be extremely dangerous to try to reach the DZ [drop zone]. However, [one pilot] disregarded my advice and had a go; [my co-pilot] and I watched him disappear into the cloud and held our breath while we waited for the fireball. Fortunately, it did not happen and we saw [the] Dakota pop out of the top of the cloud. He had not managed to drop [his supplies] but he claimed to have seen the DZ as he tried to maintain visual contact beneath a 100 foot cloud base; he did not make a second attempt.[60]

While the drop zone for Bumper South was not as majestic a venue as the Gorongosa plateau, it still required the complete attention of the Dak pilots.

John Fairey recounts that "on our way to and from the DZ we flew over Chipinga near the Cabora Bassa–South Africa power lines," to the make the drop in a valley. The DZ was not as obvious as that in Gorongosa: "I was not sure where it was. We relied on the SAS man [with a radio on the ground] for directions and when to start the drop."[61]

In addition to the often harsh flying conditions, Frelimo was becoming increasingly adept at setting up air ambushes. The Gorongosa drop zone was especially dangerous given its limited approach options with enemy small arms fire a frequent threat to the planes approaching at 500 feet. "I was the lead Dak," recalls one former Bumper pilot, "and thank goodness the ground gunners hadn't been trained in lead shooting—all the ack-ack round passed behind me. Not a round hit…but [the dispatcher in the back] was scared witless by the racket of the rounds cracking by the door."[62] Although the Dakotas were only occasionally fired on, the lower and slower flying helicopters were particularly vulnerable to mobile anti-aircraft columns using 37mm and 12.7mm weapons or 'Frelimo mobiles,' as they came to be known. Acting on reports of aircraft activity inbound into Mozambique, the Frelimo mobiles would try to position themselves along the expected return flight path in the hope of catching the aircraft returning to Rhodesia. This tactic apparently proved successful in downing an Alouette III on 17 October 1979. The aircraft was hit by ground fire and forced down in the Catandica area of Manica Province.[63] Two accompanying helicopters were able to recover the unhurt crew and passenger, but the damaged aircraft was deemed to be in an area too dangerous for recovery and had to be destroyed the next day from the air by Hunter strike fighter aircraft. The RhAF's postmortem analysis of the incident recommended that "routes do not be used more than once as tracing of [Frelimo] mobile movements is not always possible. It is considered, in light of above, that this mishap could only have been avoided by change of route."[64]

The fighting begins: Early operations, 1977–78

With the shift in Rhodesian war strategy, the Rhodesian high command or Combined Operations (ComOps) began a steady escalation of external military operations against ZANLA targets in Mozambique. First by deploying small teams of Selous Scouts and SAS troops and using air strikes to attack transiting guerrillas and their bases, but then eventually relying on larger-scale conventional incursions that grew in both frequency and size. At first the Rhodesians carefully avoided directly engaging the Mozambican army, but as the Zimbabwean guerrillas consciously sited their bases near *Forças Populares De Libertação De Moçambique* (Popular Forces for the Liberation of Mozambique) or FPLM positions, the two forces became increasingly intermingled. Thus, all military targets in Mozambique became fair game. In addition, the Rhodesian target list was expanded to include critical Mozambican economic infrastructure and lines of communications. Renamo's role in this strategy, according to Ken Flower, was "essentially to provide the opportunity for Rhodesia to deal with ZANLA in Mozambique without doing so directly, and to perpetuate or create instability in areas of Mozambique."[65]

It is safe to say that by the latter half of 1977, Commander André and his small band of men were conducting regular, yet very limited forays into Mozambique from their base at Odzi. "To start off with it was sabotage, to disrupt the population and disrupt the economy which really comes under sabotage, to come back with decent recruits at that stage and hit any Frelimo bases they came across. And if they came across ZANLA they were to take them on," said Coventry during a 1986 interview.[66] One early Renamo fighter remembers that the first CIO-trained soldiers were organized into two 15-man platoons with Matsangaissa directly commanding one platoon and his then deputy, Orlando Macomo, leading the other.[67] These units would be deployed for as short as a few weeks or up to 60 days inside Mozambique and while in the field each platoon would further break down into three five-man squads for operational purposes. Tactics were pretty simple and it was said that Matsangaissa would often initiate ambushes "by leaping to his feet, fully exposing himself with gun above head" at the start of Renamo attacks.[68] Although transported to the border by truck for infiltration into Mozambique, no Rhodesian forces accompanied the guerrillas on missions at this time and without radios (they only came into use after August 1979) the guerrillas were on their own.

All early Renamo operations were pre-planned by the CIO team and pre-operation briefs "were generally of very high standard; targets and time frames being important," according to a former CIO instructor.[69] Likewise, the returning Renamo teams would be debriefed by the CIO handlers concerning the location of ZANLA bases and movements; intelligence that was then shared with ComOps. In addition to intelligence gathering, the objective of many of these early missions was to disrupt ZANLA and FPLM supply lines in central Mozambique through the destruction of bridges, the mining of roads, and train derailments. Most early operations were conducted close to the Rhodesian frontier in the Catandica and Pungwe River basin areas and north of the Chimanimani salient in Manica Province. But by late 1978 Renamo guerrillas were ranging into Sofala Province and launching attacks along the Beira–Chimoio road and rail line, the Dondo–Inhaminga corridor, and south of Inchope.

Recruitment was another priority for Renamo in these early years and re-education camps were attractive targets, as they usually contained many imprisoned ex-Frelimo soldiers or political prisoners with strong personal grievances against the Machel government. With encouragement from the CIO, Matsangaissa implemented a rudimentary hearts and minds campaign among the peasantry of Manica and Sofala provinces by stoking the fires of opposition to Frelimo's policies of collectivization, communal villages, and the usurping of traditional authorities. Through the distribution of food, seeds, and consumer goods that were usually looted from government-run stores, the guerrillas sought to gain the trust of the people in areas where they operated. These efforts were largely successful. More important, by late 1978 Commander André was "finally given the green light [by the Rhodesians] to recruit as many people as he wanted to beef up his small guerrilla army"[70] and Renamo's ranks would swell quickly. The war was about to get a lot nastier.

The growing Matsangaissa mystique and Cristina's broadcasts served increasingly as a rallying point for anti-government sentiment. They also proved instrumental in the recruitment in July 1977 of a young Frelimo officer from Sofala Province—Afonso Dhlakama. Dhlakama, the son of a Shona-speaking Ndau traditional leader, was born in Mangunde, Chibabava

District, in the southern part of Sofala Province in 1953. He was educated by Catholic seminarians in Beira and later conscripted into the Portuguese colonial army, but deserted in 1972 to join Frelimo. During the independence struggle he served as a Frelimo commander in Niassa Province. In 1977 he was serving as a logistics officer in Beira prior to his defection to Rhodesia that July. As Dhlakama rose to prominence within Renamo, the Frelimo government claimed he had been cashiered from the army for corruption and misconduct, thus his fleeing to Rhodesia. Dhlakama has personally disputed these charges, claiming that "he felt discriminated against on ethnic grounds, and that he had even obtained the necessary travel documents" and he "could not have done this if he were guilty of misconduct."[71]

Matsangaissa apparently took an immediate liking to the short, bespectacled and bookish 24-year-old and within six months Dhlakama would become André's second in command. Much has been made by some observers of Dhlakama rapid rise and the related downfall and disappearance of Matsangaissa's previous deputy, Orlando Macomo.[72] While there is certainly a dark side to Renamo and its internal power struggles, the downfall of Macomo can more simply be traced to a failed mine laying operation that he led in August 1977. And his subsequent attempt to cover it up by lying to his Rhodesian instructors. Once the truth came out, however, Macomo was transferred to Salisbury by the CIO and never heard from again.[73] Meanwhile, after having proved himself in the field and gained Matsangaisa's confidence, Dhlakama would be named Renamo's new deputy commander by the end of the year.

Rather than wither under the dual threats of growing internal unrest and external military aggression, Machel dealt with the situation by tightening his party's grip on power and strengthening security ties with Moscow and the Eastern Bloc. At its Third Party Congress in February 1977, Frelimo transformed itself into a vanguard party of Marxist-Leninism; reactionaries, counter-revolutionaries, and internal dissenters were purged from the party. In March, Mozambique signed a Treaty of Friendship and Cooperation with the Soviet Union that included Moscow's pledge to assist Maputo in the event of a military attack on the country. With the help of several hundred Soviet and East European advisers, Mozambique began to speed up the process of transforming and re-equipping its military into a conventional force. Between 1977 and the end of 1978, the Soviet Union delivered hundreds of millions of dollars of military hardware, including 56 armored personnel carriers, 40 tanks (obsolete T-34/85s), anti-aircraft missiles (including high altitude SA-3s), 43 MiG-21 fighters, and numerous pieces of heavy artillery and anti-tank missiles, but very little in the way of useful counter-insurgency equipment.[74]

For Frelimo, Renamo activities paled in comparison to the growing intensity of Rhodesian cross-border attacks on itself and its Zimbabwean allies. Moreover, observed the renowned Mozambican historian Malyn Newitt, "since its founding in 1963, Frelimo had never been seriously challenged; dissident individuals and breakaway movements had all been isolated and withered for lack of support" and therefore "it was difficult for Frelimo's leaders even to be seen to be taking seriously a phenomenon like Renamo."[75] Thus, not surprisingly the government simply referred to Renamo guerrillas as "*bandidos armados*" (armed bandits). They were nothing more than common thieves and criminals acting as surrogates for the white minority governments and could be easily dismissed. As Machel apparently saw it, the best way to bring an end to the Rhodesian and South African threat to his country was to bring about the liberation of Zimbabwe (and eventually South Africa) by remaining steadfast in his support for Mugabe while at the same time increasing the potential cost of armed aggression by beefing up his military forces.

1979: The turning point that never was

In hindsight 1979 was a significant watershed for both Frelimo and Renamo. It was a decisive opportunity to change the course of the war, yet both sides failed to capitalize on unfolding events, or seize the initiative to shape future events to their advantage. For up until now Rhodesian security forces had carried the burden of destabilizing Mozambique through external operations in the course of their battle with ZANLA forces, and although the Renamo insurgency was slowly gaining support and growing in size, it comprised less than 1,000 men at the start of the year.[76] This would all change in the final half of the year with the establishment of permanent Renamo bases inside Mozambique that would set the insurgents on the path toward self-sufficiency, a more than doubling in the size of the guerrilla force, along with a widening in the number and scope of Renamo operations; and the opening round of South Africa's entry into the conflict. Clearly Renamo was on the rise.

Nonetheless, this period would also witness a leadership crisis within the insurgency following the untimely death of Matsangaissa; mark the ending of Rhodesian military assistance with the signing of the Lancaster House ceasefire and peace agreement opening the way for Zimbabwean independence; and see Frelimo's tentative moves toward regaining the battlefield initiative over Renamo. Clearly Frelimo was on the rise. However, neither side would be able to take advantage of their opportunities to gain the upper hand and thus the war would continue to drag on for another 13 years.

Several key political events inside Rhodesia led off 1979, with Smith and his Rhodesian Front party leading a successful referendum campaign in January on moving toward black majority rule. The referendum and subsequent elections in April were the core part of Smith's internal settlement strategy that was designed to undercut domestic support for Mugabe and Nkomo's nationalist guerrilla forces. By May the "new nation" of Zimbabwe-Rhodesia was in place with Abel Muzorewa serving as head of government, but security forces still remained staunchly under white control. The move proved to be an abysmal failure, neither achieving the international recognition, the lifting of sanctions as Smith had hoped nor in diminishing domestic support for ZANU and ZAPU.

Up to this time Renamo guerrillas had been largely been operating on their own inside Mozambique, albeit with extensive Rhodesian logistical support and operational guidance from the CIO. However, with ComOps deciding to adopt a more offensive strategy—highlighted by escalating cross-border operations into neighboring states—the SAS assumed a more hands on approach with Renamo. Flower's previous focus on intelligence collection, harassing actions, and cultivating long-term opposition to Frelimo quickly became subsumed by the larger and more immediate need of the

Rhodesian high command to ensure their country's very survival. This change in operational strategy was reflected clearly in a top secret document entitled, *Short-Term Strategy for Mozambique, 23 March to 23 July 1979*, which would guide future Renamo operations. According to this document, three of the six enumerated tasks were: to create the maximum desirable state of instability in Mozambique; to give the maximum possible support to any non-communist anti-Frelimo group; to minimize the Frelimo government's support to ZANLA and its opposition to the newly elected Muzorewa government.[77] And in Renamo, the Rhodesians had the perfect tool that was ready, willing and able.

Beginning in January, joint Renamo–SAS operations would increasingly become the norm, although both organizations still continued to operate independently of each other too. In addition to serving as operational planners, advisers and specialized trainers (in explosives and demolition for example) , small SAS call signs of three to four men would now be regularly accompanying Renamo forces, armed with AK-47s, RPG-7s, 60mm or 82mm mortars, and anti-vehicle mines on deep-penetration missions into Mozambique. Once Renamo established permanent bases inside Mozambique, larger size SAS call signs would routinely be deployed to these bases for periods of up to six weeks. Given the huge demand late in the Rhodesian war for SAS operators (not only in Mozambique but also in Zambia and Botswana) there were never enough personnel to go around and the SAS commander, Lieutenant-Colonel Garth Barrett, was never able to deploy more than two dozen men with Renamo at any one time.[78] Nonetheless, the SAS presence was felt well out of proportion to its numbers, because not only did the teams provide expertise and boost morale and confidence among the young guerrilla fighters, but they also gave Renamo units direct radio communications with Odzi for the first time. Prior to this, messages were hand-carried, which often negated their timeliness and intelligence value.

This new partnership proved immediately fruitful. In January a joint force attacked and destroyed the Mavuze hydro-electric power station at the Chicamba Real Dam 42 kilometers east of Umtali. This was followed by the high-profile sabotage of Beira's fuel storage depot on 23 March.[79] Both operations resulted in serious damage to Mozambique's economy at a time it could ill-afford it. Likewise, ZANLA's lines of communication and its logistics network increasingly became high priority targets—second only to ZANLA guerrilla camps—for the SAS and Renamo in 1979. Across central Mozambique key bridges were targeted for destruction, interdiction efforts against road, rail, and telecommunications was stepped up, and enemy supply bases sought out for destruction. The Tete–Mutarara rail line north of the Zambezi River was sabotaged in April by Renamo forces.

Meanwhile, other joint units were steadily advancing into new parts of southwest Manica Province. Here they attacked and seized the town of Machaze, just 50 kilometers north of the Save River in July. 'A' Squadron SAS and Renamo call signs were particularly active in and around the Chimoio area in late July conducting interdiction missions as part of Operation Blanket, and often found themselves playing cat and mouse games with heavily-armed FPLM units, according to SAS situation reports. One call sign came under such heavy small arms fire that it was forced to call for a hot extraction shortly after landing.[80] Another joint SAS–Renamo team, however, was successful on 26 July in attacking traffic along the road south of Inchope; ambushing a FPLM Land Cruiser with an RPG-7 and small arms that left seven dead, including what appeared to be three East German advisers.[81]

In the waning months of 1979, as Rhodesia fought for its life, military activity in Manica and Sofala provinces would spike sharply, turning most of central Mozambique into a ragging war zone. Several factors accounted for this intensification of the conflict. First, in late August Renamo began the long-anticipated process of establishing permanent bases inside Mozambique, which would permit them to conduct larger and more sustained operations. Second, given the failure to obtain international acceptance of the Muzorewa government and the lifting of sanctions, previous political constraints on direct cross-border military action by the Rhodesian military all but evaporated. Further reinforcing this trend was the rise of former South African Defence Minister P. W. Botha to the presidency of South Africa in September. Under President Botha's leadership, Pretoria abandoned any pretense of détente with black Africa and began implementing an aggressive strategy to combat the 'total onslaught' it saw coming its way. Thus, as we shall see, both direct and indirect South Africa military assistance to Salisbury increased markedly in the last four months of the year. Third, ComOps' partial implementation of Operation Manacle—designed to unleash a crippling blow on the entire Mozambican economy and once and for all end Machel's support to Mugabe and ZANLA forces—came into effect.[82] Finally, the start of the Lancaster House peace talks in London commenced on 10 September, put pressure on both Salisbury and the Zimbabwe nationalist forces to gain an advantage on the battlefield to strengthen their position at the negotiating table.

The move to Gorgongosa

The long planned move by Renamo to permanent bases inside Mozambique finally began to take place at the end of August and by 5 September, Matsangaissa and a 300-man battalion accompanied by a small group of SAS under the command of Lieutenant Charlie Buchan arrived in the Gorongosa region from Odzi.[83] Here he divided his force into three 100-man strong companies. One company stayed with Matsangaissa setting up the central base up on the mountain itself, while another was deployed southwest of the mountain and the third company was positioned to the east of the mountain in the Gravata area. Meanwhile another 300-man battalion moved to establish its presence in Manica Province just northwest of the Chimanimani Mountains in the Mussupa–Revué river basin region in early October. This shift to operational bases inside Mozambique, as well as the new priority of targeting Mozambican infrastructure and ZANLA lines of communication by the Rhodesians had an immediate impact on the scope and nature of Renamo operations. Buoyed by an influx of manpower Renamo, now numbering several thousand men, rapidly expanded its presence throughout Manica and Sofala provinces. The northern operational area ran all the way from the Pungwe–Vanduzi river basin north of the main Umtali–Chimoio road eastward through the Gorongosa region to Inhaminga and up northwesterly to Marringue–Macossa area. While the southern operational area stretched from between the Revué and the Buzi rivers, across into the Chibabava region of western Sofala Province.

Renamo's mining of roads and the laying of ambushes, combined with the nearly constant threat of air attack by armed RhAF Reims-Cessna F-337 reconnaissance flights or Hunter strike aircraft, made road travel along routes leading to and from the main Beira–Chimoio road increasingly dangerous for Frelimo forces and Zimbabwean guerrillas. In southern Manica, the Chimoio–Dombe–Espungabera road was cut repeatedly by insurgent activity, and by early October the FPLM garrison at Espungabera became increasingly isolated. To counter this heightened activity FPLM and ZANLA were compelled to begin operating in much larger and more heavily-armed units of up to 200–300 men. It was not uncommon for joint FPLM–ZANLA forces in pursuit of Renamo guerrillas to be equipped with armored vehicles (including tanks) and anti-aircraft weapons.

In addition to their combat activities, the insurgents attempted to gain the trust of the *povo* (the masses) and win them over to their cause. Matsangaissa was especially careful not to have his men become a burden on the already impoverished peasantry and set out to make Renamo's new bases self-sufficient. With the help of Operation Bumper supply flights, large quantities of food, seeds, and farming implements were airdropped into Gorongosa for use by the guerrillas and the local population. Recruitment remained a priority too, and shortly after establishing Renamo's presence in the Gorongosa region, Commander André personally lead a company of 30 men on another raid against the Sacuze re-education camp in early April. According to a former Renamo combatant, Matsangaissa took 15 men and attacked the barracks while the second group of 15 fighters freed the prisoners: "many, many people were freed; over 200."[84] Most of those liberated joined Renamo right there on the spot. A large group set off to Odzi for training, but some opted to accompany André and his men back to the Gorongosa base. Before departing, however, the attacking force and the former inmates laid waste to the camp: "we tore, really, tore it apart."[85] A Renamo communique claimed 16 FPLM soldiers were killed in the attack and a large number of weapons and other war matériel captured.[86]

Salisbury also sought to use the growing insurgency to pressure the Machel government just as the Lancaster House peace talks got underway.

Several high-profile sabotage incidents in and around Beira were launched in September. On the 12th, a Renamo unit with SAS support set off to destroy Frelimo's vital tropospheric scatter station set high up on Mt. Xilvuo, 110 kilometers west of Beira near the provincial boundary between Manica and Sofala provinces, according to a former Renamo fighter. [87] The Mt. Xilvuo communications center "was part of a communications chain linking major Frelimo bases around the country" and "cutting that chain would not only seriously disrupt Frelimo communications, it would also force them to switch ... to a system which was far easier for the Rhodesians to intercept."[88] The guerrillas were able to penetrate the FPLM defenses and seriously damage the installation, putting it out of service for some time. After a narrow escape from pursuing FPLM forces, the SAS support team was extracted by AB-205 helicopters (known as Cheetahs). Less than a week later, on 18 September, a joint SAS–South African recce team conducted a seaborne infiltration of Beira harbor, sinking two dredgers, but attacks on the main telephone exchange and a ZANLA arms warehouse had to be abandoned at the last moment. Nonetheless, with the loss of two of the harbor's three dredgers, the harbor began to silt up quickly, increasing shipping cost and negatively impacting revenues. Moreover, the sabotage team had taken care to spread Renamo leaflets along the way and thus Renamo was able to claim credit for the bold attack.[89]

Even as Renamo and the SAS stepped up guerrilla warfare in central Mozambique, ComOps was adding to Machel's and Mugabe's worries by launching Operation Miracle, a major assault against ZANLA's New Chimoio (or Chimoio Circle) base located a mere 50 kilometers northeast of Umtali from 29 September to 6 October. (Following the deadly Rhodesian assault on its old headquarters at 'New Farm' in the Vanduzi–Chimoio area during Operation Dingo in November 1977, at Frelimo's urging ZANLA had moved and dispersed its main base away from the more populated areas of Chimoio to this new location.) Although not involved in the attack itself, small Renamo teams working with SAS call signs from 'A' Squadron conducted intelligence gathering and reconnaissance on the base in the weeks leading up to the operation. What they and air reconnaissance helped uncover was a huge complex of at least five camps spread across some 64 square kilometers. Dominating the terrain was a large granite hill, nicknamed 'Monte Cassino' by the Rhodesians. The Soviet-designed defenses on Monte Cassino and other surrounding high ground included numerous gun emplacements, anti-aircraft positions, and an extensive network of well-concealed bunkers and interconnecting slit trenches.[90] The camp was believed to contain several thousand ZANLA guerrillas and trainees.

Given the size of the base and the nature of its defenses, a complex assault plan was devised. It would require mobilizing a powerful 320-man flying column equipped with Eland armored cars supported by a half dozen World War II-vintage 25-pounder artillery guns and working in conjunction with an air mobile force of Rhodesian Light Infantry (RLI) troopers and SAS commandos. The assault would be preceded by extensive air strikes from Canberra bombers and Hunters.[91] Weather delays, poor air visibility, and deployment and coordination problems hindered the operation from the start. Unexpected heavy resistance, especially from atop Monte Cassino, allowed ZANLA forces to make a fairly orderly withdrawal by day three of the battle. While the Rhodesians destroyed and captured large amounts of equipment, they inflicted only light casualties on the Zimbabwean guerrillas. FPLM also lost several armored cars and an unknown number of troops to air strikes when it tried to mount a counterattack in the latter days of the operation. For such meager results the cost was high. Five RhAF officers killed and three desperately needed aircraft lost in a single operation; a Canberra and a Hunter in fending off a FPLM counterattack on day five, as well as an Alouette III lost while taking part in a diversionary operation.[92]

Even after taking a severe pounding at the hands of the Rhodesians from Tete to Gaza provinces in the first nine months of 1979, Machel and Frelimo remained unbroken. Although still unable to prevent cross-border raids, the steady influx of Soviet weaponry gave Frelimo the growing capability to make Salisbury pay an increasingly high price for its cross-border forays. The days of external operations being a cake walk were over. Likewise Mugabe's forces had suffered thousands of casualties, but he and his field commanders continued to push thousands more across the border into Zimbabwe-Rhodesia on a monthly basis. By early October Rhodesian intelligence estimates put the number of ZANLA fighters inside the country as approaching 8,000 with probably another 10,000 undergoing training in Mozambique (not including several thousand trained guerrillas held in reserve).[93] The signal was clear—ZANLA was winning the battle of attrition.

The death of Matsangaissa: "Your Sunray got it"

On 17 October 1979 disaster struck for Renamo when the charismatic leader and the heart and soul of the insurgency, André Matsangaissa, was killed in battle. That much is certain. There are, however, almost as many accounts of the details surrounding his death and the subsequent rise of Afonso Dhlakama as there have been writers on the subject of Renamo.[94] To add to the confusion, nearly all of them contain some elements of the truth. Much of the underlying cause of these conflicting stories can be attributed to both pro-Renamo and pro-Frelimo sources that sought to use Matsangaissa's death as a way to rally their respective supporters during the war. The account presented here is one pieced together from multiple sources thought to be the most reliable, including some with direct knowledge of the events of October 1979.

As has been noted previously, Renamo fighters were extremely active in and around the Gorongosa region since the establishment of their main base atop Gorongosa mountain in early September. For defensive reasons, a 90-man Renamo company was positioned at the bottom of the mountain in the M'sucossa area. Just to the south lay the fortified FPLM garrison at Gorongosa town (formerly Vila Paiva de Andrada) some 65 kilometers north of the main Beira–Chimoio road. The roughly 400-man FPLM garrison was a particular target of Renamo's attention; roads were mined, raids on outlying outposts launched, and the threat of ambushes ever present. Apparently in response to this harassment, Frelimo mounted a retaliatory operation against Renamo positions north of Gorongosa in mid-October. Despite the guerrillas putting up a strong initial resistance they began to run low on ammunition and the attacking FPLM force was able to gain the upper hand and overrun the Renamo position. Upon hearing of the deteriorating situation, Commander André grabbed about a dozen men from the main camp and all the ammunition they could carry and "charged down from the mountain" with a SAS call sign in pursuit to rally his beleaguered forces, according to a former Renamo guerrilla fighter.[95] The Matsangaissa-led counterattack was successful in recapturing the old Renamo position and routing the weary FPLM troops. After pursuing the fleeing enemy to the outskirts of Gorongosa town itself, André paused to consider his next move (and likely to regroup his forces) when he and a group of his men were attacked by fresh FPLM troops. André was shot and "killed with a bullet to the head."[96] The SAS team immediately called for a RhAF casevac mission, but it was too late and the resulting fighting too intense to recover the body. Their message to Odzi: "Your Sunray [Renamo commander] got it."[97]

Upon hearing the devastating news, the CIO quickly dispatched Renamo's deputy commander, Afonso Dhlakama (who happened to be back at Odzi), by helicopter to the Gorongosa mountain camp to try to regain control of the situation. Although long acknowledged as the logical successor to Matsangaissa since his appointment as deputy commander in late 1977 and his battlefield experience, Dhlakama lacked the natural charisma and daring of Commander André and was viewed as somewhat bookish and more calculating by the Renamo rank and file. His reputation among some of the CIO instructors was also poor: "I thought he was a weak character," said Coventry years later.[98] Other instructors, including Danny Hartman, thought more highly of Dhlakama, who "was both highly intelligent and a natural leader" with the potential to lead a broader political movement.[99] Nonetheless, from the very beginning "Dhlakama felt he needed to assert his new position among some of Matsangaissa's closest commanders before he could consolidate his leadership," according to Cabrita.[100]

Even some six weeks after taking command the state of affairs remained dicey for Renamo's new leader. The SAS, reporting in early December, indicated that, "MNR Commander C4 [Gorongosa] told C/S 12 [the eight-man 'A' Squadron call sign at Gorongosa] that three minor commanders are planning to assinate [sic.] him and request that the three be uplifted and that general situation is serious."[101] SAS headquarters was not moved. Urging a tough love approach and informing the SAS team that "uplift will not take place and [the] leader has to sort out own problems." So not only did Dhlakama have to deal with a series of FPLM operations to dislodge him and his men from their Gorongosa mountain base in the waning months of the year, but he also had to quell a potential rebellion among disgruntled guerrilla commanders. The undercurrents of this discontent would ripple through the Renamo ranks for some time until finally resolved in late 1980.

Time running out

The last few months of 1979 saw some of the most intense fighting so far across Zimbabwe-Rhodesia, Zambia and Mozambique as the Rhodesian war neared its climax. While the politicians at Lancaster House argued over the terms of a peace settlement in London, their respective militaries attempted to deliver the coup de grâce to the enemy. While ZANLA sought to push as many guerrillas (supplemented by FPLM regulars) as they could into the Rhodesian countryside and ZIPRA prepared for a conventional thrust across the Zambian frontier to Salisbury, ComOps finalized details for Operation Manacle to cripple the Mozambican economy. Given the growing urgency of addressing the developing threat posed by ZIPRA's Soviet-equipped battalions of armored cars and tanks, the Rhodesian military turned its focus to Zambia, launching three major operations in a 45-day period. Lacking the manpower and matériel to unleash the same level of destruction on Mozambique, ComOps instead relied on the SAS and its Renamo partners to deliver the knockout blow in Mozambique and bring Frelimo to its knees.

Despite intense FPLM pressure on its Gorongosa stronghold following Matsangaissa's death, Renamo guerrillas remained on the offensive throughout much of November and December. And although Frelimo forces were able to root out the insurgents from a number of their positions in the Gorongosa region during this time, they were unable to destroy Dhlakama's forces or capture Renamo's central base despite public claims to the contrary.[102] The underlying reason for this (and subsequent failures in the months and years ahead) could be found in FPLM's changed makeup. Machel's rational need to build a new conventional military capable of at least bloodying Rhodesian and potential South African cross-border raids left him with a military that was ill-structured, improperly equipped, and poorly trained to conduct counter-insurgency warfare. The lightly-armed, but highly mobile and aggressive FPLM that had effectively fought the Portuguese, had been transformed by 1979 into a large, unwieldy and heavily-equipped, Communist-trained military force. While FPLM units fitted out with armored personnel carriers, heavy artillery, anti-aircraft missiles, and even tanks were making life increasingly dangerous and costly for Rhodesian cross-border operations, these units were also proving themselves incapable of hunting down Renamo guerrillas and their SAS partners, who were wreaking havoc on Frelimo and ZANLA logistics and lines of communication. When faced with overwhelming enemy numbers, Renamo fighters would simply melt away into the bush to live to fight another day.

Behind all the chaos was Flower's grand plan to isolate most of Tete Province and the city of Beira from the rest of the country south of the Save River by continually pushing Renamo bases and operations eastward toward the coast.[103] By early November, SAS teams and the Rhodesian Air Force had successfully destroyed or severely damaged all major bridges over the Zambezi River in the Tete–Moatize area, as well as damaged the critical Sena railroad bridge down river. Renamo units meanwhile attacked the important rail and road center at Inhaminga, northwest of Gorongosa, and cut road and telephone communications between Catandica and Vanduzi in northern Manica. In the southern operational zone, Lucas Mulhanga (also known as Lucas Mhlanga) with a 300-man battalion established a new base on the Sitatonga Mountain. Lying at the southern end of the Chimanimani salient overlooking the Lucite River it became the jumping off point for Renamo companies advancing southeasterly toward the Save River and the main Beira–Maputo road. By December, Renamo had deployed nearly two battalions (some 500–600 men) into the northern operational zone centered on Gorongosa and nearly another three additional battalions (about 800 men) into the southern operational zone.[104] Renamo was now active in about three-fourths of Manica and Sofala provinces.

Not only did the scope of Renamo operations rise dramatically in

November and December, but the complexity of its operations increased as well. To counter-balance the larger and more heavily-armed FPLM units now engaging the guerrillas, it became increasingly common place for SAS and Renamo units to call on the Rhodesian Air Force for help. Loitering Lynx armed reconnaissance or Hunter strike aircraft were regularly used to break up concentrations of threatening enemy forces. During one mid-November probe into Renamo territory, south of Dombe in western Manica, for example, a large 550-man joint FPLM–ZANLA force was posing such a threat. The Renamo commander on the scene requested an air strike on the column; Rhodesian Air Headquarters replied that it would "send Hunters on [a] seek and destroy mission."[105] An improved and highly effective radio communication network also allowed senior Renamo commanders to concentrate their dispersed forces quickly for specific operations. This was demonstrated in an early December attack on the heavily defended Buzi and Revué river bridges by the SAS and a 350-strong Renamo force.[106]

This period also saw the foreshadowing of a new kind of violence, with the Mozambican press reporting that, on 1 December, Renamo guerrillas carried out a vengeance raid on the border town of Espungabera, killing and decapitating Frelimo officials and then impaling their heads on stakes.

Renamo was also coming of age as a military force by demonstrating its capability to conduct large-scale operations on its own. This was the case in Operation Arrow, its 7 December attack on ZANLA's Toronga training camp in southwestern Sofala. The camp and an associated FPLM position were discovered earlier in the month about 20 kilometers south of the Buzi–Lucite river junction in the Chiboma area. Subsequent reconnaissance revealed it to contain several thousand Zimbabwean recruits, but that "many wanted to return [home] to Zimbabwe-Rhodesia."[107] It was initially thought that Renamo might be able to evacuate the camp without attacking it directly given the discontent among the recruits and a lightly-armed ZANLA force. The presence of at least one FPLM company near the camp and the apparent fear of discovery, however, forced the guerrillas to abandon this idea. The attack went ahead as planned that morning with some 60 Renamo soldiers assaulting the FPLM position, while an additional 50–60 guerrillas struck the camp itself. Much to their surprise the Renamo attackers encountered heavier than expected resistance from bunkers and trenches, as well as from the FPLM force apparently armed with 14.5mm heavy machine guns and 82mm mortars. After nearly three hours of fighting the camp was eventually overrun, leaving an unknown number of ZANLA and FPLM soldiers dead, Renamo capturing considerable amounts of equipment and supplies, and freeing some 100 Zimbabweans wishing to return home. After a week-long trek back to the border, 60 of this group would reach the Chipinga area of Zimbabwe-Rhodesia.[108]

Even under this blistering military campaign, Machel remained defiant, knowing the end of the Rhodesian conflict was fast approaching and confident in the resilience of his military to weather the storm. Although tacitly acknowledging the unlikelihood of being able to wipe out Renamo completely, given its Rhodesian support, Frelimo did not opt to remain passively on the defense. Soviet and Eastern Bloc weapons continued to flow into the country and FPLM forces mounted numerous search and destroy operations to keep Renamo off-balance and maintain pressure on the insurgents' Mozambican bases.

On several occasions Frelimo infantry were operating so close to the main Gorongosa drop zone that Cheetah helicopters ferrying in SAS call signs took ground fire, and a 6 November Dakota resupply flight was forced to abort due to the presence of enemy troops in the area. By mid-December FPLM beefed up its presence in Gorongosa town to 400 men and deployed an additional company, reinforced with tanks dug-in just to the west of the mountain. Dhlakama saw this "as the beginning of a squeeze" on his headquarters.[109] With SAS assistance Renamo fighters, however, were subsequently able to ease the pressure by overrunning the new FPLM company position on 30 December and in the process capturing huge quantities of ammunition, supplies, and food, including 75,000 rounds of 7.62 ammunition, 225 RPG-7 rockets, 200 82mm mortar bombs, 1,800 rounds of 14.5mm ammo, tents and blankets, canned food, and even 25 head of cattle.[110] According to intercepted FPLM communications, Frelimo mobiles equipped with 37mm anti-aircraft guns were also extremely active—although apparently unsuccessfully—in conducting air ambush operations in the Vanduzi–Catandica area of Manica Province in the latter half of December.[111] Meanwhile in the southern operational zone, FPLM maintained a heavy mechanized presence along the Dombe–Espungabera road to counter the Renamo encirclement of its Espungabera border post and hinder movement in and out of Zimbabwe-Rhodesia. Here too, low-flying Rhodesian aircraft were sought out; one flight of two Cheetahs was shot at by FPLM forces armed with RPG-7s but not damaged in the Chimanimani–Espungabera area on the 21st.[112]

And then it was over. On 21 December 1979 all the warring parties to the Rhodesian conflict formally signed the Lancaster House peace agreement that ended seven years of intense bloodshed. A ceasefire was to take hold on the 28th and elections to be held in early 1980. Of more direct impact on the fighting inside Mozambique was the message sent out from ComOps that same day. It read, "With immediate effect all external calls signs are to be withdrawn from Mozambique, Botswana, and Zambia immediately."[113] Although not unexpected, the actual announcement probably came as a severe shock to SAS call signs on the ground in Mozambique, and even more so to Renamo fighters whose fate was now uncertain. They needn't have worried. For only one day later, ComOps sent another highly sensitive message to SAS headquarters that ordered the continuation of Operation Bumper. It included the warning that, "it is stressed that a compromise of Operation Bumper could have the most serious and far-reaching effects on the cease fire" and "each cross border sortie must be planned in absolute detail to ensure minimum risks of confirmed detection."[114] The war in Mozambique would go on.

Assessment

In a mere three and a half years the political, economic, and security landscape of Mozambique had been changed by a movement, starting out as nothing more than a radio station on foreign soil effectively fanning the flames of anti-Frelimo sentiment and regionalism, that transformed itself into a potent military force of nearly 3,000 well-trained guerrilla fighters. While it is undeniable that the embattled minority regime in Rhodesia provided the means, support, and guidance that allowed Renamo to evolve as quickly as it did, the insurgency's roots were nevertheless Mozambican. It would take another seven years before Frelimo reluctantly began to acknowledge that the insurgency sprang from genuine historical factors and specific political grievances. In the meantime, Mozambicans would find themselves caught up in the cross-currents of the regional struggle against apartheid, and of the Cold War confrontation in Africa. Both these factors would be critical in fueling the evolution of the Frelimo–Renamo war.

On the battlefield Renamo had proven itself an effective guerrilla force. It had survived some difficult times—including the death of André Matsangaissa—to become a serious challenge to Frelimo. And in spite of its tainted founding, it was able to rally a degree of popular support and exploit the legacy of Frelimo founder Eduardo Mondlane by challenging unpopular and misguided government policies and what many saw as an elitist leadership. Without Rhodesian sanctuary and the accompanying training and equipment, as well as direct battlefield assistance, Renamo would almost certainly not have become the military threat that it posed by the end of 1979. More likely, rural discontent and anti-government sentiment in central Mozambique would have manifest itself, as but a series of disjointed populist rebellions led by charismatic leaders in keeping with Mozambican history. Punitive Frelimo military campaigns would probably have kept the lid on the situation, but domestic grievances would continue to simmer until some form of political accommodation was reached.

For its part, Frelimo had shown enormous resilience in the face of fierce external aggression and a growing domestic threat. Machel's unwavering commitment to Mugabe and the liberation of Zimbabwe in the face of the Rhodesian–Renamo onslaught was both a strength and a weakness. While it enabled him to pressure Mugabe into negotiating an end to the Rhodesian war and thus severing Renamo's foreign lifeline, it also caused Machel and the Frelimo leadership to misjudge the depth of domestic discontent that gave rise to the Matsangaissas and Dhlakamas of Mozambique, and seriousness that this unrest posed to Frelimo's continued rule. The FPLM took a severe beating from 1977 to 1979, finding itself overwhelmed with the Herculean task of fending off the Rhodesian military while at the same time addressing the mounting Renamo insurgency. In the end, it did neither one well. It did, however, survive and gain valuable experience.

The prospect of Zimbabwean independence was surely a source of optimism and relief for Machel and Frelimo, just as it was a time of uncertainty and fear for Dhlakama and Renamo. Neither side though could have anticipated how dramatically events would play out in the coming years. Nor could they clearly comprehend the opportunities to end the conflict they had missed. Instead the costly war would drag on for another dozen years, at even greater cost to the Mozambican people.

CHAPTER FOUR
PUNCH AND COUNTERPUNCH

The imminent independence of Zimbabwe promised not only to alter the political and security landscape of that country, but of the entire region too. In early 1980, however, nothing was assured. The Lancaster House ceasefire was holding. Nearly 18,000 Zimbabwean guerrillas were at internal assembly points awaiting the arrival of Lord Soames and 850 Commonwealth peacekeepers to oversee the transition, and elections were scheduled. Change was definitely coming, but exactly what type of change was the momentous question that all were waiting to have answered. From the Zimbabwean guerrilla forces to the Rhodesian military and from would-be political leaders of all stripes to the increasingly isolated apartheid government in Pretoria, everyone was holding their collective breath. None more so than the Renamo leadership.

The 4 March 1980 election provided the definitive answer. To the surprise of many—including the CIO and the Rhodesian military leadership—Robert Mugabe and his ZANU party won a majority of the vote. Rhodesians worst fears were becoming reality. Even more astonishing to combat-hardened Rhodesian soldiers the results were allowed to stand. Independence was set for 20 April 1980 with the swearing in of 'that Communist terrorist' Mugabe as the first prime minister of the new nation of Zimbabwe. Renamo and Dhlakama knew they were in serious trouble. Things were even more somber across the Limpopo River in neighboring South Africa. Pretoria's nightmarish vision of a Communist-inspired, African nationalist wave sweeping its way into the heartland of apartheid was now on the verge of becoming true. It was time for President P. W. Botha to circle the wagons and fortify the laager against this onslaught.

Over the next two years Frelimo and Renamo would witness new highs and new lows as the tide of war in Mozambique ebbed back and forth. Finally free of the Rhodesian menace, Frelimo was able to turn its full attention toward Renamo and inflict several serious defeats on Dhlakama's forces. But Machel's hopes of Zimbabwean independence immediately inflicting a mortal blow to

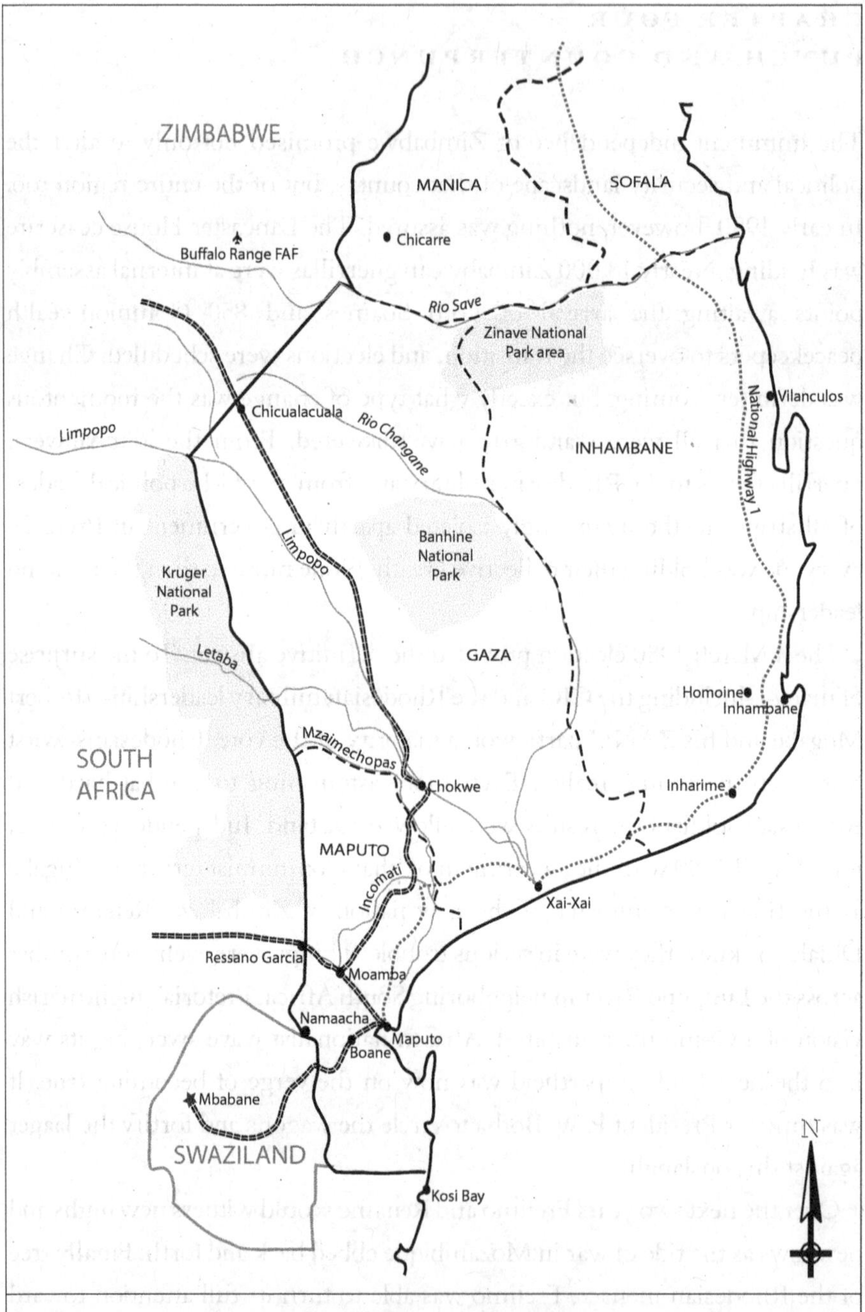

Map 4: Southern Region

the 'armed bandits' were dashed when South African military intelligence gladly inherited the CIO's operation "lock, stock, and barrel."[115] Rhodesian destabilization had been replaced by South African destabilization. Renamo for its part would be forced to weather internal dissension and external pressure, but ultimately would bounce back to become an ever a greater threat to Frelimo rule in the years ahead.

A new year: New hopes, new fears

December 1979 was proving to be a busy month indeed for Renamo and its Rhodesian allies. Even amid stepped-up combat operations in central Mozambique, joint contingency planning was underway to provide Renamo forces a golden handshake of supplies and weaponry and to formulate a post-Rhodesian strategy for the movement should a peace agreement be reached at Lancaster House. Although undoubtedly reassured that everything would turn out fine in the end, Renamo, the CIO, and the SAS decided to hedge their bets going into 1980.

As part of an effort to arm twist the warring parties into agreement at Lancaster House, British Foreign Secretary Lord Carrington announced his intention to dispatch Lord Soames to Zimbabwe-Rhodesia and have him installed as the new British governor on 12 December.[116] Not only did this move help break the log jam in London, but it energized SAS handlers of Operation Bumper to act. In a message from 'A' Squadron to SAS headquarters on 9 December it was urged "to resupply MNR [Renamo] with large quantities of supplies in view of Governor's arrival ASP. What about C-130s."[117] In less than a week, the orders went out: "Major re-supply planned for 161800B [16 December at 1800 hours] using two large aircraft [almost certainly South African C-130s[118]] each carrying approx 9,000 kg freight. One aircraft to Northern DZ [Gorongosa] and one to Southern DZ [Sitatonga area] simultaneously."[119]

Shortly thereafter, Dhlakama and two other senior Renamo commanders were flown from their Gorongosa base by Cheetah helicopter to Odzi, as was as Lucas "Luke" Mhlanga from the southern operational zone headquarters at Sitatonga, for a planning conference. Although there appears to be no written record of these discussions, subsequent accounts reveal the existence of a secret agreement between top Rhodesian and South African military officers. This gentlemen's agreement allowed for the transfer to South Africa of so-called compromised units (such as the Selous Scouts and Renamo), which the Rhodesians feared would be subject to reprisals in the event of Zimbabwe-Rhodesia's collapse.[120] This contingency, as well as operational planning in the event of a Rhodesian ceasefire was most likely discussed at this four-day conference.

Meanwhile, fighting between Frelimo and Renamo (with some apparent covert SAS assistance) kept up throughout the early months of 1980 despite the ceasefire taking hold in neighboring Zimbabwe-Rhodesia on 28 December. Frelimo was especially anxious to regain control over central Mozambique and dislodge the insurgents once and for all from their main Gorongosa base. In January it launched an offensive designed to do just that. The Soviet-planned operation called for leading elements of the 4th and 5th brigades to sweep east to west from the Dondo–Inhaminga road/rail line in eastern Sofala Province toward the Gorongosa massif, while 3rd Brigade troops moved northward along the Inchope road axis toward the mountain. At the same time other FPLM units would try to seal the area to the west of the objective to prevent Renamo fleeing in that direction. In total the FPLM probably committed some 7,500 troops, including motorized infantry backed with heavy artillery and armored vehicles, to the effort.

Before moving westward from the Dondo–Inhaminga sweep line, two battalions from the 5th Brigade were tasked with destroying the Renamo base near the town of Inhaminga. According to a former Frelimo soldier, a reconnaissance team discovered that Renamo was present in some strength, so the decision was made to shell the base with artillery prior to launching the late afternoon infantry assault.[121] Following the bombardment, the battalions moved in from two different directions and quickly overran the camp with little resistance from the guerrillas. "Renamo had so many casualties," he claimed, because of the unexpected use of heavy artillery by the attacking FPLM force. The following day, the 5th Brigade regrouped and began its move westward across difficult terrain toward Gorongosa National Park on the east side of the mountain. Poor-quality dirt tracks and seasonal rains quickly turned the advance into a slough through the mud. One vehicle and its crew were lost when attempting to ford a swollen stream. It took the column two back-breaking days to reach its next objective near the Cavalo area. Meanwhile, 4th Brigade was also struggling to make progress through the difficult terrain as it moved up from the southeast into Gorongosa National Park. Farther to the west 3rd Brigade troops were making better progress along the Inchope road. In due course the three FPLM columns united near Gorongosa town and the combined force then advanced northward onto the mountain plateau, brushing aside what little enemy resistance they encountered in the weeks ahead. In the face of Frelimo's superior numbers and heavy weaponry, Renamo appears to have opted to abandon its defensive positions and main base on the mountain. By late February Frelimo was clearly in control of most of the region and began to draw down its forces.

Renamo's new patron: South Africa

The new year was certainly off to a bad start for Renamo. And it was about to get worse, with Mugabe's electoral victory in March and looming Zimbabwean independence in April. This meant the loss of Renamo's rear base at Odzi and the ending of Rhodesian logistical and combat support. The insurgency was in serious trouble. Were it not for an extraordinary set of circumstances within South Africa's ruling National Party a mere 18 months earlier, Renamo days were probably numbered, and it likely would never have grown into the powerful national insurgency that it did. Its fate—or at the very least, a far different version—would have been sealed with Zimbabwean independence, confining the Renamo insurgency to a festering regional revolt common throughout Mozambican history.

The rise to power of P. W. Botha in South Africa changed all this. Botha's assumption of the South African presidency and the ascent of the military-intelligence establishment changed the strategic landscape of southern Africa by opening a new era of apartheid-supported destabilization against the Front Line States (Angola, Botswana, Mozambique, Tanzania, Zambia and Zimbabwe). For in Renamo, Pretoria found the perfect tool, and it could not have come at a more critical time for Dhlakama. The roots of this relationship can be traced back to before Zimbabwean independence when the CIO's Flower requested South African financial and material assistance for Renamo in early 1979. The Botha government apparently jumped at the opportunity to get involved, and shortly thereafter began supplying some limited material and financial assistance. A South African military intelligence officer, Colonel Cornelius "Charles" van Niekerk, was appointed as the liaison officer to work with the CIO's Ricky May. Pretoria was reportedly so pleased with the relationship that it was planning to provide the Rhodesians with over $1 million in funding for 1980.[122]

Although certainly not anticipated at the time, Colonel van Niekerk (or "Commander Charlie" as he would come to be known within Renamo) would come to represent the personal face of South African destabilization in Mozambique for the next decade, and as such, play a leading role in shaping the course of the Renamo insurgency. A career intelligence officer, van Niekerk served as a military attaché in Nampula, Mozambique in the early 1970s observing Portuguese counter-insurgency operations there and monitoring the limited South African involvement.[123] Like many of his Afrikaner military contemporaries he was a no nonsense officer committed to the defense of the apartheid regime. His field experience in Mozambique, plus his ability to speak Portuguese and Macua, were apparently deciding factors in his initial posting as the Renamo liaison in 1979. As time would tell, he proved to be the right man for the job.

While van Niekerk's official role would be to align Renamo's overall war strategy with Pretoria's destabilization efforts in Mozambique and to coordinate South African assistance to the guerrillas, it was his ability to develop strong personal rapport with senior guerrilla commanders—especially Dhlakama—that firmly entrenched him as the critical link between Renamo and the South African military. At times it would appear that van Niekerk had an almost caring, paternal relationship with Dhlakama, who often addressed him as "my friend Commander Charles."[124] Yet the close relationship may have had a manipulative side as well by serving to deflect responsibility away from van Niekerk onto "those officials in Pretoria." This provided an effective buffer in making unpopular decisions: "we couldn't always do what we wanted" and "sometimes [Commander Charles] had to say no to our requests," said a former senior Renamo commander.[125] Although a professional soldier carrying out his orders, van Niekerk also apparently strongly believed in Renamo's cause which "became an emotional relationship" for him, according to Cabrita.[126] Dhlakama also recalls that van Niekerk considered the March 1984 Nkomati Accord "an act of betrayal" and that van Niekerk said afterwards, he "thought about committing suicide."[127]

To Renamo's young leaders, van Niekerk seemed unshakable and "always very calm" even in the face of adversity.[128] Former senior Renamo commander, Raúl Domingos,[129] remembers an incident in 1983 when his guerrilla forces had just suffered a significant defeat at the hands of Frelimo forces. Renamo suffered serious casualties and the loss of vital supplies. As a result Domingos was on the verge of panic, but van Niekerk told him to collect and calm himself, so as to be able to think clearly about the situation and how best to address it. Said Domingos, "He taught me to be cool under pressure."[130]

The announcement of Mugabe's election victory on 4 March 1980 that would start this chain of events caught the CIO completely off guard. The seemingly impossible had indeed happened. Renamo was "given 72 hours to get out of the country" and Coventry and his team at Odzi "shoved across [the Mozambican border] everybody except for 250."[131] According to Coventry's recollection this would have brought the total Renamo strength up to nearly 2,000 men, but other evidence now available indicates that the figure was probably closer to 3,000 by this time. The handover took place in three stages over the course of several days[132] amid the post-election confusion and Lord Soames's unwillingness (or even ignorance) to prevent it. First, Orlando Cristina and the staff of the *Voz da África Livre* along with the mobile transmitter were flown out of Fylde airfield near Hartley in a South African C-130 to Pretoria. Next, an SAS team drove seven Renamo vehicles loaded with equipment and arms from Odzi to South Africa. And finally the 250 or so new trainees remaining at Odzi, along with Coventry and several other CIO officers, were airlifted from the forward airfield at Grand Reef outside Umtali to the Waterkloof Air Force Base just outside Pretoria. Upon arrival this group was then transported by road to a hastily erected bush camp near Kruger National Park along the banks of the Letaba River. Differences between the former Rhodesian CIO handlers and their new South African hosts over the management and future direction of the movement, however, soon led to a break between the two sides. Coventry and all but one of his team returned to Zimbabwe, leaving the South Africans solely in charge. Over the next six months, the South Africans would work to not only rebuild Renamo into the effective guerrilla force that it had been under the Rhodesians, but also to make it even stronger and more of a political threat to the Machel regime.

The move to South Africa resulted in several immediate changes for the insurgency. While Cristina's vision of Mozambican nationalism had been a driving force behind the creation of Renamo, he was largely marginalized and held in check by the Rhodesians, who were more interested in forging Matsangaissa's guerrillas into an effective military tool. For Salisbury the insurgents were simply a useful way of pressuring Machel into abandoning his support for Mugabe and his ZANLA forces—nothing more and nothing less. Talk of overthrowing Frelimo and installing a more representative Mozambican government was an effective recruiting tool, but it was just talk as far as the CIO was concerned. Matsangaissa, Dhlakama, and many other rank and file fighters vehemently disagreed with this stance, but they clearly understood it was the price to be paid for Rhodesian support. However, once under South African tutelage, Cristina was to assume new importance as Renamo's secretary general in November 1980. He would play a leading role in Pretoria's effort to recast Renamo as a broader and more robust political-military organization. Although not the first choice of South African intelligence officials, who had flirted with other exiled Mozambican political leaders, Cristina was able to out maneuver his opponents and gain reluctant acquiescence from Dhlakama to become the external face of the movement.[133] Lingering questions over Cristina's tainted colonial past, his association with Jardim and the expatriate Portuguese community, and allegations over diversion of funds would taint his leadership role. Moreover, it would awaken the developing fissures between the guerrilla fighters inside

Mozambique and their external political network. This last factor would end up having a very profound and negative impact on Renamo and complicate peace negotiations later on. But none of that mattered for now. It was a high price, but once again one that had to be paid to ensure Renamo's survival.

On the military front, the South Africans also had very strong opinions as to the future direction of the insurgency, as well as the extent and nature of their assistance. Despite widespread agreement within the military as to the ultimate goals of regional destabilization—to undermine support for the ANC, to counter the development and alternative use of non-South African transportation networks, to ensure continuing economic and trade dependence on South Africa, and to encourage the formation of politically friendly states on its borders—there were stark differences as how best to implement this grand strategy. One faction saw Renamo developing more or less along its current lines, as but one tool in the destabilizing of Mozambique. Proponents of this approach, such as van Niekerk and the military intelligence leadership, wanted to provide low-level, covert support to Renamo. This would entail minimal political risks, yet provide enough leverage to pressure Machel into changing his behavior. Another more hardline element within the South African Defence Force (SADF), however, wanted to provide more extensive and direct military assistance to Renamo in the hopes of overthrowing Frelimo or in forcing it to negotiate with the insurgents. In the end, the indirect approach advocated by van Niekerk and the military intelligence leadership won the day and would prove decisive in shaping the future conduct of the war.

Renamo on the ropes

Despite the glimmer of hope that came with the transfer of Renamo's rear base to South Africa, Dhlakama and his men back in Mozambique were facing long odds. Uprooted by the early 1980 Frelimo offensive around Gorongosa, running low on supplies, and feeling increasingly isolated with the disruption to Renamo communications, the tide of war had shifted in Frelimo's favor. Complicating the guerrilla's deteriorating position in the northern operational zone was the South African Air Force's (SAAF) reluctance to begin resupply flights into the Gorongosa area because of the distances involved, and what the South Africans claimed to be the high air threat to their irreplaceable transport aircraft.[134] To make matters worse, Lucas Mhlanga from his base at Sitatonga appeared to be colluding with some of his Rhodesian contacts to break away from the current leadership and become the new conduit for South African aid to Renamo, according to Cabrita.[135] So Dhlakama decided to move south. Ordering a general withdrawal from north of the Beira–Umtali transportation corridor at the end of April, he had weapons and the remaining supplies cached in anticipation of Renamo's eventual return. Then in early May, Dhlakama along with his depleted force of several hundred men moved south to Sitatonga. Those guerrilla fighters not willing to make the trek southward probably just filtered back to their homes or even took up banditry to make a living.

Once at Sitatonga, Dhlakama moved boldly to reassert his leadership and rally Renamo forces. Simmering problems within the insurgent ranks had been building for some time. The two semi-autonomous operational zone structure, the loss of Rhodesian logistics and communication support, and FPLM pressure contributed to a factionalized and disjointed Renamo command that fueled personal rivalries. As southern base commander, Mhlanga apparently tried to exploit this situation to burnish his standing within Renamo and with his Rhodesian mentors. In a 14 April letter, Mhlanga thanks Coventry for "giving us [Mhlanga and Dhlakama] the chance of settling our problems" and notes that "I have asked Alfonso to cooperate with me" in resolving differences and goes on to warn that "our failure to cooperate means the destruction of our war."[136]

The resulting showdown between Dhlakama and Mhlanga has since assumed mythical status, climaxing with the now legendary and widely repeated "shoot out" between Dhlakama and Mhlanga factions at Renamo's "Chisumbanje base ... in June 1980" that resulted in Mhlanga's death, according to multiple published histories of Renamo.[137] This story, however, is pure fiction. In reality Dhlakama had largely consolidated his position within Renamo by obtaining the overwhelming support of old line Renamo field commanders and the guerrilla ranks in the eight months since Matsangaisa's death. Moreover, although Mhlanga was able to exercise a fair degree of operational independence in the southern zone and had strong personal relationships with some of his Rhodesian mentors, he was nonetheless a fairly junior commander, having only joined Renamo in early 1979. Any attempted power grab by him would have undoubtedly faced considerable opposition from older, more experienced field commanders. Upon his arrival at Sitatonga in May 1980, Dhlakama, confronted with Mhlanga's insubordination, had him arrested and imprisoned.[138] To further underscore his position, Dhlakama was named "President and Supreme Military Commander" of Renamo in June.[139] Mhlanga was later released, helped set up the new Renamo base at Chicarre in southern Manica Province and continued to serve as a field commander until the end of 1980 when he was again imprisoned, according to a former Renamo combatant.[140] Subsequently, he was transferred to South Africa, where he then disappeared from the scene.

In addition to sorting out Renamo's internal divisions, Dhlakama and his men were confronting a dramatically changed battlefield and serious operational challenges. The loss of their Rhodesian rear base, the abandonment of Gorongosa, and the as yet unproven South African logistics support were weighing heavily on the insurgency. Even with the March influx from Odzi and the arrival of Dhlakama's Gorongosa guerrillas at Sitatonga, Dhlakama could muster just 800–900 men at the base. Another estimated 300–400 guerrillas were scattered across smaller Renamo camps in southern Manica and Sofala provinces as well. A major SAAF C-130 airdrop of 19 tons of ammunition and supplies on 20 June augured well, but the new South African supply line was still in its infancy. Moreover, Sitatonga's isolated location up high in the rugged mountainous region that was once an asset was now fast becoming a strategic liability with the hostile Zimbabwean border to the west and Frelimo forces on the move from the south and east.

Flushed with its successful Gorongosa offensive earlier in the year, FPLM was feeling its oats and with a little help from the newly-installed Mugabe government it was preparing to finish off the 'armed bandits' once and for all. Operation Leopard (April–July) was to be the final nail in Renamo's coffin.[141] Even before Dhlakama had regrouped his forces and consolidated his position at Sitatonga, Frelimo was already on the move. The plan involved deploying troops along the Save River border with Gaza Province to prevent Renamo guerrillas fleeing southward while elements of 2nd Brigade sweeping northward from the Save would drive toward the Buzi River. At the same time the main FPLM force drawn from 3rd and 4th brigades would move down from the Beira transportation corridor and push westward along the Buzi in the direction of Zimbabwe, where Mugabe promised to seal the border. A third FPLM force was given permission to transit Zimbabwe and would launch its attack from the border town of Espungabera toward Sitatonga itself. The air force would also be used to bomb suspected guerrilla concentrations and provide air support when needed. If all worked as planned Renamo would be trapped by the three converging columns and completely destroyed.

Rather than directly face this formidable force, Renamo guerrillas for the most part gave ground while mounting harassing attacks on the heavily-equipped, but largely road-bound FPLM troops. By late June, however, Dhlakama's troops were running out of territory and the Frelimo forces had reached the foot of Sitatonga Mountain. Renamo then moved to stiffen its resistance by taking advantage of the rugged favorable terrain. In response, on 30 June Frelimo unleashed a prolonged artillery and air bombardment on the Renamo positions, prior to moving forward with its infantry. Later that evening the exhausted Renamo forces abandoned their positions, and their Sitatonga base fell to advancing FPLM troops in the first days of July. Many of the fleeing guerrillas headed northeast across the Mussapa River to link up with Renamo troops under the command of Languane Vareia Manje. Others took advantage of Mário Franque's (also known as Mario Frank) diversionary attacks against FPLM troops south of Sitatonga to slip through the porous government lines. In the end, Frelimo trumpeted another major victory over the 'armed bandits' with the capture of Renamo's main southern base, the killing of 272 and the capturing of another 300.[142] Still, despite this success, Dhlakama and the majority of his men escaped and would live to fight another day.

Underscoring the point that the insurgents were battered but not beaten,

Renamo activity continued unabated south of the Beira corridor to the Save River during the latter half of 1980. Now operating from smaller size bases and formations, the guerrillas kept up a steady stream of hit-and-run attacks on towns and collective farms, sabotage of bridges and telephone lines, and ambushes of road traffic, including frequent attacks along National Highway 1 in western Sofala. In some more remote areas of Manica, they even managed to lay siege to isolated government garrisons, according to Cabrita.[143] Nonetheless, the Frelimo offensives of 1980 seriously crippled the Renamo insurgency. With the loss its key bases and critical supplies, its combat strength cut by more than half, and a vastly restricted operational area, Renamo was on the ropes. An unintended consequence of this successful campaign, however, was Frelimo's mistaken belief that the 'armed bandits' had all but been defeated. Now all that was left to do was mop up the Renamo remnants. Or so Frelimo thought.

Renamo weathers the storm

As gloomy as Renamo's immediate situation was in the remaining months of 1980, its long-term prospects were vastly improving. For by now Renamo's rear base and radio station in South Africa were firmly in place, nearly a thousand newly-trained reinforcements were ready for deployment with hundreds more in the training pipeline, and the SADF logistics tap was open with weapons and supplies flowing into Mozambique. Within Renamo itself things looked better too. Beyond affirming his dominance as Renamo president and commander-in-chief, Dhlakama made his first overseas trip in late November to drum up support within European circles sympathetic to the insurgents. All in all, things were looking up for the insurgency.

Meanwhile back in Mozambique, the guerrillas had shortened their lines of supply and communication by establishing their new main base in a hilly area about 65 kilometers south of Espungabera and north of the Save River at Chicarre (also known as Garagua). By October reinforcements from South Africa (including those previously evacuated from Odzi back in March) were moving into southern Manica Province as "farmers in southeastern Zimbabwe reported 'an armada of helicopters passing overhead' from South

Africa heading into Mozambique."[144] This influx of new fighters coincided with Pretoria's intensification of its destabilization campaign. First, the SADF encouraged the insurgents to broaden theirs attacks on the country's infrastructure to include all major transportation links between Mozambique and it neighbors as part of South Africa's wider regional objective of ensuring its continued economic dominance.[145] In addition, van Niekerk was urging Dhlakama to shift his operational focus southward across the Save River into Gaza and Inhambane provinces. This would allow Renamo to put more direct pressure on the Mozambican capital and carve out an insurgent controlled zone along the South African border. A 'liberated zone' would secure Renamo supply lines and act as a buffer against ANC infiltration. (Apparently the idea was to recreate the successful strategic position Jonas Savimbi's anti-government guerrillas had established in southern Angola to protect South African-controlled South West Africa against guerrilla infiltration.) At the same time Dhlakama was pressed to undertake a campaign of urban terrorism in Beira and Maputo.[146]

Escalating its sabotage of major road, rail, and communication links sat well with Renamo's military stratagem. Dhlakama, however, was reluctant to commit major resources south of the Save River until he had shored up his position in central Mozambique and seized the initiative back from the FPLM. Moreover, the operating environment in the south, especially in Gaza Province, was ill-suited for guerrilla warfare with its largely flat terrain, limited cover, and scarcity of water. The Mozambican air force would also pose a substantial threat to Renamo operating in any significant numbers. In the end, Dhlakama opted for a cautious approach that prioritized the central region of the country while carefully expanding operations north across the Zambezi River and south across the Save. National Highway 1 in southern Sofala was singled out for special attention by small Renamo ambush groups launching hit-and-run attacks. Soon road traffic between Beira and Maputo was restricted to vehicles traveling in military convoys during daylight hours and eventually closed all together.[147] In November the Beira–Umtali oil pipeline and the Cahora Bassa Dam transmission lines were sabotaged and several towns in western Manica were assaulted at the end of the year.[148]

Low-level insurgent and bandit activity (it was often hard to tell one from the other) in northern Manica and Tete provinces near the Zimbabwean border also began to increase as larger groups of Renamo fighters filtered back north of the Beira corridor. A former FPLM intelligence officer recalls in December 1980 locating a large Renamo camp "believed to hold over 100 men; maybe up to 200" in northern Manica, opposite the Nyanga area of Zimbabwe.[149] Some 850 FPLM troops from Chimoio, along with elements out of Tete, launched an early morning assault on the camp. Using artillery, rocket propelled grenades and small arms, the attackers quickly overran the camp. "We were not sure of how many we killed, but there was a lot of blood spoor and we managed to capture some men and weapons," recalled the officer. One of the captured prisoners turned out to be a radio operator and subsequently revealed the location of the Renamo new base at Chicarre to his captors. (Frelimo would mount a major attack on this base in December 1981.)

Clearly by the beginning of 1981 Renamo was well on the path to recovery thanks largely to timely and critical South African support, and Frelimo's failure to maintain the military momentum it gained earlier to keep Renamo on the run. The recovery, however, was far from complete. The insurgents still had a long way to go before they would regain the strategic initiative. Renamo had yet to re-establish a permanent base of operations north of the Beira corridor, or re-assert its presence in Tete Province. And while recruits were flowing into its ranks thanks to *Voz da África Livre* broadcasts and South African press-ganging of illegal Mozambican immigrants, they still needed to be trained and tested on the battlefield. Although several accounts claim Renamo had between 6,000 to 7,000 trained fighters at the end of 1980,[150] the actual figure—even counting the influx of end-of-the-year reinforcements from South Africa—was most likely closer to 4,000 given desertions, sickness, and battlefield casualties. Higher estimates of "close to 10,000 men under arms" at this time are even more obviously inflated.[151] Thus, it would be several more years before the insurgents gained enough strength and capability to seriously challenge Frelimo's grip on the country.

Seemingly confident that a vulnerable Renamo had weathered the worse

Frelimo could throw at it, Dhlakama reportedly boasted, in April 1981, the overthrow of Machel by 1985 and promised there would be no further food shortages because adequate supplies would come from South Africa.[152] What may be more remarkable, however, was that the speech took place not far from Renamo's old Sitatonga base—in an area that had been cleared of insurgents only ten months before. As the guerrillas flowed back north, new bases were set up along the way at Jambe along the Revué River in Manica and at Grudja farther downstream in Sofala. Fighting erupted along the border with Zimbabwe near the Chimanimani salient and at Espungabera from mid-June to August. The Espungabera district once again was chosen for special retribution by the guerrillas; Frelimo officials were reportedly killed and mutilated and collective villages laid waste with the refugees fleeing into Zimbabwe, according to news reports.[153]

The SADF also stepped up its own activities along the Beira corridor. Using Renamo as a cover, its teams sabotaged the rail, road, and oil pipeline. Some operations were highly successful, such as the 29 October attack by recce commandos on a vital bridge over the Pungwe River near Beira that effectively blocked a large arms shipment to Zimbabwe's notorious 5th Brigade. Others, like the deaths on 15 October of four commandos, including Lieutenant Alan Gingles, killed while trying to set explosives, brought unwanted attention on growing SADF involvement in Mozambique. Pretoria of course denied any involvement.[154]

The final month of 1981 marked a major watershed for Renamo's homecoming north, not only operationally but also symbolically with the return of the insurgents to the Gorongosa area. In early December a 300-man battalion from the Grudja base crossed the Beira corridor and established its main base of operations to the east of Gorongosa mountain. Located some 30 kilometers from Renamo's original Rhodesian-era base on top of Gorgongosa Mountain itself, the new base was sited near the Nhandugue River in the Sadjunjira area that lies just west of the Panda hills. It would become Renamo's future main headquarters, which came to be known as Casa Banana. An accompanying airstrip would later be hacked out of the bush along the eastern side of the Panda hills as well. Symbolically, the insurgents pledged never to leave the area again, noting that "their credibility was at stake" and "If we did not stay put, we would never regain the trust and respect of the local residents."[155]

Shortly after their arrival, Renamo forces captured John Burlison, a British ecologist, and his assistant in the Gorongosa National Park. Burlison's 150 days in captivity would later yield much useful information about Renamo and its level of popular support.[156] Although there were some scattered reports of alleged guerrilla activity by jittery Frelimo forces in Zambezia and Niassa provinces in late 1981, Renamo would not actually cross the Zambezi River and commence operations until mid-1982.

Feeling more secure now with the steady stream of South African supplies and instructors coming into Chirrare and other provincial bases by mid-1981, an energized Dhlakama turned his attention southward. In early July he ordered a 300-man battalion under the command of Vareia Manje to cross the Save River and open a new front in Inhambane Province.[157] The Save was a formidable natural obstacle that FPLM's 2nd Brigade commander relied on to bar any Renamo advance southward, but he lacked the manpower and capability to effectively guard more than 300 kilometers of the river's length. Nonetheless, Manje's force found the going rough and "clashes [with FPLM] occurred almost daily" until he and his men were able to cross the river into the thick bush of the Zinave National Park.[158] Shortly afterward a base was set up near the Chicholane swamps of the park, not far from the provincial border with Gaza. Near-constant pressure by Frelimo forces in the area restricted Renamo's freedom of movement at first, but the dense and difficult terrain of the park also prevented FPLM from effectively massing its firepower against the guerrillas. Another battalion, including female guerrillas, under the command of Mário Franque joined Manje's forces briefly in November before moving southwestward into Gaza Province.[159] Over the coming months and into 1982, Renamo would reinforce its units south of the Save as the insurgents expanded their activity ever closer to the capital. The war was finally coming to Frelimo's southern heartland.

With Renamo's successful expansion of operations, came a decision by Dhlakama to relocate his headquarters and staff from Chirrare back to

Gorongosa. Just as final preparations were underway, Frelimo struck on 4 December.[160] Major-General Tome Eduardo's battle plan, Operation Punishment, called for an air strike to lead off the attack, which would then be followed by a two-pronged assault on the base. Eduardo's FPLM force of nearly 1,000 men would drive down from the northeast while elements of 2nd Brigade, having crossed the Save River, would move in from the south. Once again, the Zimbabwean army would be asked to seal the border to prevent Renamo escaping westward. The air strike by MiG-17 fighters went off as scheduled, but from then on nearly everything went wrong. The southern column never made it across the Save. Eduardo's force was slow in covering the ground and once at the foot of the mountain ran into stiff resistance. "We found mines had been placed along the approaches to the base," recalled one Frelimo officer, and the enemy was well placed in defensive positions behind large rocks and thus "we lost a lot of people here."[161] Over the course of the next two days the attacking force laid siege to the Renamo base and rained shells on suspected insurgent positions.

Chicarre fell to Frelimo on 7 December 1981. Despite the intensity of the fighting, Renamo suffered only a handful of casualties and nearly all the 520 guerillas at the base simply dispersed. FPLM casualties were not reported. The operation was not a total failure as large quantities of South African military equipment, supplies and ammunition, along with over 3,000 small arms were captured by Frelimo. The biggest prize was not a military one, but the discovery of documents (since known as the Garagua Documents) outlining internal Renamo matters, as well as military planning discussions between Dhlakama, van Niekerk, and other SADF personnel.[162]

Despite its growing commitment of men and material to the fight against the 'armed bandits', Frelimo was able to secure only fleeting success against Renamo. What was becoming increasingly clear by the latter half of 1981, however, was that not only was the structure and training of the now 48,000-man Mozambican army completely ill-suited for fighting an insurgency, but that a comprehensive counter-insurgency strategy was desperately needed. To address the first part of the problem, President Machel in May called upon the Tanzanian government to help reorganize and restructure the FPLM.

Training would also be revamped to focus on counter-insurgency tactics and operations. Notwithstanding the sense of urgency it would be almost another year before these changes were implemented. Even less progress was made on developing a counter-insurgency strategy, although some local commanders apparently experimented with using rural resettlement programs to win the hearts and minds of the peasantry. Unfortunately, the widespread unpopularity of these forced resettlement programs and the new villages' vulnerability to Renamo attacks undercut any potential socio-economic benefits. Moreover, Frelimo officials for the most part refused to believe that any of their policies might be to blame for fueling the insurgency and instead focused almost entirely on imposing a military solution.

The war escalates

Over the next two years the fighting would vastly intensify, spreading like wildfire to all corners of the country and in doing so transform the Renamo insurgency into a grave challenge to Frelimo's very survival. Thus, by early 1984 the war would reach a decisive turning point. But once again neither side could take advantage of their opportunities to end the fighting. Renamo had grown stronger, but it was first and foremost a military organization that had yet to find its own political identity outside the long shadow of its apartheid patron and Pretoria's self-serving regional security agenda. Frelimo, on the other hand, was a victim of its own propaganda and self-delusion, too internally fragile and militarily weak to acknowledge, let alone address, its shortcomings. Neither side was ready for peace. And both remained convinced that victory would only be found on the battlefield.

By now the overall pattern of the conflict was well-established. Rainy season insurgent gains were followed by dry season government counter-offensives. Towns were lost and recaptured. Lines of communication cut only to be restored. Frelimo overran Renamo bases, but the insurgents simply scattered to fight another day, as rising numbers of civilians found themselves caught in the crossfire. Despite the regular mobilization of large numbers of men and equipment by the government and its allied forces—frequently exceeding 10,000 men plus supporting artillery, tanks, and aircraft—for large-scale offensive operations, the often difficult terrain, logistical shortfalls, and the unwieldiness of operational plans repeatedly prevented Frelimo from inflicting significant casualties on the insurgents. Renamo could strike at will, but could not take and hold major cities. Ultimately the fighting evolved into a classical war of attrition as Frelimo and Renamo sought to outlast the other both militarily and politically. This meant an endless series of small unit engagements, rarely exceeding several hundred combatants on each side. It was a soldier's war that would grind on into a survivor's war.

Renamo strikes back

As is often the case in war, fortunate timing plays a significant role in shaping military events. And so it was to be for Renamo's rebound from 1982 onward. The FPLM's capture of Renamo's Chicarre base and its treasure trove of supplies in December 1981 should have been a major disruption to the insurgents' efforts to return to the offensive, were it not for the fortunate departure months earlier of Renamo columns to the south and to the north. As previously noted, at least some 600 guerrillas had already crossed the Save River into southern Mozambique at the time of Chicarre's fall,[163] while another 600 Renamo fighters moved north across the Beira corridor; one battalion into the Gorongosa area and the other battalion on route to the Zambezi River. These timely movements, along with a new found SAAF willingness to commit air assets back into resupplying the new Casa Banana base, provided Dhlakama with the forces and equipment necessary to return quickly to the attack in both southern and central Mozambique at the beginning of 1982.

Since their arrival south of the Save, "there was an explosion of Renamo activity" recalls a Frelimo commander, [164] as the guerrillas steadily marched southward along the coast of Inhambane Province and across central Gaza Province toward the Limpopo River during 1982 and 1983. Although not adverse to attacking government garrisons and towns to capture arms and supplies, the smaller, lighter-equipped but fast-moving guerrilla units generally avoided engaging the numerically superior and well-entrenched FPLM forces. Instead, they focused their attention on soft targets, cutting

Frelimo's lines of communication and disrupting economic activity. Traffic along the all-important National Highway 1 between Maputo and Beira came under constant assault. Ambushes, bridge sabotage, and raids of shops and towns along the road were the order of the day. The coastal plain south of Inhambane city was especially hard hit with the road and rail line being repeatedly attacked in mid-1982 and the town of Inharime attacked and looted.[165]

Civilians as well as government forces were frequently caught up in these attacks as the guerrillas sought to capitalize on Frelimo's inability to safeguard its citizenry or lines of communication. Renamo's goal was to create a climate of insecurity and fear. This strategy had the added benefit of tying down large numbers of FPLM forces in static positions, while giving the guerrillas increased freedom of movement across the hinterlands. It also highlighted the indiscriminate nature of war and would foreshadow an escalating spiral of violence and brutality that would come to be a defining hallmark of the conflict in the south.

A former Frelimo officer recalls one grisly incident in February 1982 in the Mabote area of northern Inhambane Province:

> We mounted an operation to rescue a group of civilians that had been abducted and taken into the interior. After successfully freeing them, we brought supplies and health workers to their village. The bandits attacked one resupply convoy, burning the trucks, looting the supplies, and killing 17 people. We buried them in a mass grave near the ambush site. I never got over that. We were very angry and pursued the attackers, but they got away. A few days later we discovered that the bodies had been unearthed from the grave and their heads cut off. The bodies were lying along the road. And the heads were on stakes like a fence of human heads along the road. It was done to scare the people. It was hard [for me] to believe how a human being could do such a thing.[166]

Operating in small groups across the bare and inhospitable terrain of northern Gaza Province guerrillas steadily worked their way southward, reaching the Limpopo River and more populous districts by January 1982. Just as in neighboring Inhambane, road and rail links in southern Gaza began to come under Renamo attacks. The northern part of the rail line from Maputo to Chicualacuala on the Zimbabwean border was first attacked in December and then regularly thereafter. In the ensuing months, road and rail traffic around Xai-Xai in southern Gaza would come under repeated Renamo attack too, forcing Frelimo to institute military convoys to safeguard traffic.[167]

By the end of 1982, Renamo had a well-established provincial base at Tome in central Inhambane and several smaller camps from which to operate. The insurgents were reinforced by a SAAF airdrop of 100 South African-trained Renamo troops in September. This likely brought the total number of insurgents in southern Mozambique to nearly 2,000 men.

By November the leading elements of a Renamo force crossed the Mazimechopes River into northern Maputo Province and began to operate in the Maguda–Chokwe area. The first reports of guerrilla activity began filtering into Maputo by early December 1982.[168] To counter this rising threat in the south and to the capital itself, Frelimo could on paper field more than ten times that number of men under arms, it had overwhelming superiority in heavy weapons, as well as uncontested control of the skies. Nonetheless, many Frelimo units, such as those belonging to the *Tropas de Guarda Fronteira* (Border Guard Brigades) or the TGF and People's Militia, were of dubious quality and capability. The lack of air-support coordination was also a serious shortcoming. Moreover, Frelimo's conventional force structure and it reliance on heavy equipment left it highly road-bound and ill-prepared for irregular warfare.

As the war grew ever closer to Maputo, the fighting north of the Save River was heating up too. The return to the Gorongosa area by Renamo at the end of 1981 and the establishment of its Casa Banana headquarters presaged some of the most severe fighting of the war to date. Operating from this new command and logistics hub, hundreds of guerrillas fanned out across northern Sofala and Manica provinces to raid communal villages, collectives and towns and strike isolated FPLM garrisons. They mined roads, bridges and rail lines and attacked state-owned enterprises and other economic targets. By November 1982 Renamo forces were reported to be operating on the very outskirts of Beira, the country's second largest city.

From 1982–1984, nearly every town and Frelimo garrison in central Mozambique would be attacked, and often smaller towns were briefly occupied by Renamo. With rising confidence, the insurgents made off with looted supplies, arms and ammunition, and even heavy weapons (including 14.5mm anti-aircraft guns, BM-21 multiple rocket launchers and even an armored car or two) that they brought back to defend their bush camps. Despite periodic counter-insurgency operations, even well-equipped Frelimo forces were proving inadequate at stemming this onslaught. Renamo guerrillas became adept at selecting strong natural defensive positions and concentrating their defenses along probable enemy lines of advance given the FPLM's reliance on motorized transport. During a September 1983 operation to clear a number of insurgent outposts east of the Gorongosa mountain, for example, the attacking FPLM force had to fight its way across the Macosa River, which "took three days and used up all our supplies," according to a former Frelimo officer.[169] The force also lost a number of men to anti-personnel mines as well. Despite regrouping, resupplying and relying on the extensive use of air attacks and shelling by 130mm towed artillery and BTR-60s, the FPLM attacking force was unable to dislodge the Renamo defenders. It was eventually forced to withdraw to Gorongosa town.

Just as elsewhere in the country, lines of communications and critical economic infrastructure were a high attack priority. In particular, the road, rail, and pipeline network of the Beira corridor that ran across the center of Sofala and Manica provinces from the port of Beira to the Zimbabwean border town of Mutare (formerly Umtali) was the focus of repeated Renamo attacks and sabotage. In January 1982 the rail and pipeline were hit. Another large-scale assault on Maforga pumping station in the Gondola area in October produced considerable damage to the critical facility, raising concern in Harare. Frelimo responded by committing an additional 3,000 troops to protect the corridor. But the growing Renamo threat was not just to Frelimo's lines of communication, but also to one of Zimbabwe's key economic lifeline and this would spur Zimbabwean intervention. In December 1982 the Zimbabwe National Army's (ZNA) 3 Brigade out of Mutare began deploying some 1,500 to 2,000 troops into Mozambique with the task of patrolling and protecting the western half of the Beira corridor from Mutare to Chimoio. This was the beginning of Operation Lifeline.[170] It was also the beginning of Zimbabwe's entry into Mozambique's escalating conflict and the shouldering of an ever-rising responsibility to the faltering Machel regime. No one could imagine at that time that it would be more than ten years before the last Zimbabwean troops would leave Mozambican soil.

The second half of 1982 also saw an expansion of the war across the Zambezi River for the first time. Before the fall of Chicare, Dhlakama had dispatched a battalion under the command of Calisto Meque northward in October 1981 with orders to open a front in Tete Province. After a grueling 600-kilometer march across enemy-controlled western Manica Province, the lead elements of Meque's depleted force crossed the Zambezi west of Tambara in August 1982 and began operations. Quickly road and rail traffic east of Tete came under insurgent attack. The main road between Tete and Zobue on the Malawi border received special attention, as did the main rail line linking the Moatize coal mines to the town of Sena down river. The war had come to Tete Province.

At about the same time, a Renamo force of 485 men under the command of Abel Tsequete, left Casa Banana and crossed the Zambezi River in the Caia area with the assistance of Meque forces. The war was now coming to Zambezia Province too, the country breadbasket and most populous region. After establishing a base at Pinda on the east bank of the Shire River, guerrilla forces started to filter eastward attacking vehicular traffic, raiding towns, sabotaging bridges and the Mocuba–Quelimane rail line. The important transportation hub of Milange on the Malawi border was attacked for the first time on 27 September. As elsewhere, the guerrillas focused their efforts on disrupting lines of communication and hindering economic activity, but they were not averse to engaging smaller FPLM units as targets of opportunity to secure weapons, ammunition, and supplies. The province would also become a fertile recruiting ground for the insurgents in the years ahead. It was also during this time that Renamo formally merged with Gimo (Jimo) Phiri's small guerrilla group, the *Partido Revolucionário de Forças Moçambique* (PRM), which had long been conducting an anti-Frelimo insurgency in the area, but with little success.[171] The new Renamo provincial base for Zambezia was established at the old PRM base in the Namuli mountains.

As 1982 drew to a close things looked bright for Renamo north of the Beira corridor and throughout southern Tete and Zambezia provinces, but to the south Frelimo was trying to turn the tables on Renamo and inflict a major blow against the newly energized insurgency.

Frelimo responds: Operation Cabana

By 1982 Frelimo could no longer ignore the growing threat the insurgents (still publicly referred to as 'armed bandits') were posing to the country. In March President Machel created ten provincial semi-autonomous commands and then appointed ex-Frelimo guerrilla commanders to these posts as senior party officials "to lend cohesion to the war effort."[172] They were tasked with mobilizing the masses under the banner of a 'patriotic call' to service and were to raise and train new provincial militias. These local militias would be used to supplement the army's defensive mission, thereby reducing the strain on the logistics network and freeing up the regular combat brigades for offensive operations.[173] In addition, the army was restructured and reorganized into the new *Forças Armadas de Moçambique* (Armed Forces of Mozambique) or FAM and provided better training by hundreds of Soviet, Eastern Bloc, and Tanzanian military advisers. New commando-type units were also formed for small unit operations and reconnaissance. Logistics and equipment were improved along with an overall effort made to raise morale.[174]

The newly restructured FAM went on the offensive in late 1982. In what was to become the largest counter-insurgency campaign so far, Frelimo mobilized a vast array of infantry brigades, mechanized and heavy artillery units, commandos, and border guards in an extremely ambitious effort, named Operation Cabana. It was designed to deal a mortal blow to Renamo in the south.[175] An estimated 10,000 men in all would be committed over the course of nearly a year. The campaign plan called for the sealing of the South African–Swazi border by Frelimo's 2nd and 5th TGF brigades, while the cooperating 1 and 4 ZNA brigades would help seal the Zimbabwean frontier with northern Gaza and Manica. Meanwhile elements of FAM's 1

Mechanized Brigade along with two motorized brigades would deploy along the north bank of the Limpopo River and form a defensive line that ran along National Highway 1 through Gaza and Inhambane provinces. Other FAM infantry brigades supported by artillery were tasked with conducting sweep operations from the Limpopo River valley northward toward the Save River and simultaneously from the Beira corridor southward toward the Save. The objective was to drive Renamo into a killing ground in northern Gaza, where the trapped insurgents would be hammered relentlessly by combined air and ground FAM assaults. An ambitious plan indeed.

Operation Cabana kicked off in August 1982 with some initial success in the south because drought conditions caused food shortages for the guerrillas and Frelimo's relocation of villagers exposed Renamo movements and made insurgent bases easier to detect. In short order the FAM swept westward into the more remote reaches of southern Inhambane over running Renamo bases and putting the guerrillas to flight. Similar progress was made in southern Gaza as Frelimo forces pressed northward. Although few insurgents were killed, large amounts of supplies were captured and Renamo's network of bases seriously disrupted. By September FAM infantry and artillery units in southern Manica Province launched their phase of the operation with a series of attacks from points south of the Buzi River with the aim of capturing Renamo's important Jambe base. Rather than stand and fight in the face of this all-out powerful assault, Renamo units gave ground and "opted for a strategic withdrawal from the occupied areas," according to a Renamo communiqué.[176] In addition, Dhlakama sought to relieve the pressure on his southern forces by ordering diversionary attacks in Tete and Zambezi provinces, compelling Frelimo to redeploy northward to face the new guerrilla threat.[177]

Despite the lack of success in inflicting significant casualties on Renamo, Frelimo kept up the pressure on the insurgents going into 1983. And no quarter was given. Heavy artillery was used against suspected Renamo concentrations. Water wells were poisoned. In January the first public executions of captured Renamo soldiers took place in Macia and Magude in Maputo Province.[178] President Machel, the next month, gave a stark warning to any potential sympathizers: "Those that give information to the bandits will die with the bandits, those who feed the bandits will die with the bandits, those who deal with the bandits will die with the bandits."[179] The loss of key operational and supply bases in the south[180] and parts of Manica produced a sharp decline in insurgent activity in the first half of 1983, particularly in Inhambane and Gaza. It also allowed Frelimo to re-establish its presence in areas previously ceded to the insurgents. Accordingly, President Machel would publicly trump the 1982–83 campaign as a success, claiming the FAM "had captured 3,500 bandits and thousands more [had been] killed or wounded." In reality Renamo escaped, suffering only minor casualties and the insurgents' losses in weapons and supplies were quickly make good by the South Africans. An unforeseen consequence was the relocation of large numbers of guerrilla fighters to new areas of the country. Maputo Province and the capital itself came under increasing attack and the war north of the Zambezi River began to escalate.

Assessment: The road to Nkomati

In the twelve months following Mugabe's March 1980 election victory, Renamo found itself in upheaval and fighting tooth and nail for its very survival. From internal factionalism, political maneuvering and personal jealousies, to battlefield problems fueled by the lost of its Rhodesian lifeline and a re-energized Mozambican military, Renamo was certainly facing the most dangerous crisis of its heretofore existence. It was also a period of missed opportunities for Frelimo to nip the insurgency in the bud. In the euphoria that accompanied Zimbabwean independence and of having survived the Rhodesian military onslaught, Frelimo clearly found itself distracted from addressing its own shortcomings and the simmering discontent within the country. Moreover, a near myopic preoccupation with the regional factors feeding the insurgency colored the government's perception of the Renamo threat adversely. 'Armed bandits' as agents of hostile states were far easier to deal with than were insurrectionist grievances rooted in unpopular government policies.

The South African assumption of the Rhodesian role was critical in allowing Renamo to survive, but it came with a heavy price tag—continued foreign dependence, loss of legitimacy as a nationalist movement, and being used as a foreign policy pawn of South Africa. Moreover, Pretoria's attempts to micromanage the insurgency would ultimately inflame underlying political fissures within Renamo and hinder its development into something more than just a guerrilla army. But none of this mattered for now. Dhlakama and others in Renamo still considered themselves true Mozambican nationalists, and politics, they naively believed, could wait until after the war was won.

Despite its problems, the military situation at the end of 1983 offered improving prospects for Renamo. Dhlakama's forces had taken all that Frelimo could throw at them and survived. They were expanding their geographic reach and were now at the doorstep of the capital itself. New bases were established to compensate for those lost, the South African and internal training pipeline was churning out new guerrilla fighters, SADF advisers and commandos were now operating with Renamo, and weapons and supplies were flowing freely. Renamo still lacked the capability to contest large-scale FAM offensives directly, but its forces were well-suited to wage a war of attrition against Frelimo.

The mood in Maputo was far less upbeat. While the newly-reorganized and restructured FAM had proven its mettle in battle and still remained a potent force, the Frelimo leadership asked far too much of it. The events of the past four years had repeatedly demonstrated the military's ability to mobilize large forces, mount major offensives, overrun Renamo bases and recapture lost territory. Nonetheless, the FAM's conventional military structure with reliance on overwhelming firepower, road movement, and extensive logistics and communications support made it ill-suited for the war it was increasingly forced to fight. Beyond its somewhat questionable ability to bomb Renamo troop concentrations, the air force lacked the necessary lift capability to support a counter-insurgency effort. Tactically, Frelimo forces also lacked any useful counter-insurgency doctrine, and instead focused on seizing specific objectives while trying to inflict maximum casualties on the enemy. Decentralization of provincial command authority in 1982 had allowed Frelimo to put more men in the field and provide a more localized response to the insurgency. But the increased burden of sustaining this force structure would create long-term problems of equipping, supplying, and maintaining morale that would come to the fore in the years ahead.

Seven years of war, first at the hands of the Rhodesians and now with Renamo, had left the country and its economy in shambles. Thousands of schools, clinics, and shops had been destroyed, rail and road infrastructure crippled and businesses had ground to a halt in some parts of the country. Hundreds of thousands of people had been displaced as a result of years of fighting and drought. Untold thousands of other civilians had died. War damages in 1982 and 1983 alone likely topped $425 million. And South African economic pressure was squeezing Frelimo too. Maputo port traffic was down by 75 percent since 1979 and the combined impact of drought and South African destabilization had cost Mozambique more than $1.85 billion by 1984.[181] The country was $930 million in debt. Machel and Frelimo were at a crossroad. They would make their decision three months later in March 1984 on the banks of the Nkomati River with the signing of an 'Agreement on Non-Aggression and Good Neighbourliness' (better known as the Nkomati Accord) with South Africa.

CHAPTER FIVE
THE SOUTH AFRICAN FACTOR

The story of the Renamo insurgency is inescapably intertwined with the struggle against apartheid, Pretoria's regional destabilization efforts, and the Cold War in Africa. For more than a decade and a half, the Mozambican conflict was buffeted by forces beyond the control or influence of either Frelimo or Renamo. The most powerful and influential of these actors was clearly South Africa. South African involvement in the war is a complicated narrative of opportunism and selflessness, of exploitation and cooperation, of loyalty and betrayal in the pursuit of the ultimate power to shape the future of Mozambique.

Neither Frelimo nor Renamo, however, stood passively by but rather sought to use their relationship with South Africa to advance their own objectives. This came at a steep price. For Samora Machel it meant making deals with the devil to ensure Frelimo's continuing economic and military survival. For Renamo it meant tainting their claim to be the legitimate heirs to Eduardo Mondlane's Mozambican nationalism; this would haunt Renamo long after the relationship with South Africa ended.

Understanding the central role of South Africa is essential in gaining a clear understanding of the war itself. The ebb and flow of the South African–Renamo relationship—more than any other external factor—influenced the ebb and flow of the war itself. And as such, its telling has routinely been subject to distortion and political manipulation from Renamo's supporters as well as its opponents.

One commonly held belief, for example, that "there was no dramatic change in the pattern of supplies, command or communications at any time from the assumption of South African control in 1980 until the end of 1988" is simply not true.[182] Change certainly did occur. Sometimes this change was significant and at others more subtle, but the relationship clearly underwent multiple evolutionary phases. And all of them ultimately had an impact on the course and direction of the war. Likewise, post-war claims by Renamo that it "didn't really need outside help" are also highly misleading.[183]

Background

The source of Pretoria's involvement in the Frelimo–Renamo war can be traced to the rise of P. W. Botha to the South African premiership in September 1978, and South Africa's growing military role in the waning years of the Rhodesian civil war. Following the collapse of Portuguese rule in Angola and Mozambique and protracted unrest in South Africa following the Soweto riots in 1976, the apartheid government found itself increasingly alone and isolated. This fueled a growing belief within the South African defense establishment that the country was now on the front lines of a Communist-inspired onslaught in the form of radical, violent African nationalism.

What was needed, chief of the SADF General Magnus Malan and others argued, was interdependent and coordinated action in all fields—military, economic, political, psychological and diplomatic—to combat this threat. Thus the 'Total Strategy' concept was born. It called for the role of the military to be expanded beyond its traditional function, linked conflict in southern Africa to the Cold War struggle, and made no distinction between an external and an internal threat to national security. Later formalized by then Defence Minister P. W. Botha in a 1977 white paper, the 'Total Strategy' approach would form the basis of Botha's security and defense thinking as prime minister and state president for the next decade. For Mozambique the consequences would be profound, as this reasoning provided the perfect rationale for unleashing armed proxies in a war of economic and political destabilization.

South African involvement in the Rhodesian bush war was crucial yet challenging; at times more like a rocky relationship between overly competitive cousins than staunch allies working together. While sharing a common ancestry and national interests, they often found themselves at odds over the best way to achieve a common goal. Pretoria's initial involvement dated back to 1967 when it dispatched police and helicopters to Rhodesia to assist Salisbury in combating Zimbabwean and ANC guerrilla infiltration. As the war heated up, some 2,000 South African police, army, and air crews were actively engaged in the Rhodesian counter-insurgency effort by the early 1970s. Badly needed war supplies and equipment, as well as economic assistance, were also flowing northward thanks to Pretoria. None of this historical involvement, however, prevented South Africa from turning the screws on the Smith government in a failed effort to shore up its own international position by supporting an American-sponsored peace settlement in Rhodesia. Pretoria publicly withdrew its men and equipment in August 1975 (although under Operation Polo helicopters and crews remained behind[184]), cut oil shipments to Rhodesia the next year, and put military cooperation on hold as a way of pressuring Smith.

Fortunately for Rhodesia, the advent of P. W. Botha to power and the rising influence of the SADF leadership at the end of 1978 resulted in renewed and reinvigorated military and political support for the embattled Smith government. And it was not a moment too soon. By early 1979 Pretoria's troops returned, South African helicopters and bombers were engaging in cross-border operations, joint training was underway again, and military supplies and equipment were once again helping to fuel the Rhodesian war machine. At the time of the December 1979 ceasefire there may have been as many as 6,000 troops and more than a dozen aircraft fighting alongside Rhodesian forces. However, it was far too little and far too late to turn the tide of the war. Nonetheless, South Africa's military engagement during the final year of the Rhodesian war put in place essential mechanisms and intelligence relationships that would allow Renamo not only to survive the Frelimo military offensives of 1980–81, but to expand enormously in the years to come.

What would eventually be a more than decade-long relationship between the South African military and Renamo would be tempestuous yet rewarding for both sides. It would also be highly dynamic and complex, driven by the changing scope and nature of SADF involvement and the political maneuverings of Pretoria in advancing its own foreign policy agenda. Accordingly, the relationship would undergo a series of significant transformations from 1980 to the end of the decade. Initially, in March 1980 following the relocation of Renamo's rear base and radio station to South Africa, military assistance increased dramatically. Pretoria also moved energetically to help burnish Renamo's image and build an effective political structure and network of overseas representatives. This level of engagement remained largely unchanged even after South Africa's signing of the Nkomati Accord in March 1984. It was only in late 1984, after public revelations of ongoing support to the guerrillas, that Pretoria actually began to scale back its assistance.[185] This second phase witnessed the continual involvement of certain elements within the SADF and military intelligence along with private covert participation by pro-Renamo elements in South Africa. By the start of the 1990s, however, the South African-Renamo relationship had atrophied, although some private South African supporters would continue to provide marginal aid up until the Rome peace accords in 1992.

Without a doubt, the political-military relationship between Pretoria and Renamo was a crucial factor in shaping the course and intensity of the war. While Renamo, or some version of its anti-Frelimo rebellion, most likely would have been able to sustain itself in the 1980s, the insurgency would never have grown so quickly or expanded as rapidly as it did without the extensive external support of South Africa. Renamo leaders, however, still downplay this support during the war: "The South Africans helped a bit more [than the Rhodesians] but only with small arms. We didn't really need outside help," said Dhlakama in a 1996 interview.[186] Denials to the contrary, Pretoria's direct involvement in the 1980s was indeed the catalyst that made Renamo the military threat that it became to Frelimo.

The Rhodesian war period

The mid-1979 appointment of Colonel van Niekerk to serve as the SADF's liaison with the CIO's Mozambique Desk was unremarkable at the time. Just another South African military officer taking note of the lessons of the bush war first hand, as the CIO team went about their business of preparing another batch of Renamo recruits for the rigors of guerrilla warfare. Yet in providing van Niekerk an overview of their "little enterprise," Coventry and May were making their case for a South African commitment of material and financial assistance to the CIO's cash strapped operation. Such assistance, they reasoned, would be essential if Renamo was to grow and expand its activities in the months and years ahead. Van Niekerk must have been favorably impressed, because shortly thereafter Pretoria began supporting Renamo operations. Thus commenced a decade-long relationship between the insurgents and the South African military (and van Niekerk personally) that would change the face of the conflict in Mozambique, although no one at the time had any inkling as to its magnitude.

The most immediate impact of the new South African role was in the area of logistics support to Renamo via Operation Bumper. Since Renamo established permanent bases inside Mozambique in September, the Rhodesian Air Force No. 3 Squadron's nine Dakota cargo transports[187] were stretched to the limit. In addition to their normal fireforce and transport duties, pilots and planes were given the added burden of now flying regular resupply missions into Mozambique. It was a great relief that by early October 1979 SAAF C-130 transports began routinely flying Bumper missions. With their larger payload the C-130s were able to airdrop large quantities of arms, ammunition, food and supplies to Renamo bases. A typical C-130 load, for example, would consist of 300 AK-47s, 98,000 rounds of 7.62mm ammo, 75 82mm and 100 60mm mortar bombs, 4 RPG-7 launchers and 40 rockets, and 24 Claymore mines, plus several thousand kilograms of food and other supplies.[188] Operating out of the more remote Fylde airfield near Hartley (now Chegutu), the SAAF aircraft and crew normally would arrive in the early afternoon for the loading of supplies and a pre-flight briefing. Although they would fly missions to both Renamo's northern and southern operational bases, they more commonly were used for larger supply runs to Gorongosa in the northern zone.

A former RhAF pilot describes one such December 1979 flight:

> The SAAF aircraft was a Hercules [C-130], which arrived at Fylde and was loaded up with supplies. After the Dak [Dakota], the Hercules was enormous and it could easily take as much supplies as three of our Daks. We climbed up to 25,000 feet and descended almost immediately after the top of the climb. As we approached the [Gorongosa] plateau, which we did from the south, the rear doors opened and the supplies were pushed out. As we were carrying out the drop, one of the SAS men on the ground reported there was a lot of gun fire aimed at us, but none of us in the front heard any

> of it. The drop completed ... we climbed away ... and arrived at Fylde after dark. The captain made a very hard landing; he left the flare far too late.[189]

Even after Operation Bumper officially ended with the Rhodesian ceasefire taking hold on 28 December, Pretoria continued to provide important logistics support on its own to the insurgents inside Mozambique. In early January 1980, for example, two SAAF transports (most likely C-130s) were cleared by the Rhodesian Air Force for a resupply mission from South Africa across southeastern Zimbabwe-Rhodesia to Renamo's main southern operational zone base at Sitatonga.[190] Some of these stockpiled supplies would later be captured by FPLM forces following the fall of the base in mid-1980.

Other support given by South Africa included the provision of weapons, ammunition, and other military supplies, as well as some financial assistance. Toward the end of 1979, van Niekerk reportedly agreed to supply the CIO with 4,500 small arms (mainly AK-47s) to meet the growing needs of Renamo.[191] The weapons were apparently obtained from Eastern European sources via Pretoria's sanctions-busting network. South Africa also supplied uniforms and personal kit items to the guerrillas, which Frelimo forces routinely recovered when overrunning Renamo bases. To assist in the infiltration and exfiltration of guerrillas across the border, the SADF supplied some seven vehicles, including heavy duty trucks, to the Odzi base. Although the amounts are unknown, South African intelligence also provided some level of funding to the insurgents in 1979 via the CIO; Pretoria was also planning to commit over $1 million in 1980, according to Coventry.[192]

Finally, the SADF played an indirect role in assisting the Renamo war effort through its joint military operations with the Rhodesian SAS in Mozambique. As noted earlier, the 23 March 1979 sabotage of the Beira fuel depot and 18 September 1979 sinking of two dredgers in Beira harbor were actually the work of SAS–South African recce commando operations with no Renamo involvement. Nonetheless, the *Voz da África Livre* was able to have the insurgents claim credit for these attacks and thus score significant propaganda wins for Renamo. Despite some unsupported claims by Colin Legum, there is no evidence that SADF personnel "were present at the MNR [Renamo] camp in Gorongosa, Mozambique from 1979" or ever deployed with the guerrillas during the Rhodesian war period.[193] Given the CIO's strong resistance to the Rhodesian SAS working directly with Renamo until mid-1979, it seems inconceivable that Flower would consent to having such external—and unnecessary—involvement in his closely run and controlled operation. Moreover, in the dozens of Rhodesian operational cables reviewed, there is not a single reference to a SADF call sign working with Renamo forces in 1979.

Across the wide Nkomati

With the transfer of Renamo's support structure to South Africa, Pretoria's assistance to the insurgents entered a new phase that would last well beyond the signing of the Nkomati Accord. After overcoming some initial organizational obstacles and chain-of-command issues within the SADF, an elaborate set of mechanisms were put in place under the Directorate of Special Tasks (DST) within South African military intelligence. Colonel van Niekerk, as officer commanding DST-2 [Eastern Operations], would be in charge of running Operation Altar—South African aid to Renamo.[194] This was a massive undertaking that included providing everything from logistics, training, communications and intelligence, and operational support to the provision of strategic military guidance, the creation of secure rear areas, and most importantly funding. This extensive amount of South African aid was instrumental in facilitating the dramatic expansion of the insurgency from 1982 onward. It also permitted Renamo forces in the field, who were now largely unhindered by logistic restraints, to gain and maintain the battlefield initiative against the Frelimo government well into 1985.

Logistics

By the end of 1981, a robust military supply chain was in place reaching from South Africa to Renamo bases as far north as the Zambezi River and helping the expansion of the insurgency northward into Zambezia Province, as well as south of the Save River and eventually to the doorstep of the capital itself. Utilizing South Africa's significant airlift capability, along with periodic seaborne deliveries by the navy, Operation Altar was able to deliver an estimated 170–180 metric tons of war matériel per year to Dhlakama's guerrilla forces.[195] In addition to the routine supply of weapons and ammunition, these shipments would also include a substantial amount of non-military items ranging from medical supplies, clothing, and even soap to office supplies, hoes, and seeds. This level of logistics support would remain relatively constant—probably never rising above 200 metric tons per year from 1982 to 1984. It would then peak in early 1984 when the SADF sought to build up Renamo's war stockpiles prior to the signing of the Nkomati Accord. After late 1984 there was a steady decline in Pretoria's covert support to Renamo, which would finally be terminated in 1988. Unofficial and private assistance out of South Africa would continue right up to the end of the conflict.

The bulk of the resupply to Renamo forces over the years was done by SAAF airdrops. Flying out of Waterkloof airbase outside of Pretoria, C-130 transport aircraft from 28 Squadron would make regular monthly flights into Mozambique to predetermined drop zones, according to a former SAAF officer.[196] The monthly supply drops were normally to key provincial bases, as well as to the main Gorongosa headquarters that received the bulk of the tonnage. Although 28 Squadron carried the burden of the logistics effort, additional sorties by 44 Squadron's DC-3 and DC-4 aircraft were used to meet pressing operational needs and supply smaller outlying insurgent bases. In addition to carrying cargo, these smaller aircraft were also used to ferry Dhlakama and his staff, senior Renamo commanders, South African VIPs, and specially trained guerrillas into and out of bush landing strips. Despite some claims to the contrary, C-130 aircraft never landed inside Mozambique because "the C-130 was too big and valuable to put into bush strips that they had in Mozambique."[197] A source familiar with Operation Altar (later renamed Mila), also reports that besides these SAAF aircraft the DST had a DC-3 under contract with Frama Inter Trading Company (later taken over by Wonder Air) that flew out of Wonderboom airport just north of Pretoria. This aircraft was especially useful for sensitive missions in the years after SAAF assistance was officially suspended in March 1984.[198]

A typical C-130 resupply mission in the early 1980s would be a dark-moon sortie involving three to four aircraft, each carrying 12,000 to 14,000 kilograms, for take-off from Waterkloof in the late evening hours, according the former SAAF officer. The palletized loads were "fairly constant from month to month" that would include 500 AK-47 assault rifles, over one million rounds of 7.62mm ammunition, 1,200 60mm and 600 81mm mortar bombs, 800 hand grenades, and 400 anti-tank and 300 anti-personnel mines, along with large quantities of explosives, detonators, and timers, according to a source familiar with the operation.[199] In addition, the shipment would contain 1,200 kilograms of medical supplies, A76 field radios and battery packs, uniform clothing, and propaganda material. The propaganda material consisted of Renamo posters and pamphlets, 10,000 manila envelopes containing corn, bean, and sorghum seeds, hoes, and consumer goods such as soap, sugar, tobacco, writing materials, and batteries that were intended for distribution to the local population in insurgent-controlled areas.[200]

Flying southeast from Pretoria toward the Durban/St. Lucia area and then swinging far out to sea and northward up the Mozambican Channel, the tight Hercules formations stayed below radar level and flew in complete darkness, only using single quick scans on their radars so as to avoid detection. Usually less than an hour before the drop, the formation would bank left and turn inland over Mozambique for the final approach to the designated drop zone. "We sometimes carried two navigators per aircraft, because we had to be on the ball, flying below hilltop level in the starlight," recalls a former SAAF C-130 navigator.[201] The guerrillas on the ground used a series of predetermined bonfires in a line, which were lit after a radio call from the aircraft when it was ten minutes out, to visually signal the drop zone. "We dropped loads from about 1,000 feet above ground" and "the whole load [normally 15 pallets] went in about three seconds using an extraction parachute. As it crossed the back ramp the aircraft pitched up uncontrollably under the weight shift."[202] The return flight was also at low level back down the Mozambique Channel or on occasion crossing the southeastern Zimbabwean lowveld, touching down at Waterkloof just as the sun was rising.

Although the pilots and crews of 28 Squadron now make the missions sound routine, it was anything but, given the number of things that could go wrong. As one officer recalls:

> The monthly nighttime resupply mission to Gorongosa was a 'max effort' using four C-130 aircraft out of Waterkloof air base. The inward leg down the Mozambique Channel and then turning inland at the mouth of the Save River was uneventful. We made the approach up to the Gorongosa DZ [drop zone] in a line of four, along the main north–south highway and one could see the glow of Beira go by to the right. During the pre-flight briefing in Afrikaans the crews were instructed *'reg uit'* or 'right on, continue ahead' for two minutes after their drop before doing a right hand 180 degree turn for home. The third aircraft, however, misheard the instruction as *'regs uit'* or 'turn right and depart the scene' and began an immediate 90 degree turn for two minutes after making his drop. We, in the fourth aircraft, saw the stars go black for a brief second as the 36-ton plane ahead cut directly across in front of us at the same altitude and in total darkness. I still shudder today when I think of it.[203]

Amazingly, no C-130 aircraft were lost that night or during the entire Operation Altar/Mila resupply missions; 44 Squadron also recorded no aircraft losses during its Mozambican service.

Although largely unreported, the South African Navy (SAN) played an active, but little-known role in Operation Altar/Mila. As early as October 1980, Colonel van Niekerk was pressing Dhlakama to expand insurgent operations into coastal Inhambane Province to facilitate seaborne resupply. Resupplying Renamo this way could be done cheaper than by air and in larger shipments, according to the Garagua Documents.[204] Once the insurgents established their presence in Inhambane Province in late 1981, identifying suitable coastal landing sites became a priority. In February 1982 a recce training team reportedly assisted in locating suitable sites near the mouth of the Save River.[205] Other seaside resupply locations included the area south of Maputo Bay, where 100 cases of AK-47s and ammunition were unloaded on 30 December 1983, as well as several points along the coast from Beira north to the mouth of the Zambezi River, according to Renamo documents.[206] One of these latter landing sites was Baia M'culuine (sometimes referred to as Culemine Bay) about 85 kilometers north of Beira and south of the Chinizua River, where in February 1983 Renamo arranged to meet a South African ship carrying 40 tons of supplies and 60 recently-trained 'specialists.'[207]

This stretch of the barren northern Sofala coast appears to have been the primary zone for seaborne resupply until late 1984 given its close proximity to Renamo's Gorongosa headquarters.

Although Mozambican press reports of the time indicate the use of everything from fishing boats to submarines to deliver supplies to Renamo, the 18,980-ton replenishment ship, the SAS *Tafelberg*, and the 2,750-ton hydrological survey ship, the SAS *Protea*, almost certainly carried the bulk of the supplies and personnel landed by sea from 1982 to 1984. Submarines were occasionally used to infiltrate or exfiltrate specialized personnel or senior leaders, but their small cargo capacity made them ill-suited for resupply runs.[208] Some scattered seaborne deliveries may have continued after the signing of the Nkomati agreement; one SAS *Tafelberg* sailor recalls a large nighttime resupply of small arms and ammunition "north of Beira" as late as 1987.[209] Zimbabwean soldiers operating in the area after 1985, however, reported finding past evidence of seaborne resupply but failed to uncover any ongoing activity from 1986 onward.[210]

While using sealift was a highly effective way to deliver large shipments, the associated difficulty for Renamo of then having to break down and transport large loads of over 40,000 kilograms by porters from the coast undetected may have diminished the effectiveness of this method somewhat. Thus, airdrops remained the preferred method of resupply. It is nearly impossible to determine the amount of tonnage that arrived by ship from South Africa, but it was probably not insignificant. Moreover, it certainly came at a critical time in Renamo's military expansion.

The biggest resupply push came in late February and early March 1984 on the eve of Pretoria's signing the Nkomati agreement with the Frelimo government. Closely informed of the secret negotiations and well aware of its potential implications for the DST's Renamo operation, van Niekerk and his team sought to provide Dhlakama with a golden handshake of 350 to 400 tons of war matériel prior to any signing of an agreement. A 16 January 1984 entry reads, "because of the commitment which the South Africans will make to Machel, the resupply for the first six months of 1984 will all be delivered in the first few months" in 25 resupply deliveries.[211] Others claim that Pretoria was hoping to stockpile enough supplies to see the guerrillas well through 1985. [212] Nevertheless, the objective remained the same that should South Africa be required to cut its military support to the insurgents, Dhlakama would still be well-positioned to prosecute the war for some time.

Operational planning for this effort was well underway by early February with an 11 February entry listing the proposed resupply dates and locations along with a listing of the cargo to be carried.[213] The list was staggering in its detail and quantities. Included of supplies to be delivered were 1,730 AK-47 assault rifles and over six million rounds of ammunition, 300 RPG-7s with 6,672 RPG-7 rockets, 120 mortars ranging in size from 60mm to 82mm and nearly 1,000 mortar bombs, 550 anti-vehicle mines and 16,400 kilograms of explosives and over three tons of medical supplies. All this was to be delivered by air and sea from 23 February to 14 March.[214] It is unclear as to how much of this matériel was actually provided, as there are vastly differing estimates by authors as to the final tonnage. But suffice it to say that Renamo was well provisioned going into 1984.

Training and operational support

A priority of Renamo and SADF leadership in the early 1980s was to put as many well-trained and well-equipped guerrillas in the field as quickly as possible. If the insurgents were to successfully step up the pressure on Frelimo they needed to not only increase, but to maintain a high level of activity. Of paramount importance were the politically critical southern provinces and the economically and demographically important Zambezia and Nampula provinces in the north. Accordingly, urgency was given to recruitment and training in both South Africa and Mozambique that allowed the insurgency to swell to an excess of 12,000 men by early 1984.

The first Renamo training camp in South Africa was established along the banks of the Letaba River in the eastern Transvaal in March 1980. It was a hastily erected and crude camp set in the bush just outside Kruger National Park and about 50 kilometers from the 5 Recce Commando base at Phalaborwa and was used to house the 250 or so recruits transferred from Rhodesia's Odzi base.[215] Following the training of this Rhodesian group in October 1980 the camp was closed and 5 Recce's Captain David Scott-Donelan, a former Rhodesian SAS and RLI officer, was ordered to construct a new, more permanent camp. Scott-Donelan selected a spot farther south of the Letaba in a more isolated part of the Gazankulu homeland's Letaba Ranch Game Reserve. With no time to waste as Scott-Donelan was told "to prepare for 200–300 Renamo," he and his team of some 25 recces went about carving the training facility out of the virgin bush. "We built everything by hand from scratch," recalled Scott-Donelan.[216] When completed, the camp, known locally as Letaba Ranch, or Zobo City by DST, consisted of a large training area with a firing range and an obstacle course, a trainee billeting area under canvas and a kitchen, a parade ground, and an armory.

In due course, the South African trainers would be supplemented by 12 Renamo instructors. This allowed the base to handle over 200 soldiers at a time undergoing a roughly three-month course, according to an Operation Altar/Mila source.[217] Training included weapons handling, marksmanship, basic guerrilla tactics and developing leadership skills; both raw recruits and veteran fighters were run through the course. The trainees apparently responded well to the recce instruction: "they were tremendous material, who became superb soldiers" with good morale and were physically tough, remembers Scott-Donelan.[218] A good part of the training was also designed to identify potential platoon leaders and those for advanced training. A small percentage of each class would be selected to attend specialized training in communications, intelligence, medicine, and demolition and explosives. Some 30–40 female soldiers were also trained as nurses at the camp.[219]

Lack of records make it difficult to determine the precise number of Mozambicans trained in South Africa in the early 1980s, but episodic accounts indicate groups of several hundred insurgents regularly leaving Gorongosa and other parts of Mozambique for training in South Africa. The first group arrived at Letaba Ranch in early 1981 and consisted of 250 men. In February 1982, 230 raw recruits from northern Inhambane Province were marched off under armed Renamo escort for basic training in South Africa, according to a recce officer.[220] And Scott-Donelan recalls a group of about 500 men traveling overland all the way from central Mozambique to reach Letaba Ranch in the early 1980s.[221] Although the main training effort clearly took place at Letaba, there has also been mention of other smaller Renamo training camps scattered throughout South Africa. One of these camps was reportedly at Potgietersrus (now Mokopane), about 50 kilometers south of Pietersburg (now Polokwane) that provided rudimentary military training to press-ganged Mozambicans who were rounded up while illegally in South Africa and then handed over to Renamo.[222] In all, the numbers of Renamo soldiers trained in South Africa over the four-year period from March 1980 to March 1984 probably never exceeded 2,500, which is far below the 'thousands' commonly cited in most accounts of the war.[223]

Just as, if not more important was SADF support for training inside Mozambique. This training apparently began in earnest in late 1980 with the deployment of a large 35-man recce team to Renamo's Chicarre base in southwest Manica Province.[224] (In later years much smaller SADF training teams, ranging from five to 15 men, would be the norm and deployed not only to the headquarters, but also to larger provincial bases.) The Chicarre team was under the command of Captain Scott-Donelan and consisted largely of black and white ex-Rhodesian SAS and Selous Scout members, several of whom had previously worked with Renamo. During his 13-week stay at Chicarre, Scott-Donelan believed the team trained "several hundred recruits" in basic weapons handling of AK-47s and RPG-7s, targeted fire, and guerrilla tactics.[225] A SADF doctor (medical staff were routinely deployed with the recce teams) also worked with Renamo commanders to improve health and hygiene at the base. Since 'basic training' for most new insurgents consisted of little more than a few weeks of weapons familiarization before being handed an AK-47, the recces often had their hands full. As this early 1982 account shows:

> They were not often easy to teach. They were instructed on ground appreciation and how to find proper cover during ambushes and to stay down. But they had their own fixed ideas and during practices would sit out in the open, completely exposed to the enemy. They insisted their personal experiences had taught them that when an ambush was sprung the enemy fired at the cover ... not at the open spaces. "Frelimo always shoots at the bushes."[226]

As needed, more advanced training in communications, first aid, and heavy and anti-aircraft weapons was given. In addition, there was a conscious effort to develop a core cadre of Renamo military instructors.[227] For example, in January 1984 plans were underway to dispatch "a team of South African instructors to train 100 Renamo instructors and 200 infantrymen in Zambezia Province," according to captured Renamo documents.[228]

Beyond basic guerrilla tactical training, Renamo early on sought to develop more conventional and specialized warfare capabilities. This was so important a goal that Dhlakama was willing in December 1983 to pull 600 highly-experienced combat veterans out of operational areas across the country for "conventional forces" training in South Africa.[229] And another group of eight Renamo instructors was sent off to South West Africa to take a heavy weapons course in early 1984.[230] Likewise there was a serious push to develop special forces operators, demolition experts, and parachutists. In 1983, 5 Recce ran 300 Renamo guerrillas through special forces training at their base in South Africa; 200 were re-infiltrated back into Mozambique, but 100 of the best served with 5 Recce until the signing of the Nkomati Accord.[231] By 1984 Dhlakama probably had developed a core of at least 800 to 1,000 highly-trained soldiers, including a couple of hundred parachutists, who would eventually form the nucleus of Renamo's semi-conventional battalions from 1985 onward.

In stark contrast to the widespread and extremely active Rhodesian SAS operational involvement with Renamo, the South African recces were used sparingly in direct support. This undoubtedly was a deliberate decision, designed to minimize the risk of public exposure of SADF involvement with Renamo. However, cross-border raids against ANC targets in Mozambique could be more easily justified as either pre-emptive or punitive actions and thus maintain the veneer of international acceptability. Nonetheless, SADF teams did operate with Renamo forces to sabotage high-profile infrastructure targets in central Mozambique, including the late 1981 attack on the Pungwe River rail and road bridges northwest of Beira[232] and the later sabotage of the huge Dona Ana rail bridge over the Zambezi River at Sena. Recces operating from the SAS *Tafelberg* were also responsible for destroying eight of nine marker buoys in Beira harbor in November 1981, and followed that action up with a return to the city a year later on 9 December 1982 to destroy the Zimbabwean fuel depot, which caused up to $20 million in damages.[233] Renamo naturally claimed credit for this attack too. With the signing of the Nkomati agreement, however, the recces appeared to have disengaged from assisting Renamo, much to the consternation of many: "I was upset about our withdrawal out of Mozambique ... very fed up," said one recce.[234] Despite this apparent cutting of ties there would continue to be sporadic reports and sightings of alleged SADF personnel and 'white soldiers' at insurgent bases inside Mozambique until the end of the 1980s.

Communications and intelligence

One of the most significant investments Pretoria made in the Mozambican insurgency was the equipping of Renamo with a state of the art military communications network that was far superior to anything Frelimo was able to field throughout the war. All company-size Renamo units were equipped with radios, which permitted secure communications between far-flung field commanders in all ten provinces and Renamo headquarters, as well as from Renamo headquarters to the insurgents' rear base in South Africa. In addition, the network gave Renamo the ability to collect timely signals intelligence on the Mozambican military. These capabilities provided a tremendous tactical advantage on the battlefield that Renamo would enjoy throughout nearly the entire course of the war. It also permitted Dhlakama and his senior commanders to exercise a high degree of centralized control and coordination over their forces and to adapt quickly to changing battlefield situations. Without such capabilities it is unlikely that the insurgency would have spread as quickly and effectively as it did after 1981.

Thanks to South African help, Dhlakama and his general staff were able to cope with the potentially devastating loss of both their Gorongosa and Sitatonga headquarters following Frelimo offensives in 1980 without missing a beat. From March 1980 until February 1983 Renamo's rear headquarters in South Africa at Sawong (or Savong) base, about ten kilometers south of Phalaborwa along the Olifants River, served as an essential communications nerve center and administrative base. It was home to a small Renamo and SADF staff that helped coordinate military assistance and keep Dhlakama in daily contact with van Niekerk in Pretoria via secure radio or telefax.[235] It also housed Dhlakama and his visiting staff when he was in South Africa for periodic meetings with SADF officials. Fear that the base had been discovered by Frelimo, however, led to its evacuation and later re-establishment in April 1983 as St. Mielie base in a western Transvaal nature reserve that was located about 70 kilometers from Potgietersrus, according to an Operation Altar/Mila source.[236] Prior to the signing of the Nkomati Accord Renamo staff at St. Mielie and its South African-provided communication network were quietly relocated to Gorongosa. Before their departure they were provided with a detailed transmission and receiving schedule for maintaining daily contact with DST's offices in Pretoria.

Although it is difficult to assess the extent of Pretoria's intelligence support to Renamo in the early 1980s, the SADF clearly passed along both political and military reporting on Frelimo. Of particular usefulness to Renamo were operational reports on Frelimo troop and aircraft movements. The primary source of this information appears to have been intercepted Frelimo military communications (which were notoriously insecure) collected by the SADF's listening post at Skietog, near the Mozambican border.[237] Other relevant information gained from special forces operations, South African agents inside Mozambique, and police interrogations of Mozambicans caught illegally crossing the border was also used to supplement DST intelligence assistance to Renamo.

Other assistance

Beyond its efforts to strengthen Renamo militarily, Pretoria sought to burnish the insurgent's political image both inside Mozambique and abroad. Orlando Cristina and his staff of the *Voz da África Livre* hardly missed a beat following their relocation from Rhodesia in March 1980. Regular radio broadcasts prepared at Vofal farm north of Pretoria were delivered to the DST for transmission into Mozambique.[238] The DST also assisted with the printing of Renamo literature, pamphlets, and posters to enhance the insurgents' anti-Frelimo and anti-communist image.[239] More important from DST's perspective, was the need to help Renamo develop a more sophisticated political awareness, and build a robust political leadership to complement the military side of the organization, something the Rhodesians had deliberately avoided doing. Beginning in November 1980, with Dhlakama's first overseas first to Europe and the formal elevation of Orlando Cristina to the newly created position of secretary-general, van Niekerk and his staff funded an extensive overseas network of Renamo representatives. These representatives were tasked with building ties to conservative, anti-communist elements in Western Europe and North America. By 1984, Renamo had representatives in Portugal, West Germany, Canada and the United States working to promote the cause.

While successful in raising the profile of the insurgents and garnering some additional international financial support as well, this effort also fueled serious—and often deadly—divisions within the insurgency that would plague Renamo to the end of the war. In the early 1980s Renamo was first and foremost a military organization that had evolved from its Rhodesian roots. And although it certainly showed an ability to tap into popular anti-Frelimo sentiment, politics was the last thing on Dhlakama's mind. Facing setbacks on the battlefield following Zimbabwean independence, Renamo's survival was at stake. Politics could wait. Thus, it is not surprising that Dhlakama abdicated much responsibility in the political arena to Cristina (and later to his successor, Evo Fernandes) while relying on the guiding hand of van Niekerk.

Unfortunately for Renamo, Pretoria's short-term motivation and attempted micro-managing of the insurgency's political development would hinder the natural evolution of an indigenous political-military leadership so critical to any successful insurgency. Moreover, it would fuel— progressively violent—factionalism within Renamo's political wing. Over the coming decade this external wing would be plagued by expulsions, defections, and assassinations. The assassination of Orlando Cristina on 17 April 1983 at Renamo's Vofal base would be the first, but certainly not be the last.[240] In time, Dhlakama would be forced by necessity to develop his own internal political structure to transform a guerrilla movement into a political movement that was capable of challenging Frelimo. But this would take years to happen and Dhlakama had a war to fight in the meantime.

All this logistical, operational, and administrative support would have been impossible without the extensive financial largess of the South African government. At its peak in the early 1980s, aid to Renamo was R14 million (approximately $9.6 million) per year, according to van Niekerk.[241] This was, however, a mere pittance when compared to DST's R300 million (approximately $205 million) annual budget, which was in turned dwarfed by the SADF's multi-billion rand defense budget of the time.[242] In fact, van Niekerk once reportedly boasted that while it required millions of rands, hundreds of troops, and tons of equipment to counter the Marxist government in Angola, he was able to do the same thing in Mozambique "with R250,000 a year and a few national servicemen."[243] Although an obvious exaggeration of the facts, the point is salient—with a relatively small investment, Pretoria was able to create a highly effective tool of regional destabilization.

The post-Nkomati show in three acts

Despite a strong sense of betrayal within some quarters of Frelimo, and especially within the ANC, the March 1984 signing of the Nkomati Accord between Maputo and Pretoria was hailed as a victory for peace by Frelimo. With a binding agreement in hand that prohibited both parties from allowing their territory "to be used as a base, thoroughfare or in any other way by another state, government, foreign military forces, organizations or individuals ... to commit acts of violence, terrorism or aggression against the territorial integrity or political independence of the other," Machel believed Renamo was finished.[244] Now that Renamo was denied South African assistance, the insurgency was a good as done. Just as the loss of Rhodesian support four years earlier had crippled Renamo, many in Frelimo believed that cutting the South African lifeline would be the final nail in the coffin. What Machel and his party hadn't bargained for, however, were the deep divisions to implementing the accord within the Botha government, as well as the resilience of the insurgency that was now deeply entrenched in large parts of the country. This miscalculation would cost Mozambique dearly in the years ahead.

Ever so reluctantly, Nkomati forced the SADF to cut ties with Renamo. The main Renamo training camp at Letaba Ranch was closed by April 1984.[245] Likewise Renamo's rear headquarters, now at St. Mielie base, was shut down in advance of the agreement and transferred to Gorongosa with Raúl Domingos and the southern front headquarters staff parachuted into Maputo Province on 5 March.[246] Recce units operating with the insurgents were withdrawn within weeks of the signing. The *Voz da África Livre* that played such an integral part in the formation of the insurgency closed down for good, along with Renamo's Vofal base north of Pretoria, housing Renamo's political secretariat. DST funding of Operation Altar/Mila would still continue, but at a much reduced level as South African stockpiles were used up and not replenished.

While it was fairly simple to end the more overt aspects of South African assistance, the actual process of military disengagement would prove more complex and would be characterized by double dealing on Pretoria's part, lingering unofficial covert assistance, and the growing involvement of an ad hoc and private South African support network.

Act One: Under the Table

Repeated denials to the contrary, South African military support to Renamo continued unabated following Nkomati. The flow of arms, ammunition, and other supplies, as well as technical support remained steady from March 1984 until the Zimbabwean army's overrunning of Renamo's Casa Banana headquarters in August 1985. This period of South African involvement did nonetheless witness a shift in modus operandi rather than an actual change in substance.

Operation Altar/Mila transformed itself from a SADF military assistance program into a covert DST intelligence operation, albeit still with the full endorsement of the SADF leadership. Top SADF leaders took great pains to reassure the Renamo leadership of their continued support, and to distance themselves from the South African politicians willing to sell out the insurgents. For example, at a 23 February 1984 pre-Nkomati planning session in Pretoria between Dhlakama and senior South African officers, Lieutenant-General Pieter van der Westhuizen pledged to "ensure resupply even after the agreement by SA [South Africa] with the communist Machel, especially ammunition and radio transmitters."[247] Moreover, correspondence between Dhlakama and senior SADF officers clearly shows that both sides viewed Nkomati as little more than a tactical ploy, with General van der Westhuizen saying, in September 1984, that the military was "always side by side with Renamo and that we shall study and work together, since our common purpose is to rid southern Africa of communism both militarily and politically."[248] Pretoria could claim to be defusing the Frelimo–Renamo conflict by accepting political accommodation with Maputo, while the insurgents would be maintaining military pressure on the Machel government to bring about its collapse.

Essential to the success of this plan was the ability to keep the insurgents well-supplied, especially with ammunition, and for Dhlakama to be able to effectively direct Renamo's military operations. Sensitivity to the discovery of the general's complicity, however, required modifications as to how this would be done. Warning Dhlakama, van Niekerk wrote in June 1984: "The political climate here ... is still bad for continuing to supply Renamo. Any violation of the Incomati [sic] Accord on our part will prejudice South African attempts at peace" but the "situation could change at any moment."[249] Thus the large and regularly scheduled SADF resupply shipments of the past were replaced by smaller, ad hoc operations run by DST directly rather than through the SADF chain of command. Large SAAF C-130 airdrops were replaced by DST's use of smaller D-3 and D-4 civilian aircraft. "Colonel Vanikerke [sic: van Niekerk] will go to Gorongosa on 22/8/84 ... to organize landing strips to make it easier to use civil aircraft that can land and not drop parachutes so as to avoid under-using capacity,"[250] noted a Renamo document. Nonetheless, even supplies for these flights steadily declined with van Niekerk acknowledging, prior to a June 1985 visit to Gorongosa, that "we have cargo but not very much."[251]

This shift clearly caused problems for Renamo early on. "We no longer have the war matériel to go on squeezing Machel," pleaded Dhlakama in a 16 June 1984 letter to van Niekerk. He went on to warn "as we are now without war material to fight him he will recover" and "could cause a bad situation to occur for us identical with that of 1980 when we were so badly hit by Rhodesia abandoning us."[252] Stepped up deliveries in August helped to alleviate some of this concern, as did the last significant SAAF operation: a planned series of six so-called humanitarian flights of C-130s to Gorongosa and Zambezia, Inhambane, and Maputo provinces in September and October 1984, according to Renamo documents.[253] Overland routes across the South African frontier into southern Mozambique, and especially into Maputo Province, steadily gained in importance along with the use of Malawian territory as a valuable resupply and transit point for covert assistance. Nonetheless, adapting to this new reality was a challenge, but van Niekerk counseled patience and pragmatism: "Avoid combat with the FAM, giving more attention to destroying the economy, infrastructure and controlling the population."[254]

Concern over maintaining regular contact led to the establishment of a highly-secure communication link between Gorongosa and DST's Pretoria office. This included agreeing that "two RNM [Renamo] men will be trained in ultra-secret communications between RNM and Pretoria," according to minutes of a February 1984 meeting.[255] The link reportedly used an advanced British Racal frequency hopping system, which neither Mozambique nor Zimbabwe were able to monitor and was in use up until early 1988. In mid-1985 van Niekerk was reportedly working personally with Dhlakama to set up a series of four transmitter-receiver relays inside Mozambique to enhance internal communications, as well as to provide the capability of broadcasting messages abroad. Van Niekerk told Dhlakama that he could "guarantee the possibilities of radio transmitters" because "we still have them in store."[256] Providing intelligence and warning information of pending FAM or Zimbabwean attacks to Renamo also appeared undiminished, thanks to the efforts of Operation Altar/Mila staff, who weekly collated intelligence material for passage onward to Gorongosa.[257] Some degree of this tactical intelligence support appears to have lasted into 1987.

Act Two: Under Cover

The public disclosure by Frelimo in September 1985 of documents (now known as the Gorongosa Documents) detailing continuing South African aid and involvement with Renamo after Nkomati, compelled South African intelligence and van Niekerk to once again modify the type and nature of their support to the insurgents. This second stage of South African disengagement would last until mid-1988 and witnessed a further constricting of support. Official SADF assistance would be cut, the use of third parties increased, and greater emphasis placed on helping Renamo secure other external aid, particularly financial assistance.

By 1986 the once bountiful South African supply pipeline was a thing of the past. However, thanks to DST funding and van Niekerk's creativity, some supplies were still getting through. These appeared to consist mainly of ammunition, explosives, some weaponry, and other highly valued items such as medicine and communication spare parts. Provincial bases outside of central Mozambique were now only getting resupply once a year.[258] Guerrilla commanders had standing orders to use up captured weapons and ammunition first, and cache the newer South African supplies for emergencies according to a former Renamo logistician.[259] Although sporadic sightings of 'South African ships,' including fishing boats, offloading supplies and personnel along the central and southern coast continued to be reported,[260] this method of resupply was erratic and largely abandoned by late 1987. Likewise, a Mozambican claim that Pretoria was planning to resupply Renamo with "250 tons [the equivalent of nearly 18 C-130 loads] of armaments to central Mozambique by sea and air" in late 1986 was clearly exaggerated and improbable given the SAAF's removal from Operation Mila by this time.

To counterbalance this declining aid, a re-energized political action plan took shape using covert funding from Operation Mila coffers. Rather than focus on the battlefield in Mozambique now that all eyes were upon them, DST sought instead to burnish Renamo's political image abroad and open new avenues of financial and material support to the insurgents. Soon news reports began to surface regularly of new support from private businessmen, conservative Arab states, right-wing political parties in Europe, and private anti-communist and evangelical groups in the United States.[261]

In Africa, the governments of Kenya, Malawi, and the Comoro Islands were repeatedly identified as providing either direct or tacit political, material or transit support to Renamo in varying degrees. The DST also reportedly facilitated the movement of senior Renamo military and political personnel into and out of Mozambique, as well as across Africa and Western Europe through the provision of counterfeit Swazi and Kenyan travel documents. Visits by pro-Renamo Western journalists into insurgent-controlled areas of Mozambique were also tacitly encouraged by Pretoria. Not only were these measures designed to grow Renamo's political acumen and improve its image abroad, but they provided Pretoria with a non-military source of leverage and influence within some Renamo circles. In addition, DST regularly exploited the insurgents' dependence on South African technical communications support to maintain direct access to Dhlakama and push its own agenda concerning potential peace initiatives. For example, in June 1987 van Niekerk and a team of DST technicians reportedly traveled to Lisbon to install a radio network to facilitate communication between Renamo and its Secretary-General Evo Fernandes's office, according to a Renamo defector.[262]

This activity, however, was a two-edged sword for Pretoria. On the one hand it helped widen the base of international support for the insurgents. On the other it provided Renamo with new opportunities outside the control of South African intelligence. In addition, continuing DST meddling in Renamo's political wing also certainly fueled divisions between those wishing to maintain South African links and those desiring a clean break with Pretoria once and for all. Several mysterious deaths in the late 1980s, including the assassination of Fernandes in Portugal in April 1988, were probably linked to this infighting and/or Frelimo's manipulation of internal Renamo divisions.

Act Three: Under the Microscope

Although difficult to see at the time, Renamo was steadily weaning itself—not by choice but by necessity—away from Pretoria. The once well-resourced Operation Mila was a thing of the past. It had given way, by late 1988, to a collection of loosely organized private and ex-officio networks operating out of South Africa, as well as other African and non-African countries. South Africa's politics of rapprochement and persistent Western efforts to lure Frelimo away from its more radical Marxist-communist roots were finally bearing fruit. Thus, the anti-government insurgency was becoming increasingly irrelevant to regional and international calculations. Moreover, it was the dawning of a new era. The fall of the Berlin Wall and ultimate collapse of the Soviet Union in 1989 removed the *raison d'être* for backing Renamo in the eyes of many South African and Western officials.

Even as the two sides continued to slug it out on the battlefield, 1988 would prove to be a significant turning point for Pretoria, Renamo, and Frelimo as it marked the end game of South African assistance to the insurgency. The opening of a South African trade office in Maputo in April was followed by bilateral discussions over security arrangements for safeguarding the Cahora Bassa power lines from Renamo attacks. This was followed by a face-to-face meeting between Botha and new president, Joaquim Chissano, at Songo, Mozambique in July where Botha promised to cut off, once and for all, any lingering South African aid to Renamo. The spirit if not the letter of Nkomati was being resurrected. Although it took more than four years after the original agreement was signed, the politicians had triumphed over the generals. Aid to Renamo would now be a thing of the past.

The tap had been shut off. Extremely limited and sporadic assistance would trickle across the border thanks to private and non-official networks in South Africa. But this largely consisted of support to insurgents in the south with the occasional resupply flight by private operators, often out of Malawi, to Renamo's central Mozambique headquarters. Press accounts, Renamo deserters, and later court testimony indicate a loose pattern of involvement between some SADF soldiers and South African policemen posted along the border with Mozambique; the Kruger National Park and the remote Kosi Bay area of northern Natal were frequently used to trans-ship supplies of food and small quantities of ammunition.[263] Renamo units also reportedly relocated a number of their camps adjacent to the border area to facilitate resupply, medical treatment, and escape if attacked by Frelimo forces. Thus, by mid-1989, the United States and most diplomatic sources in South Africa were confirming that "official support for the rebels from the SADF has ceased," but that some assistance is coming from "private elements of the SA [South African] military or by the private sector."[264] A detailed investigation by the *Weekly Mail* at the end of 1989 reached a similar conclusion finding that "the picture that emerges is one in which private businessmen and farmers are used to carry out the logistics to support Renamo with some help from elements in the military."[265]

This situation clearly had a very direct impact on the course of the fighting and subsequent peace negotiations. Renamo was forced to become largely militarily self-sufficient or what a CIA report termed "a self-sustaining fighting force" by 1990.[266] And one that was compelled to modified its operations and tactics to cope with severe ammunition shortages in the later years of the war. The deterioration of Renamo's heretofore effective communications and command network due to lack of maintenance, spare parts, and overall wear and tear not only impacted operational readiness but also complicated Dhlakama's ability to communicate with his negotiation team during future peace talks. Although various individual South African officials and military officers undoubtedly tried to maintain contact with Dhlakama after 1989, "South Africa's once considerable influence over Renamo has diminished" and strains in the relationship had emerged, according to the CIA.[267] As evidence of the deteriorated relationship, Dhlakama reportedly moved his family, which had resided in South Africa since March 1980, to central Mozambique in November 1989.[268]

Assessment

As with many similar Cold War conflicts, the Renamo insurgency became unavoidably part of the global superpower confrontation. In this, South Africa was able to brazenly manipulate its regional position by billing itself as a bastion of anti-communism and defender of the West against a Soviet-inspired takeover of southern Africa by radical African nationalists. Proxy wars, thus, became another tool used in combating the international communist threat to the continent. Although the United States did not ultimately back anti-government insurgents in Mozambique or align itself with South Africa as it did in Angola, the policy debate in Washington over the Mozambican conflict was highly contentious and in flux throughout most of the 1980s. Nonetheless, Washington's Cold War agenda in Africa served as an enabler of Pretoria's regional destabilization of Mozambique, and thereby fanned the flames of what would most likely have remained a low-intensity internal conflict.

Without a doubt the role of South African aid to Renamo was instrumental in dictating the course and intensity of the war in Mozambique. Pretoria's willingness to assume the role of an external sponsor following Zimbabwean independence in 1980 permitted the young and embattled insurgent movement to weather Frelimo efforts to crush it at its most vulnerable moment. Although it is probably likely that some form of anti-Frelimo insurgence would have continued to survive in central Mozambique without South African assistance following Zimbabwean independence, it most certainly would not have assumed the same character and capability of the Renamo insurgency in the early 1980s. Without the extensive logistics, training, communications and intelligence, and operational support to include the provision of secure rear bases and financial assistance, Renamo would not have been able to increase in size and capability nor expand the range and scope of its operational activities as rapidly as it did from 1982 onward. Here, Pretoria's assistance was the critical factor. It allowed Dhlakama to seize—and maintain—the battlefield initiative and dictate the course of the war for most of the 1980s. This source of leverage also enabled the SADF to insist that Renamo bring the war south in 1982–84 as quickly and forcefully as it did. This military pressure, along with South African unilateral military and economic pressure, proved key in pushing Machel to sign the Nkomati Accord in March 1984. Furthermore, the final cut off of aid at the end of the 1980s forced Renamo to become increasingly self-reliant and adapt its tactics to cope with the new logistics constraints. More importantly this changed operational environment probably gave the insurgent leadership the impetus to reach a negotiated, rather than military, settlement to the war.

The prolonged—and often reluctant—process of the SADF breaking ties to Renamo in the post-Nkomati era almost certainly lengthened the war and crippled prospects for an early peace settlement. It is apparent that Pretoria's generals got caught up in the insurgency's initial success in the years leading up to 1984 and lost sight of the larger political and strategic objective, which was to force Frelimo into modifying its behavior. The goal was never to have Renamo take over the reins of power. For ultimately, the insurgency was simply a tool and, as one South African senior intelligence officer chastised his colleagues, "you don't fall in love with your operations" because "you have a goal to achieve; we fell in love with Renamo and it became the be all and end all."[269] Thus, as long as South African military officers facilitated (both in terms of material and moral support) Renamo's dream of 'winning on the battlefield,' true compromise leading to a political solution was next to impossible to achieve. So the fighting continued. It was only many years later, after the insurgents were finally forced to become self-reliant that they could realistically assess their prospects for achieving their goals via not military, but political means. And only then could the prospect of peace become a real possibility in Mozambique.

All this military assistance came at a high political price too. It gave van Niekerk and his superiors in the SADF undue influence over Renamo, which they often tried to micro-manage much to the long-term detriment of the insurgency. The most significant impact of South African aid during the 1980s may have been, unintentionally, to hinder the insurgency's growth and development as a Mozambican political movement. Renamo's lack of a strong political leadership and agenda was a legacy of its Rhodesian CIO roots and surely one that would need to be rectified over time. However, Pretoria's heavy-handed involvement in trying to graft a political organization of its own design onto the existing military one proved counterproductive and divisive. Much of the infighting—and even deaths—among those in the external wing of Renamo can be blamed on DST's attempts to handpick and manipulate the political leadership. The result was disorder, a climate of distrust, and a largely dysfunctional political structure out of touch with the realties and needs of those fighting inside Mozambique. In addition, this bifurcated structure stymied what should have been the natural growth of a strong political leadership within Renamo's guerrilla ranks. It also meant that the insurgents were never really able to effectively mobilize and politicize the population, even in areas of strong anti-Frelimo sentiment. This failure, and the South African legacy, would haunt Renamo and Dhlakama through peace negotiations in the 1990s, as well as in the first post-war election.

The fact that as South African assistance waned, Renamo was able to garner some degree of African and international support clearly shows that other avenues of support were available to the insurgents. Admittedly, these tended to be more financial and political in nature, but this assistance also came with fewer strings and probably would have allowed Renamo to evolve along a much more Maoist political-military path after 1984. Realistically, the enormous pressure of the Cold War and South Africa's regional destabilization policy, would have made this extremely difficult to attempt in 1984, let alone achieve. Renamo had become addicted to SADF support and the withdrawal process, as we have seen, for both addict and supplier, would prove to be harder than either imagined. Ultimately the break did take place and the long-term future of both parties was better off for it.

André Matsangaissa, Renamo's first military commander; killed in action in October 1979.
Photo courtesy of André Thomashausen

A young Afonso Dhlakama, then Renamo's deputy commander, talking with CIO officer Danny Hartman in 1979 at Odzi.
Photo courtesy of Danny Hartman

Orlando Cristina (center) would rise to become secretary-general and head Renamo's political wing from November 1980 until his assassination in April 1983.
Photo courtesy of André Thomashausen

Regarded as a brave and charismatic leader, 'Commander André' instilled great loyalty among Renamo cadres by personally leading troops in combat. *Photo courtesy of Danny Hartman*

Below: Thanks to Rhodesian largess, the ranks of the Renamo guerrillas swelled from a few dozen men in 1977 to nearly 3,000 well-trained men by early 1980. *Photo courtesy of Danny Hartman*

Following Mozambican independence in June 1975, Frelimo sought to transform its guerrilla forces into a conventional army with Soviet and Eastern Bloc assistance to counter the Rhodesian and South African military threat.
Photo courtesy of Centro de Formação Fotográfica, Maputo, Mozambique

An abandoned tobacco farm at Odzi served as Renamo's rear base and the CIO's training and support facility until Zimbabwean independence.
Photo courtesy of Danny Hartman

Samora Machel, guerrilla fighter, leader of Frelimo and future president of Mozambique in the early 1970s. *Photo Times Media*

Machel's granting of safe haven to ZANLA guerrillas following Mozambican independence in 1975 brought the wrath of the Rhodesian military down on his country from 1976 to 1979. *File photo*

The challenging drop zone high atop Mt Gorongosa.
Photo courtesy of John Reid-Rowland

Samora Machel, president of Mozambique from independence until his death in a controversial plane crash in October 1986.

Rhodesian Air Force Dakota transports prepare to drop supplies to Renamo forces at Gorongosa as part of Operation Bumper, October 1979.
Photo courtesy of John Reid-Rowland

Rhodesian Air Force Dakota transport conducting Operation Bumper resupply flight in October 1979.
Photo courtesy of John Reid-Rowland

By 1979 Rhodesian security forces were conducting regular, large-scale, cross-border raids into Mozambique to disrupt ZANLA forces and infrastructure.

A heavily-armed Selous Scouts flying column during a raid into Gaza Province in late 1979.

Afonso Dhlakama assumed leadership of Renamo following the death of André Matsangaissa in October 1979 and oversaw the enormous expansion of the insurgency during the period of South African military assistance. *Photo Times Media*

Under the leadership of P. W. Botha, apartheid South Africa engaged in an aggressive campaign of regional destabilization in the early 1980s. This included military assistance to anti-government insurgencies in Angola and Mozambique.

Flying out of Waterkloof airbase outside Pretoria, C-130 transports from 28 Squadron carried the burden of supplying Renamo force from 1980 to 1984. *File photo*

General Magnus Malan commander of the SADF at the height of South African assistance to Renamo in the early 1980s. *File photo*

Machel had hoped that the ending of the Rhodesian war with the Lancaster House agreement in December 1979 would spell the end of the Renamo insurgency, but it was not to be. *File photo*

Lieutenant Alan Gingles (back row, third from left) and two of his men of 5 Recce Commando along with new recruits at Renamo's Chirrare base in 1981. *Photo courtesy of David Scott-Donelan*

Above: Frelimo rallying the population in 1985: "Let us make the year of the 10th anniversary a decisive occasion in the struggle for the total liquidation of the armed bandits!" *Photo Robert Botha / Times Media*

Major Frelimo offensives often resulted in the overrunning of Renamo bases and the capture of large quantities of weaponry and ammunition, but these operations rarely inflicted significant casualties on the guerrillas. *Photo courtesy of Centro de Formação Fotográfica, Maputo, Mozambique*

South African and Mozambican delegations negotiating the treaty of non-aggression on the banks of the Incomati River in March 1984. *Photo courtesy of Centro de Formação Fotográfica, Maputo, Mozambique*

Celebrating the signing of the "Agreement on Non-Aggression and Good Neighbourliess", better known as the Nkomati Accord, on 16 March 1984. *Photo courtesy of Centro de Formação Fotográfica, Maputo, Mozambique*

SAS *Protea. Photo Times Media*

Backed into a corner, Machel tried to put the best face on the Nkomati Accord. *Photo courtesy of Centro de Formação Fotográfica, Maputo, Mozambique*

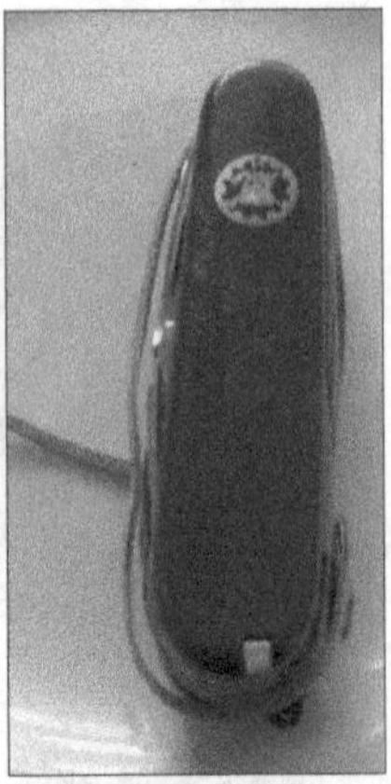

Above left: President Machel awards gifts to Zimbabwean officers following the capture of Renamo's Casa Banana headquarters in August 1985. Operational commander, Lieutenant-Colonel Lionel Dyck (foreground right) looks on. *Domingo, 5 September 1985.* Above right: The Swiss army knife with the Frelimo crest awarded to Dyck by President Machel. *Photo Author*

SAS Emily *Hobhouse. Photo Times Media*

Beginning in August 1985 the ZNA began carrying an increasingly heavy burden of the fighting in central Mozambique. *Photo courtesy of Centro de Formação Fotográfica, Maputo, Mozambique*

Renamo guerrillas resting at a stream in Maputo Province, 1987. *Photo Cloete Breytenbach*

Renamo soldier equipped with an RPG-7 near Maringue, Sofala Province, 1988. *Photo Cloete Breytenbach*

As the war dragged on, the quality and training of troops began to noticeably decline. *Photo Cloete Breytenbach*

FAM troops prepare for operations in southern Możambique, the scene of heavy fighting in 1987–89. *Photo courtesy of Centro de Formação Fotográfica, Maputo, Mozambique*

Toward the latter years of the war, Frelimo forces increasingly found themselves relegated to a passive defensive role and thereby ceded the strategic initiative to Renamo forces. *Photo courtesy of Centro de Formação Fotográfica, Maputo, Mozambique*

Frelimo forces entering a destroyed village following a Renamo attack. The civilian population increasingly found itself caught in the crossfire of the war.
Photo courtesy of Centro de Formação Fotográfica, Maputo, Mozambique

Wreckage from the crash of President Machel's aircraft is strewn across the South African countryside, October 1986. *Photo Times Media*

Female Renamo soldier, central Mozambique, 1988. *Photo Cloete Breytenbach*

Renamo child soldier, central Mozambique, 1988. Child soldiers, some as young as 13, were dragooned into the ranks of both guerrilla and government forces, especially in the later years of the war. *Photo courtesy of Paul Moorcraft*

By the end of the war millions of Mozambicans had been made refugees in Malawi, Zimbabwe, and South Africa and millions more were internally displaced. *Photo Newscom.com*

President Chissano's diplomatic offensive: May 1987 meeting with Prime Minister Thatcher at No. 10 Downing Street. *Photo Newscom.com*

President Chissano's diplomatic offensive: October 1987 meeting with President Reagan at the White House. *Photo Reagan Library*

The Rome peace talks lasted from July 1990 to October 1992 and would ultimately require the active involvement of regional leaders to hammer out an acceptable agreement.

The Renamo delegation, October 1992: Afonso Dhlakama (second from left), Vicente Ululu, and Raul Domingos.

Bottom: The Frelimo delegation: Alberto Chissano (second from right), Amando Guebuza, and Pascoal Mocumbi; Archbishop Jamie Goncalves is to Chissano's left.

All photos courtesy of Centro de Formação Fotográfica, Maputo, Mozambique

Frelimo President Chissano signs the General Peace Agreement on 4 October 1992.

Renamo President Dhlakama signs the General Peace Agreement on 4 October 1992.

"The war is over. Peace at last."

All photos courtesy of Centro de Formação Fotográfica, Maputo, Mozambique

Derailed train near Lamego, Sofala Province. Attacking road and rail infrastructure was a central part of Renamo's strategy to sever Frelimo's lines of communication and to immobilize the country. *Photo Ersnt Schade, www.ernstschade.com*

Above: Rural villages and their inhabitants were often targets of Renamo raids. *Photo courtesy of Centro de Formação Fotográfica, Maputo, Mozambique*

The heavily damaged Dona Ana railroad bridge at Sena on the Zambezi River. Strategic towns along the Zambezi River witnessed some of the most brutal fighting of the war. *Photo courtesy of USAID*

Derailed and looted train in Maputo Province. In an effort to isolate the capital, rail lines to and from South Africa and Swaziland came under constant attack by Renamo forces from 1987 onward.

Heavy fighting in and around Caia, Sofala Province between 1986 and 1990 destroyed nearly all the town and much of the surrounding infrastructure.

Bottom: Vehicles traveling the main north–south highway were under constant threat of ambush and hundreds of civilians died in these attacks.

All photos courtesy of Centro de Formação Fotográfica, Maputo, Mozambique

CHAPTER SIX
ZIMBABWE TO THE RESCUE

The signing of the Nkomati Accord in March 1984 was a humbling experience for Frelimo and one that caused much angst behind the scenes. Machel tried to put the best face on the agreement, but it was a bitter political pill for Frelimo to swallow. Foreign governments, particularly those of the Front Line States, were shocked and stunned by Frelimo's apparent capitulation to the apartheid regime, although they remained supportive in public. But Machel had little choice in early 1984. The war was going badly. Large-scale government offensives had failed to inflict serious causalities on the insurgents and, thanks to South Africa, Renamo had a seemingly unending source of supplies and war matériel. Moreover, the once localized insurgency was now on the verge of engulfing the entire country. Thus in return for denying the ANC use of, or access to, Mozambican territory, the Pretoria government would be required to curtail its support to Renamo. As long as Maputo adhered to the agreement, Pretoria would suspend its destabilization efforts and thus allow Frelimo to concentrate on ending the Renamo threat once and for all.[270]

Unfortunately, it was not to be. The war not only continued, but intensified in many parts of the country as South Africa pushed men and supplies across the border in the form of a golden handshake to Renamo. The capital and its environs in particular came under increasing pressure throughout 1984. Once across the Zambezi, the insurgency quickly spread to engulf every province by the end of 1984, forcing Frelimo to spread its forces even thinner. Renamo not only consolidated its position in northern Sofala and Manica provinces, but came to dominate most of the countryside in the center of Mozambique. Frelimo found itself limited to isolated garrisons, major transportation arteries, and larger towns and cities. The situation was rapidly deteriorating and Frelimo needed help.

A special relationship

Not surprisingly, Machel turned to Mugabe for assistance. This of course was not the first time the lives and interests of both men and their respective

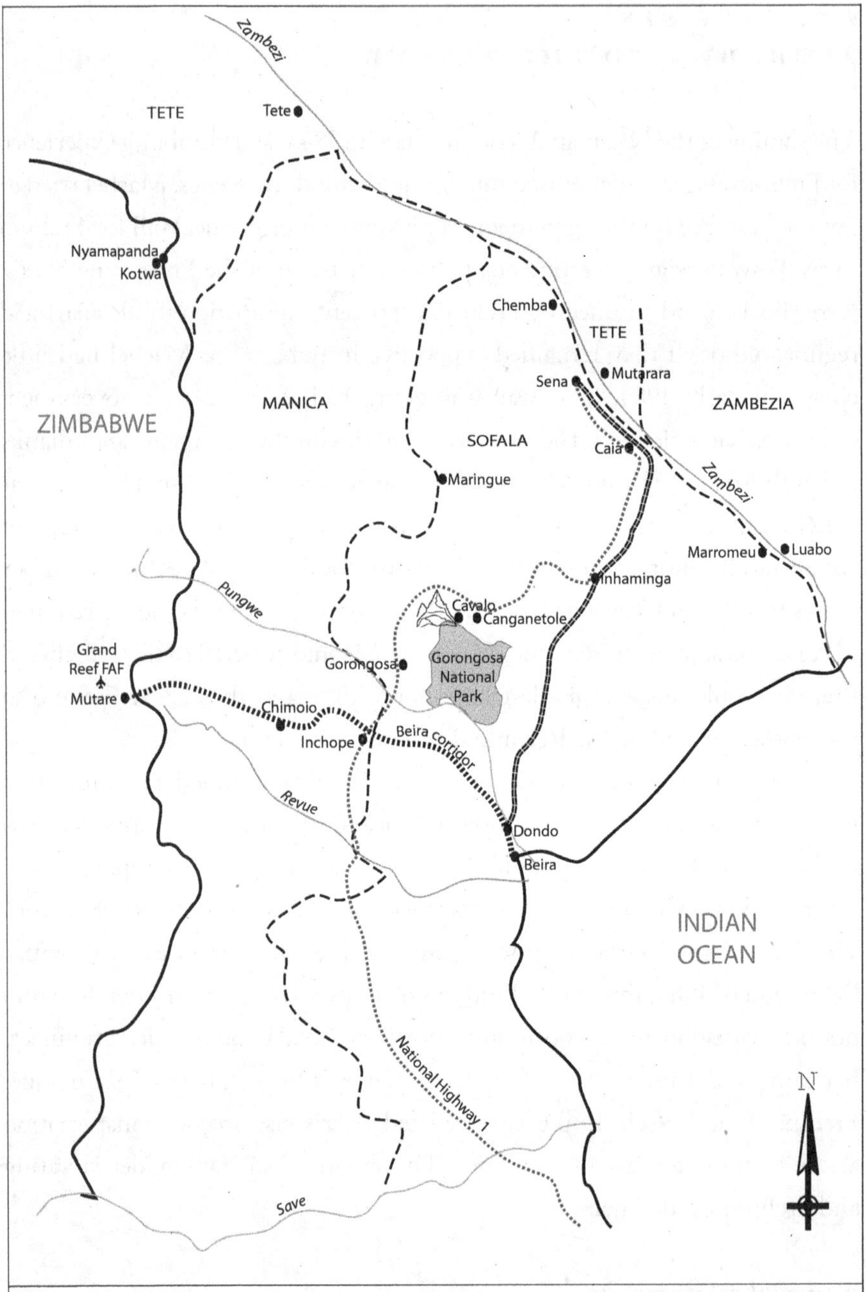

Map 5: Central Region

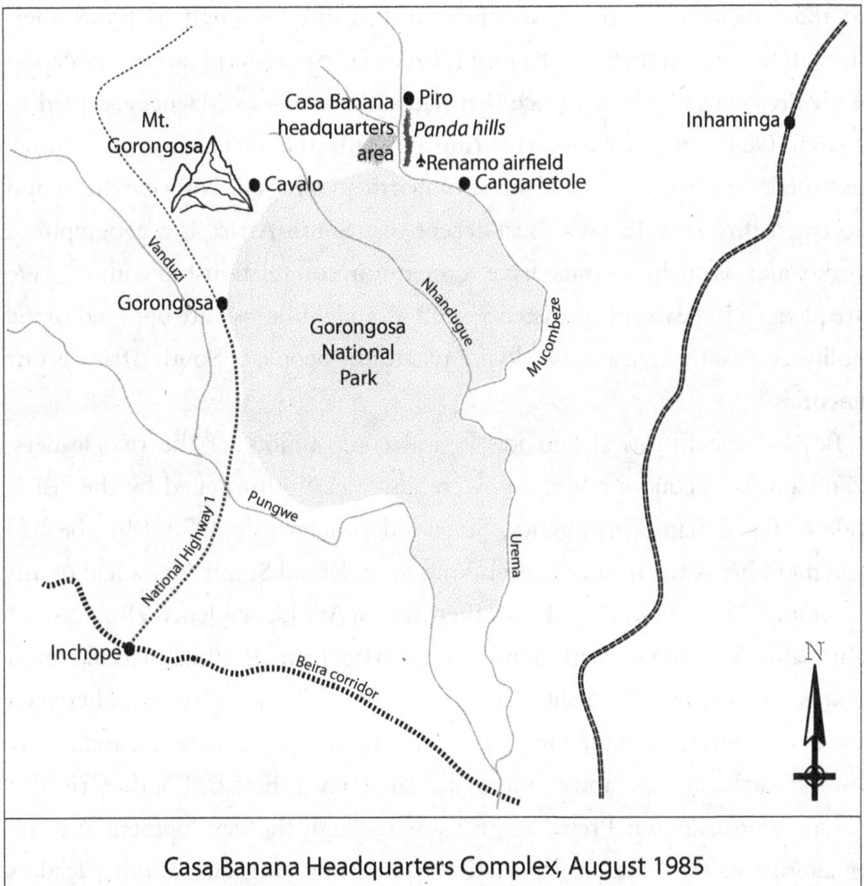

Casa Banana Headquarters Complex, August 1985

countries found themselves intertwined. Zimbabwean nationalists owed much to Frelimo for its assistance during their own liberation struggle, and Mugabe's personal rise to power in Zimbabwe could not have been done without Machel's unwavering support. And, as we have seen, Mozambique paid dearly for this support at the hands of the Rhodesians. Moreover, both men clearly understood the ominous threat that the apartheid regime posed to their social revolutions, yet they were realistic enough to know their limitations in directly confronting Pretoria. Short-term accommodation with Pretoria was often a price that had to be paid—as Machel accepted in March 1984—in return for ensuring not only the survival of his regime, but the long-term success of the anti-apartheid struggle. Mugabe knew and accepted this as well: "We must accept that South Africa is a geographical reality and, as such, we must have some minimum relationship with it." "We are pledged to peaceful coexistence with it" and while "we are opposed to the politics of South Africa ... we do not regard the people of South Africa as our enemies."[271]

Beyond the historical and ideological compatibility of the two leaders, Zimbabwean economic interests were also clearly threatened by the rising tide of the Renamo insurgency. Since independence in 1980, Mugabe had sought to break the historical economic stranglehold South Africa had on his economy. The numbers spoke for themselves: At independence 91 percent of Zimbabwe's trade was with South Africa, 41 percent of all its manufactured goods were exported to South Africa, a preferential trade agreement between the two countries provided millions annually in foreign currency, and nearly three-fourths of Zimbabwe's international debt was held by South Africa.[272]

One way to loosen Pretoria's grip was through the development and use of alternative trade and transportation routes. For Mugabe and other leaders of the Front Line States, Mozambique's rail, road, and ports held the key to building economic independence and, as such, became both a political and financial priority. Beyond the long-term political benefits to Zimbabwe of using the Mozambican routes, the immediate economic windfall was even more pronounced. For example, the National Railways of Zimbabwe (NRZ) estimated that use of the Chicualacuala rail line from southeast Zimbabwe to the port of Maputo would cut freight expenses of the country's primary exports by a half to two-thirds.[273] Savings exceeding 40 percent in some cases were also possible by using the port of Beira instead of the South African port of Durban.[274] Enhanced revenues from the increased use of its transportation and port facilities would also bring substantial economic benefits to Mozambique, and lessen its financial dependence on South African goods exported through Mozambique.

Of course the powers that be in Pretoria were well aware of these facts too. As we have seen previously Mozambique's transportation, lines of communication, and economic infrastructure were priority targets of not only Renamo forces, but of direct South African covert action. Here the mutual interests of Dhlakama and Pretoria aligned. Renamo's military strategy of attacking Maputo's vulnerable lines of communication overlapped nicely with South Africa's geo-political goal of keeping Harare an economic hostage. Accordingly, the Beira corridor and the Chicualacuala rail line received special attention. They were constantly under attack from 1981 onward, with the Chicualacuala rail line being closed down completely by August 1984. Road and rail bridges were destroyed or seriously damaged. The oil pipeline and pumping stations across central Manica and Sofola were repeatedly sabotaged. And vehicular traffic from Beira to Mutare was under constant threat of ambush.

Just as their enemies had found common cause in their attacks, so too did Machel and Mugabe increasingly come to see their national security interests as one, and the defeat of Renamo would not only be a victory for Frelimo, but for Zimbabwe as well.

The final straw for Mugabe appears to have been the early December 1982 SADF commando attack on the Zimbabwean fuel depot in Beira, resulting in the loss of two and a half months' supply of petroleum which precipitated an acute fuel shortage in Zimbabwe. The country was nearly brought to a standstill for lack of fuel. At one point there was but one day's supply of petrol available and Zimbabwe became entirely dependent of South Africa for fuel.[275] Shortly thereafter, Mugabe ordered additional reinforcements—several hundred troops had recently deployed in late November[276]—into

Mozambique to assist Frelimo in protecting the western half of the Beira corridor from insurgent attacks. Enough was enough.

Into the breach

Although a 1981 security pact between Mozambique and Zimbabwe provided the basis for military cooperation, the deployment by the end of 1982 of some 1,000 Zimbabwe National Army (ZNA) troops inside Mozambique on a permanent basis represented a new milestone. Up to now the Zimbabwean military had played a largely passive role in the war, limiting itself to intelligence exchanges, sealing its side of the border, or granting the FAM free movement through Zimbabwean territory in support of past offensives. Its assumption of responsibility for safeguarding the road, rail, and pipeline network from the Zimbabwean border town of Mutare to the central Mozambican transportation hub of Chimoio in December 1982, dubbed Operation Lifeline, put it squarely in the thick of the war.

Initially troops for Operation Lifeline were drawn from the ZNA's 3 Brigade under the command of Brigadier-General Vitalis Zvinavashe based out of Mutare with each one of the brigade's three battalions rotating in and out of Mozambique. Zvinavashe was a strong proponent of Zimbabwean intervention. Based on his close personal ties with a number of Frelimo commanders he was well aware of the FAM's deteriorating military condition, but felt his men were up to the task. However, with the expansion of the mission by 1984 to include patrolling and protecting the considerable length of the corridor from Mutare to Beira, the entire brigade of 3,000 men plus supporting elements found itself on constant deployment in Mozambique.[277] This unrelenting burden had a telling impact and strained 3 Brigade to breaking point.

To ease the burden, the ZNA began rotating each of its regular infantry brigades into Mozambique for six to nine month deployments, and established a Special Task Force (STF) at Chimoio by mid-1985 to serve as the headquarters for the rotating brigades. Each rotating brigade commander served as STF commander with responsibility for protecting the corridor. According to a ZNA officer, the headquarters "was set up on a swamp south of the airfield so no-one wanted to stay there; senior officers stayed in town with their wives and girlfriends while junior officers ran the headquarters."[278] At first no Air Force of Zimbabwe (AFZ) aircraft were permanently based at Chimoio airfield, but deployed for short periods from Zimbabwe as needed for operational support to the army. By March 1986, however, the requirement for a more immediate response time caused the AFZ to position an air detachment of three helicopters and one transport aircraft at the airfield, along with a 65-man support team under a wing commander.[279] In later years the significant presence of relatively well-off Zimbabwean soldiers and airmen in the Chimoio area would lead to tensions with the FAM and local population.

Even as Harare moved to enhance security along the Beira corridor, another of Zimbabwe's important economic corridors to the north came under increasing insurgent pressure. Since moving into Tete Province at the end of 1982, Renamo activity had steadily expanded northwestward to the rest of the province. By mid-1984 the insurgents were threatening the primary commercial link between Zimbabwe and Malawi—the 263-kilometer highway running from Nyamapanda on the Zimbabwean border through Tete to Zobue on the Malawi frontier. Vehicles were being ambushed. Trucks looted and burned. Roadside villages burnt to the ground and the road repeatedly mined by the Renamo forces. In response, a joint security committee was established in June 1984 between Mozambique, Malawi and Zimbabwe to counter the threat, but the ZNA would carry the heaviest load as part of Operation Cob Web. Elements of the 1st Mechanized Battalion under the command of Major Jesse Hickman were dispatched to provide armed convoy escorts. Using their Brazilian-made Cascavel armored personnel carriers for the so-called 'Gun Run' across the province, the troops patrolled the road to pre-empt insurgent activity and provided fast-reaction forces in response to Renamo attacks. Headquartered at Tete, the roughly 600-man unit was also charged with securing and protecting the key rail and road bridge crossings over the Zambezi River there.[280]

Live and let live

The ZNA's deployments along the Beira and Tete corridors from the end of 1982 until the middle of 1985 were largely defensive in nature and done with the intent of freeing up FAM units for offensive operations, but this situation also gave rise to a strange strategic accommodation between Renamo and Zimbabwean forces.

While Renamo would continue to probe Zimbabwean defenses, strike targets along both corridors, and periodically clash with ZNA troops, a clear *modus vivendi* began to take shape, particularly along the Beira corridor. Both sides appeared to develop a 'live and let live' approach to the conflict. Despite the occasional disruption, for the better part of two and a half years Zimbabwean goods and fuel flowed steadily from Beira to Mutare, while Renamo guerrillas were free to operate unhindered by the ZNA outside the corridors. The notable exception to this informal arrangement was along the Mozambican–Zimbabwean frontier where both sides often directly challenged each other.

How exactly this situation came to be and what exactly the understanding entailed is difficult to determine. Moreover, like most controversies surrounding the war, the evidence is often conflicting. According to one ZNA officer, "we had no problems with Renamo over the pipeline and corridor early on, as Renamo informed the ZNA of its crossings"; there was "an informal arrangement."[281] Likewise, a senior Renamo commander claims there was "an agreement" in the early 1980s whereby Zimbabwean forces would only operate 20 kilometers on either side of the corridor. "Tiny Rowland had brokered the deal with Dhlakama."[282] But, another former senior Renamo commander says, there was no such agreement and the pipeline and road "was sabotaged and attacked all the time."[283] Most likely 'an understanding' evolved along the lines of maintaining the status quo between local commanders on the ground, that was periodically broken at the direction of higher command authority, or as new forces rotated in. Once these flare ups passed, however, there was a return to the old status quo of live and let live.

The reference to Tiny Rowland (chief executive of Lonhro, the UK-based multinational with extensive financial interests in southern Africa) points to a degree of pragmatism on Renamo's part, as well as the duplicity of others with an interest in the operations of the corridor. Rowland was well known for his ability to navigate the treacherous waters of Africa conflicts to advance Lonhro's business interest. Reportedly he would work with anyone from apartheid capitalists to Marxist African liberation movements. Thus, it comes as little surprise that a Lonhro subsidiary, which was part owner of the Beira pipeline, entered into "a secret protection agreement with Renamo" to prevent insurgent sabotage of the pipeline in June 1982, according to Alex Vines.[284] Vines cites Lonhro documents showing payments to Renamo totaling $500,000 per month over a three-month period from June to August 1982. Attacks still continued however. Possibly because "symbolic" insurgent attacks under the terms of the agreement were permitted, to placate Renamo supporters in Pretoria.[285] Alternatively, Renamo could have used the attacks as a reminder to Lonhro, or Zimbabwe, of its capability or even simply because some Renamo units took their own initiative to launch raids from time to time. Ultimately, what stands out is the apparent willingness of Renamo and its adversaries to find some mutual form of accommodation that served the particular interests of all parties at the time.

Frelimo under pressure

By the latter half of 1984 it was becoming increasingly apparent that Machel's gamble at Nkomati was a failure. Rather than contain the insurgency, it had worsened. Insurgent attacks were now averaging 100 a month,[286] with every province affected. Renamo guerrillas were operating at the doorstep of the capital. Repeated FAM offensives had produced only limited, short-term relief from this onslaught while depleting material and manpower. The widening violence and repeated droughts were sending to the cities hundreds of thousands of desperate people that the government could not afford to feed, shelter nor protect. Even Pretoria's diplomatic efforts to broker meaningful peace talks were proving fruitless. Frelimo was in deep trouble.

Although Renamo had been operating in Maputo Province since the end of 1983, the post-Nkomati period saw a sharp rise in activity across the province. The closure of South Africa's Letaba Ranch training camp pushed several hundred newly-trained guerrillas across the border into southern Mozambique. One of these groups included Raúl Domingos, the new

Southern Front commander (responsible for Gaza, Inhambane and Maputo provinces), who along with 60 men and five women were airdropped into northern Maputo Province just prior to the signing of the Nkomati Accord. It was here, just south of the Mazimechopes River along the Maputo–Gaza provincial border, that Domingos established Renamo's main operational base for the province.[287]

Over the next 15 months Domingos and his guerrilla forces would tighten the screws on Frelimo, moving increasing closer to the capital. As usual heavy emphasis was placed on interrupting supply and transportation routes. Rail and road networks north and west of the capital, including the strategic hub at Magude about 100 kilometers north of Maputo, were repeatedly subject to attack. The Chicualacuala rail line closed down completely in August. National Highway 1 north of Manhica became an increasingly deadly stretch of road. In an operational shift, Renamo also began operating in larger groups of 60–80, even occasionally up to 200 or more. These larger company-size formations were used to assault vulnerable FAM and militia positions with the goal of capturing significant supplies and munitions. By June 1985 Renamo was claiming to capture thousands of weapons and more than 100 tons of supplies each month from government forces.[288]

To support this rising level of operational activity, Renamo turned increasingly to forced recruitment in the south to fill its ranks. Many of these were young children abducted from schools and villages. They were forced to carry away looted or captured supplies and then marched to remote bush camps near the South African border for several months of military training. By some estimates "around 40 percent of Renamo combatants were under the age of eighteen" at the time of recruitment: eight percent were between ten and 14 years old.[289] (Comparable figures for Frelimo combatants show that just over 12 percent of those recruited were under the age of 17, while another 6.5 percent were under 15 years old, according to a confidential 1992 government report.[290]) It was difficult for most. "Close to 90 of us were taken" following Renamo putting the local garrison to flight and "we were forced to walk for two days," recalls one 14-year-old Renamo recruit. Life at the Spartan camps was hard and food shortages common: "anything we could find, we ate."[291] By 1985, Renamo probably had around 2,000 guerrillas operating in the south.

Meanwhile, in central Mozambique the insurgents were not only consolidating their grip on large parts of the rural countryside, but were pushing farther north well beyond the Zambezi River valley. Even Frelimo's hold on larger towns was now in jeopardy. The district capital of Maringue changed hands on a regular basis, the vital railway town of Inhaminga was repeatedly raided, and Gorongosa town kept virtually under siege. Assaults on FAM positions increased, including one on the Pungwe bridge garrison in June that left 79 FAM dead, according to Renamo claims. And since entering southern Niassa and Nampula provinces in mid-1983, Renamo columns moved ever eastward toward the provincial capital of Nampula throughout 1984. The Ncala corridor—containing the main road, railway, and communication lines from the port of Ncala to Malawi—fell under heavy attack as did the key transportation hub at Cuamba. By May 1984, the insurgents reached Cabo Delgado Province, where they quickly gained a following among the Makonde people and other long-standing anti-Frelimo elements in the province. Renamo now had an established military presence in every province of the country.

Secret South African-brokered peace talks in September and October 1984 failed to gain any traction. Neither Frelimo nor Renamo trusted Pretoria and its ultimate agenda for the future of Mozambique. South Africa's failure to rein in its military or staunch the flow of private aid to the insurgents from across the border, only further fueled Frelimo charges of Pretoria's complicity in continuing to support Renamo. Within a year of signing, both the Nkomati agreement and any hope for peace were dead. The war would go on.

Harare goes on the offensive

To rectify the deteriorating situation Machel called upon his closest allies—Zimbabwe and Tanzania. Both countries agreed to triple the number of their troops in the country.[292] Following a June 1985 meeting between Machel and Mugabe, Mugabe agreed not only to commit more troops, but to go on the offensive against Renamo forces in central Mozambique. For his part, President Nyerere pledged to train new Mozambican recruits at its Nachingwea, Tanzania training base for operations in the north.[293] In August, Mugabe would publicly vow that ensuring access to the sea through Mozambique was worth any price to Zimbabwe—even a commitment of "20,000 to 30,000 men."[294] By early August 1985 the Zimbabwean military presence along the Beira corridor had grown to between 5,000 to 6,000 troops and support personnel. And planning was well underway "to annihilate the Renamo bandits and restore law and order in Manica, Tete and Sofala provinces."[295] The stage was set for a considerable escalation in the war.

The attack on Casa Banana[296]

The main Renamo headquarters, known as Casa Banana, was located in the savanna scrub forest between the town of Cavalo (lying on the eastern edge of the Gorongosa massif) and the Panda hills just northwest of the village of Canganetole. It occupied a large area just north of the Rio Nhandugue near an old factory, and contained an extensive collection of crude buildings housing a command and communication center, radio and mechanic repair shops, tailor shops (making tents and other articles from old parachutes) and a bush airstrip.[297] Most important of all in August 1985, it housed the senior Renamo leadership, including Dhlakama and many of his senior lieutenants, not to mention large quantities of weapons and ammunition. Estimates of the number of insurgents, including trainees, at the Casa Banana complex and its various outlying camps at the time vary widely—even among those present. But it would appear that some 400–600 fighters were at Casa Banana itself, and upwards of perhaps another 1,000 were spread across the Gorongosa area, bringing the total Renamo forces to between 1,400 and 1,600 at the time of the attack.[298]

Despite knowledge of the base's general location for some time, the FAM had been unable to effectively attack it. With the Zimbabwean military decision to go on the offensive against Renamo, however, capturing Casa Banana and inflicting a costly defeat on the insurgents became a top priority target. Once the orders were given, it didn't take long for a squad of Patrols Company from Lieutenant-Colonel Lionel Dyck's 1 Para Group to pinpoint the base's exact location, and estimate the Renamo strength at about 300 men.[299] Much to the consternation of Zimbabwean unit commanders in the field, however, senior Mozambican and Zimbabwean generals including General Dai and Major-General Zvinavashe (now ZNA Chief of Staff) and their staffs took it upon themselves to do most of the pre-operational planning for what promised to be the largest joint operation of the war. The result, according to one field commander at the time, was "an unworkable plan that had no chance of succeeding."[300]

The attack on Casa Banana (code name Operation Grapefruit) was to be spearheaded by the Zimbabwean army and directly supported by Mozambican infantry, artillery, and air assets. It was designed to deliver a crippling, if not mortal, blow to the insurgents and their command structure. As initially conceived, the plan called for moving thousands of combat troops by air, vehicle and foot into the area east of Gorongosa mountain. Western intelligence services believed that some 8,000–10,000 Zimbabwean and Mozambican troops were to take part in the massive operation.[301] Once these troops were in position, a Zimbabwean strike force with close air support would directly assault the Casa Banana camp to either kill or drive the fleeing guerrillas into the waiting arms of the encircling Zimbabwean and Mozambican troops. At least that was the plan.

The reality of actually mounting and coordinating such a huge undertaking quickly proved to be too much. Both militaries were compelled to dramatically reduce the size of their forces. Large numbers of Zimbabwean troops were simply not available. An entire brigade was already tied up defending the Beira corridor, other units were protecting the Tete corridor or involved in convoy duty, and the unsettled situation in Zimbabwe's far western Matabeleland region tied up at least two additional infantry brigades. More critically, the promised Mozambican forces were never released. The 5th Brigade out of Beira with its heavy weapons remained in garrison, and Mozambican air force planes remained on the ground, according to a Zimbabwean source familiar with the operation.[302] In the end Operation Grapefruit would be an entirely Zimbabwean affair conducted only by the units of the Presidential Guard Brigade and 1 Para Group with support from the AFZ. All totaled, the attacking force would ultimately number less than 600 men and a handful of aircraft.

Despite the massive cut in combat strength, the original operational plan remained in place. Soldiers from the Presidential Guard and 1 Para began to assemble at the STF base at Chimoio by mid-August. Operational orders were issued for the Presidential Guard's three badly understrength battalions (totaling 500 men) to advance on Cavalo, on the eastern side of the Gorongosa massif. From here they would deploy by 27 August into three stop lines ringing the Renamo headquarters complex. One battalion would position itself north of Cavalo forming the western stop line, while another battalion would deploy along the south bank of the Rio Nhandugue and the third battalion would force march from Cavalo eastward through some 60 kilometers of rugged bush to form the eastern stop line running just east of the Panda hills. Meanwhile some 65–70 troopers from 1 Para, under the direct command of Lieutenant-Colonel Dyck, would be airdropped to the north of the Casa Banana location. Dyck's men, along with planned Zimbabwean air strikes, would drive the guerrillas into the awaiting arms of the Presidential Guard troops.[303] D-Day was set for 28 August and would commence with air strikes and the para drop.

Given the tactical requirement to move hundreds of Presidential Guard troops quickly and silently across miles of difficult terrain and then effectively position them prior to the main attack, Dyck was fearful of losing the element of surprise. So Dyck took it upon himself to modify the operational plan, relying instead on 1 Para's air mobility capability and its well-trained soldiers to strike the Casa Banana compound directly.[304] He was taking quite a gamble. The small group of paratroopers would be going up against a Renamo force estimated at least five times its size and, while the Zimbabweans had air superiority, the assault force would be on its own for many hours before any additional ground reinforcements could reach the battlefield.

When D-Day arrived on 28 August, Dyck first deployed a small group of about 20 men in an ambush position along a track about 20 kilometers north of the camp in anticipation of Renamo using it as a likely escape route. Then, flying out of 1 Para's forward base at Chimoio some 125 kilometers distant,

Dyck recalls, "the main attack force of two Daks worth (28 men) were dropped directly south of the camp, in a dry river bed ... about 300 meters from the edge of the camp. I was overhead with the K-car and had two helicopters for trooping dropped paras for repositioning stops [along] the track to the north of the camp."[305] Although vastly outnumbered, the bold air assault caught the guerrillas completely off guard. "There was panic everywhere" as "we were caught by surprise," remembers one former Renamo soldier.[306]

Individual guerrillas fought as best they could amid the ensuing chaos, while others were told to destroy all materials and supplies before escaping. Once on the ground the paratroopers formed sweep lines in an attempt to drive the fleeing Renamo soldiers toward the northern ambush position. AFZ Hunter strike aircraft meanwhile pounded the area northwest of the main headquarters complex to subdue any resistance and kill any insurgents fleeing in that direction. In short order the main base and the adjoining airfield just east of the Panda hills were overrun and captured by the Zimbabwean paratroopers. Sporadic fighting would continue throughout the day as isolated pockets of resistance were overcome or the insurgents retreated.

The success of the air assault, however, was not accompanied by similar success on the ground by the Presidential Guard troops. The planned encirclement was never achieved and only one of the Guard battalions was to get into a blocking position west of the camp and cut off retreating Renamo forces. The two other battalions got lost in the heavy bush south of the Rio Nhandugue and never found their starting positions before the attack.[307] It would take more than a week for them to find their way out of the area, all the while having to be resupplied by air from Chimoio with ration packs.

Despite the significance of the battle, there appears to be no official record of Zimbabwean casualties[308] and only a small number of Renamo were killed or wounded. Most insurgents just fled in the face of the surprise attack. Frelimo would publicly claim that 500 insurgents were killed in the combined ground and air assault.[309] Dhlakama escaped unscathed—by motorcycle to the north—as did all his senior commanders. While the enemy death toll was disappointing, the discovery of key documents detailing ongoing South African support to Renamo (which would come to be known as the Gorongosa Documents), as well as the capture of "huge amounts of supplies"[310] and the disruption of Renamo's command and control structure, handed President Machel's flagging forces a major psychological victory. "We have broken the back of the snake," said Machel. "The tail will still thrash around for a while. Now we are pursuing the head of the snake."[311] Machel was in fact so impressed with the result that, during his 5 September visit to the battlefield, he personally thanked Dyck and his men. He then presented Dyck with a Swiss army knife emblazoned with the Frelimo crest, which Dyck still has in his possession more than 25 years later.[312]

The capture of Casa Banana on 28 August 1985 was a significant victory for Harare and Maputo. Its capture, combined with the destruction of the main Renamo base south of the Beira corridor at Muxamba in Manica Province a week earlier, put the insurgents on the defensive.[313] Renamo was on the run, at least for now. And the war had entered a new phase. Direct Zimbabwean military intervention would alter not only the operational environment for both Frelimo and Renamo, but also the strategic direction of the war—and the search for peace—itself.

Maintaining the pressure on Renamo

In the months following the fall of Casa Banana, Zimbabwean and Mozambican forces continued to operate aggressively in the Gorongosa, Maringue, and Macossa districts of northern Sofala and Manica provinces to keep Renamo off balance. Insurgent bases at Indoro and Nhamatanda in northern Sofala fell to FAM forces in mid-September.[314] By mutual agreement, however, the FAM assumed more of a supporting role in this effort. The ZNA would take the operational lead in central Mozambique south of the Zambezi River, while Frelimo would redirect its focus south of the Save River to shore up the government's position in southern Gaza and Inhambane provinces and around Maputo.[315] Meanwhile, the newly enlarged Tanzania People's Defence Force (TPDF) contingent of approximately 2,000 men would shoulder the burden of training and supporting the FAM north of the Zambezi River. The TPDF contingent, headquartered at Quelimane, would increase to 3,000 men by 1987 and go on the offensive with FAM forces to regain lost territory in Zambezia Province.[316]

But Dhlakama and his men were not sitting still. Just as with past large-scale government offensives, Renamo forces simply filtered out of the ZNA operational zones and shifted their attacks to new and more vulnerable districts. A number of smaller guerrilla units remained behind to maintain a presence, harassing ZNA and FAM patrols and garrisons, raiding supply lines, and striking targets along the Beira corridor as a reminder that they were far from defeated. The waning months of 1985 and into 1986 also saw a major increase in Renamo activity along the Zambezi River valley and Zambezia Province. The lower Zambezi towns of Sena, Mutarara, Caia, Mopeia, and Luabo came under Renamo control, as did the important crossroads city of Morrumbala in Zambezia by the end of 1985. In addition, substantial quantities of arms, ammunition, and supplies were captured from the retreating FAM garrisons.[317] Fighting also increased in parts of southern Tete Province as well.

This turn of events was especially disheartening for Frelimo and its allies given their recent success in dislodging Renamo from its central Mozambican stronghold. The unexpected loss of Marromeu, the center of the Zambezi valley's sugar processing industry and the sprawling Sena Sugar Estates, and the flight of the nearly 300-man garrison on 9 January was especially troubling and spurred the ZNA and FAM to action. A previously planned reinforcement mission now would become a joint effort to recapture the city and its important airfield, codename Operation Octopus.[318] In charge of coordinating the planning and leading the assault would be Colonel Flint Magama. Magama, who erroneously has been called "one of the most famous soldiers in the ZNA,"[319] was in reality a politically well-connected staff officer (intelligence). He had little combat experience, but sought to make a name for himself by inflicting a crushing defeat on the Renamo forces occupying Marromeu.[320] His lack of field experience, poor situational awareness, and personal recklessness, would end up costing him and five others their lives.

Magama's plan called for securing the airfield outside the city as a bridgehead for the recapture of Marromeu. A swift air assault would take the airfield. Reinforcements would then be flown in and the attack on the city would commence. The entire operation would be over in a day, two at the most. It was planned for 24 January.

Things began to go wrong from the start. Despite the presence of an SAS call sign on the ground, the scouts were unable to operate effectively given the heavy Renamo presence in the area. Thus, without adequate reconnaissance, Magama had no reliable information as to the terrain, landing zones, or insurgent strength and defensive deployments. Logistics were inadequate too. There was no fuel for the helicopters and the anticipated AFZ aircraft were not available. Nor was there a communications plan in place. But, rather than abort the operation, a Casa 212 transport on a routine supply run to Chimoio was commandeered and loaded with paratroopers who were to capture the airfield. In support of the airdrop, "an overly keen" Magama flying in a Mi-25 Hind helicopter gunship decided to conduct an aerial reconnaissance of the area.[321] Once over the airstrip the Hind came under heavy insurgent fire and the helicopter crashed along the bank of Zambezi killing Magama, two SAS soldiers and the three-man Mozambican air crew, according to the official ZNA after-action report.[322] The newly-dropped troops were taking heavy fire as well, and unable to either secure the airfield or the crash site.

Shortly thereafter, Lieutenant-Colonel Dyck was ordered to recover Magama's body as quickly as possible "for the good of the nation."[323] It took two days, however, for Dyck to assemble a follow up force at Inhaminga because of unserviceable AFZ aircraft and the difficulty in then assembling Mozambican helicopters and transports as replacements, according to official AFZ documents.[324] Moreover, the weather turned worse, grounding the Mozambican aircraft, as the situation deteriorated for the small ZNA force pinned down in Marromeu. On the 27th Dyck made the decision to use two Dakota transports to air assault the airfield at dawn with 32 of his men. Dyck would command the operation from a Casa 212. The insertion was conducted "in atrocious weather—rain, low scudding clouds—[and the pilots] had a devil of a time staying visual with the ground at 500 feet above ground level for the drop," according to a former Zimbabwean officer.[325] Some insurgents were also using captured tanks to bombard the drop zone.

But the bold move succeeded. The airstrip was quickly secured and soon additional reinforcements were flowing onto the battlefield. The Renamo forces put up an initial fight, but the weight of the new ZNA troops forced them to abandon the town. By the afternoon Marromeu was back in government hands. The body of Magama and the other crash victims were then recovered. Official Zimbabwean casualties for Operation Octopus were eight killed and eight wounded, while the insurgents were believed to have lost 150 of the estimated 1,300 men in the Marromeu area. More important was the recapture of "a large assortment of arms and ammunition" including tanks and heavy weapons taken from the FAM garrison.[326]

At the end of January 1986, the Zimbabweans began withdrawing from their forward positions at Marromeu, Inhaminga, Casa Banana, and other locations in the Gorongosa area and returning to Chimoio as part of a major redeployment. FAM troops then took up defensive positions at these locations. In five short, but intense, months of fighting the Zimbabweans had clearly tipped the military and political balance back in Frelimo's favor and they had proven their ability to effectively conduct counter-insurgency operations. Nonetheless, the strain on Harare's experienced but limited personnel, its aging equipment, and logistics capability was telling and it would severely impact the Zimbabwean military's ability to conduct sustained offensive operations inside Mozambique.

Even as the Zimbabweans pushed north toward the Zambezi valley, growing numbers of Renamo guerrillas began quietly infiltrating back into the Gorongosa region with the onset of the rainy season. On 14 February Renamo attacked. The FAM garrison at Casa Banana was quickly overrun by some 400 insurgents, scattering the defenders and sending them fleeing to Cavalo and Gorongosa town.[327] Renamo not only regained its old headquarters, but captured large quantities of supplies and heavy weapons from the FAM as well. In short order, the insurgents were laying siege to other FAM positions in the area and conducting harassing raids against Frelimo supply lines.

The speed of the Renamo recovery and the collapse of the FAM in early 1986 caught the Zimbabweans completely off guard and ill-prepared. Not only was the Zimbabwean high command still redeploying its troops, but it was in the midst of a major restructuring of its Mozambican operations. The role and operation of the STF was still being fined-tuned and an STF air element only just added in March. Training and equipping of regular ZNA brigades for combat deployment was still a work in progress. And a revamped operational doctrine had yet to be put in place alongside the appropriate force structure. Thus, it took almost two months for the Zimbabweans to put together an attacking force with the capability to recapture Casa Banana, in what was codenamed Operation Zero.[328]

Delayed briefly by bad weather both at Chimoio and at Grand Reef forward airfield outside Mutare, Operation Zero launched at dawn on 12 April. Including elements of 3 Brigade, 1 Commando, and other units, the attacking force probably numbered no more than 1,000 men in total.[329] Using both fixed wing and helicopter air assets, the first wave of the recently designated 'STF Strike Force' began dropping into the Casa Banana base. The air assault was preceded by a heavy aerial bombardment of the base and it's supporting defensive positions. Meanwhile at the STF headquarters in Chimoio, Major-General Zvinavashe and several of his Frelimo counterparts anxiously monitored the situation. Early reports indicated that fighting was particularly heavy in the northern part of the base, with insurgents entrenched in the Panda hills to the east. Once the airfield was secured, however, second wave reinforcements and additional supplies were flown in by Dakota transports from Chimoio and the fight was all but over by midday. At 1400 hours Casa Banana was officially back in Zimbabwean hands.

Although Casa Banana and its airfield were quickly retaken, it would be several days before all the outlying Renamo outposts would be recaptured and the region secured by follow-up units. The reoccupation of Cavalo and other Renamo defenses along the eastern edge of the Gorongosa mastiff by elements of 3 Brigade's 2nd Battalion, for example, proved to be challenging.[330] Despite a preparatory AFZ airstrike against the defending Renamo force, the attacking ZNA force became bogged down, losing a vehicle to an RPG attack and exhausting nearly all its ammunition in skirmishing with the insurgents before reaching the objective. It took an additional day of fighting and the support of two more companies uplifted from Casa Banana before Cavalo was taken on the 14th and Operation Zero came to a close.[331]

The surprisingly quick and easy reconquest of Casa Banana and its supporting outposts came with few casualties on the Zimbabwean side—three dead and seven wounded. Few Renamo dead were found afterward, but areas of the battlefield were so heavily cratered as a result of the air bombardment that making an accurate assessment was all but impossible. There were also some indications that Renamo had warning of the pending operation and that most of the insurgents withdrew in the days before the assault,[332] thus accounting for the low number of casualties. Much of the previously abandoned FAM heavy weapons and equipment was recovered and Frelimo gained an important propaganda victory with the recovery of the base. However, to avoid a repeat of this cycle, the ZNA would maintain a battalion-size presence in the Casa Banana area until the 1992 ceasefire.

By the second half of 1986, the bulk of the ZNA's 6,000–8,000-man force in Mozambique had pulled back to the defense of the Beira and Tete corridors (with the exception of the Casa Banana base presence). Henceforth, offensive operations would largely become the responsibility of specialized units such as 1 Para Group, 1 Commando and SAS or the Strike Force contingent operating out of Chimoio or from forward airfields in eastern Zimbabwe. This reflected a shift in operational strategy. Rather than mount large, resource- and manpower-intense operations periodically as the FAM did, the ZNA adapted a harassing strategy. Relying on mobility and air power, Zimbabwean forces would undertake multiple small-scale actions against known or newly identified Renamo bases and troop concentrations. The goal was to keep Renamo off balance and prevent it from massing its forces for large-scale offensives. More than 40 of these ZNA operations would take place from Tete in the north to Gaza in the south by the end of the war.[333]

Renamo adapts

While Renamo's war aims remained unchanged—weaken Frelimo by attacking the country's economic infrastructure, confine the government to major population centers, and wage a demoralizing war of attrition against the FAM—Renamo had no choice but to change its heretofore successful operational and tactical approach to the new reality of the Zimbabwean military threat. The Zimbabweans "were bad for Renamo"—they were well-trained and prepared "unlike the Frelimo soldiers," recalls one former guerrilla fighter.[334] The use of helicopter-borne troop insertions of small squads along with air strikes and gunships, initially caused Renamo serious problems. Morale dipped very low. "It was hard. They really hurt us," recounts one senior commander.[335] So Renamo adapted.

Some of the biggest changes occurred in the insurgent controlled areas of the countryside. The ZNA capability to utilize its air mobility to launch quick, pinpoint strikes made Renamo's past use of large, fixed bases a liability. Not only was there the potential to suffer serious casualties, but the potential loss of critical supplies of ammunition and weapons was something the insurgents could ill-afford in the post-Nkomati era. The loss of Casa Banana had been a lesson well learned. Although Renamo did not abandon the use of a centralized headquarters or the use of provincial bases by any means, the layout and defense of these bases changed markedly, especially in central Mozambique. For example, the new Massala headquarters in the Maringue District northwest of Gorongsa was deliberately spread out over a wider area. The central command area was surrounded by multiple smaller camps that often contained civilian populations. This layout was not only harder to detect from the air, but also provided an advance warning system of an approaching enemy.[336] Permanent structures were few and very crude in construction. Numerous underground storage caches and bunkers were also built. In other more distant operational areas, the bases became little more than bush camps of wood and thatch.[337] Often with only a single generator and few improvements, they could be quickly abandoned at the first sign of trouble.

Likewise, Renamo units, including the large, semi-conventional battalions that were established after Nkomati, were dispersed into smaller formations to make them less attractive targets. The Dragon Battalion, for instance, spread its 1,097 men across eleven different positions, some with as few as six men and the largest being 475, according to a Renamo situation report.[338] Companies were often split into more platoons and then the platoons into five-man squads, called *equipas* (teams) and deployed as sentries.[339] Larger formations set up all-round defensive positions by carefully positioning B10 recoilless rifles and 82mm mortars. Heavy 14.5mm or 12.7mm machine guns were sited in an air defense role that, in the ultimate twist of irony, were very similar to the ZANLA guerrilla bases of old.[340] The downside to this dispersion of units was the increasing difficulty in command and control as communication problems set in later in the war.

The aggressive, harassing nature of Zimbabwean attacks from early 1986 onward also forced Renamo to adapt its defensive tactical doctrine. To counter the Strike Force raids the guerrillas learned to avoid immediately retreating in the direction of the stop groups. Instead they scattered sideways or even moved toward the advancing ground forces to try to break through their lines. There were instances, recalls one Renamo guerrilla, when "the enemy soldiers ended up firing at each other since none of us were in the middle as they had expected."[341] Air attack was a constant concern too. But soon the insurgents discovered that whenever the first air strike was launched it was best to remain motionless on the ground or hide behind a tree or a rock to avoid detection. "This worked perfectly, especially where the terrain was of a more barren type," recalled Renamo's former chief of staff.[342] Renamo would later go on to claim that the AFZ became increasingly indiscriminate in their bombings of suspected insurgent positions, which often led to the deaths of many civilians.

Opening the eastern front

The biggest shift in Renamo strategy came on 20 June 1987 when Dhlakama 'declared war' on Zimbabwe and commenced sustained military operations in eastern Zimbabwe. Although Renamo guerrillas had long crisscrossed the porous border in search of supplies or to seek safe haven among their Shona kinsmen in the face of Frelimo offensives, the fighting had remained confined to the Mozambican side of the border. This was about to change as Harare had to pay a price for its military intervention in Mozambique. According to a former Renamo general, the strategic goal was to force Harare to defend its own territory and thus pull troops out of Mozambique.[343] Five- to 15-man units began infiltrating northeast Zimbabwe from Tete Province as early as

May 1987 and soon alarm bells were ringing all along the eastern frontier. From Kotwa in the north to Chipinga in the south, the insurgents unleashed a wave of attacks on commercial farms, schools, health clinics, shops, and villages. Property was looted or destroyed and panic set in. Five attacks in August alone, including an attack on the Jersey Tea Estates south of Mutare that left four ZNA soldiers dead, produced the first military casualties on Zimbabwean soil. By September the insurgents claimed to be operating as far as 50 kilometers inside Zimbabwe, and were averaging three to four major attacks per month. Over the course of the next two years more than 450 people (including several dozen ZNA soldiers) would die from these attacks, while others would be abducted into the insurgent ranks.[344]

To counter the Renamo raids Harare quickly instituted counter-insurgency measures. It rushed additional troops to the border region and reinstituted the Rhodesian-era protected village concept in the hardest hit areas to isolate the guerrillas from the local population. The Renamo threat also provided Harare with a ready-made rationale to crack down on Ndabaningi Sithole's opposition ZANU-Ndonga party in the Chipinga area and discredit other nascent political discontent with the Zimbabwean military involvement in Mozambique. So much so, that the new counter-insurgency effort in the east was codenamed Operation *Ndonga Chirenje* (Remove Ndonga) and would coincide with the deployment of the newly-trained 6 Brigade to the frontier at the end of 1987.

Beyond the psychological impact and the brief boost in Renamo morale, Dhlakama's eastern offensive had little impact on the war inside Mozambique. The raids, while annoying and instilling fear, did little real damage to the Zimbabwean economy. They failed to divert large numbers of Zimbabwean troops already in Mozambique or force Mugabe to reassess his commitment to Frelimo. In point of fact, the Zimbabwean military presence in Mozambique would expand by the end of 1987 to include not only operations in the central region but also in the south.

Renamo on the attack

The real response to Zimbabwean intervention would be the escalation of the war in Mozambique itself. But rather than challenge the Zimbabweans directly in central Mozambique, Renamo directed its operations northward toward the Zambezi River valley, expanded its activity in Zambezia and Nampula provinces, and put pressure on the Mozambican capital again. It was designed to send a clear message to Frelimo and its allies that the insurgents were far from being defeated.

Accordingly, the second half of 1986 saw several thousand Renamo insurgents go on the offensive all along the Zambezi valley from lower Tete Province to the Mozambican coast, where they "made unprecedented gains," according to a CIA assessment.[345] By September Renamo was in control of a number of large towns along the Zambezi River from Mutarara to Chuabo, including the key towns of Caia and Marromeu (again). Hundreds of Frelimo soldiers were taken prisoner. Other FAM river garrisons were under siege, forcing civilians to flee the deteriorating situation into neighboring Malawi or farther afield. The newly captured towns were looted of anything of value and Caia soon looked "as though vultures had picked clean its carcass," according to a journalist's account.[346] Rather than pin themselves down or expose themselves to air strikes, Renamo established defensive positions and camps outside the vacant towns.

Renamo made significant gains in other parts of Zambezia Province as well, taking control of nearly all the district capitals.[347] Gile, nearly 500 kilometers from Gorongosa, had fallen in July and Morrumbala would come under insurgent control in August. The strategic western Zambezia border town of Milange was cut off, forcing some 1,700 FAM soldiers and their families to take refuge in Malawi.[348] It would later fall to Renamo in October. By early October the Malawian government was reporting that more than 70,000 Mozambicans had fled the recent fighting in Zambezia and Tete and crossed the border into Malawi.[349] This number would swell to over 200,000 within a month. The deteriorating situation pushed Mugabe and Machel to increase the pressure on Malawian President Banda in mid-October to stop aiding and abetting the Renamo insurgents, who they claimed were operating from bases inside Malawi, or suffer the consequences. The reality, however, was that Renamo had no permanent bases but—like Frelimo—conveniently made use of Malawian territory for transit and to obtain non-military supplies, and southern Malawi had also become a key trading hub for looted goods.[350]

Much has been made of Renamo's grand plan to split the country in two in late 1986 by gaining control over the Zambezi River and its adjoining districts, and thus laying the ground for the establishment of a "Free Mozambique" (similar to UNITA's enclave in southeastern Angola) during the so-called October offensive.[351] None of the senior Renamo generals interviewed, nor Dhlakama himself, identify this as their goal. Rather, the push northward was part of their longstanding military strategy of gaining control over the countryside, and denying Frelimo access to a key economic and population heartland north of the Zambezi. And while a number of towns would fall under Renamo control, the insurgents carefully avoided establishing a permanent large-scale presence in them, because of their vulnerability to FAM and ZNA counterattacks and air strikes. For Dhlakama, the critical military weakness of Frelimo's army was its morale: "not training, not equipment, but poor morale."[352] Renamo's ability to overrun FAM garrisons seemingly at will and capture larger towns was a way to target this vulnerability and bring about a collapse of the FAM.

Although not as desperate a situation, Renamo activity in the south was continuing to create problems for Frelimo too. Since early 1986 the rail line from Maputo to Swaziland came under regular insurgent attack, as did the main highway just north of the capital. Renamo units would rely on a system of spies to inform them of convoy movements, so they could deploy ambushes and then quickly withdraw after their attacks.[353] By March, guerrilla teams were infiltrating the Matola area outside the capital and clashing with Frelimo forces and police. Renamo would also claim responsibility for a car bombing in a residential neighborhood of Maputo later in the year. Anti-personnel land mines on beaches north of the city injured several people and fueled panic. And the frequent sabotage of powerlines made power outages a regular feature of city life throughout 1986.

As pressing as the military situation was for Frelimo, it would be overshadowed by an unexpected political change. On 19 October 1986 a Soviet-piloted aircraft returning from Lusaka and carrying President Machel crashed inside South African territory near the Mozambican border.[354] There were some survivors, but Machel was killed. Frelimo's long-time leader and bitter opponent of Renamo was gone. In his place Joaquim Chissano assumed the reins of power. Despite some serious internal challenges to his leadership of Frelimo and growing calls for a negotiated end to the war, Chissano was quickly able to not only secure his hold on the party, but win over the military leadership as well. Using his diplomatic skills he accelerated Machel's rapprochement with the West, shored up the economy with help from the international community, and reconciled with Banda by signing of a joint security agreement in December. All this would pave the way for Frelimo to once again go on the offensive at the beginning of 1987 and attempt to reverse the Renamo gains of the past year.

Assessment

The entry of Zimbabwe directly into the conflict clearly altered the strategic landscape of the war. It also most likely prolonged the fighting and hindered any chance of a negotiated end to the war. Albeit the reality was that neither Frelimo nor Renamo were ready (or more importantly willing) to talk peace in late 1985. Both sides still held out hopes of a victory on the battlefield. It would take another seven years, and a downward spiral of increasing brutality and violence with no end in sight, that ultimately would force both parties to the negotiating table. It was then, and only then, that real progress could be made in bringing the war to an end. Renamo demands for the withdrawal of all Zimbabwean troops from Mozambican soil would be a key issue in peace talks, but one Mugabe and Chissano were willing to concede when the time was right.

As traumatic and unexpected as Zimbabwean military intervention, and capture of Renamo's Casa Banana headquarters, was to Renamo in August 1985, it is interesting to note that not a single senior Renamo commander considered this to be a potential turning point in the war. There could be several explanations for this mindset. Possibly after having experienced the similar loss of their headquarters in 1980 and 1981 to government offensives, or having to cope with the cutback in South African support after Nkomati, or simply having the confidence that they had lived to fight another day, made them somewhat immune to how close they came to disaster. Renamo's ability to regroup, restructure and go on the offensive by early 1986, shows that this confidence was well placed. It also underscores the missed opportunity by Harare and Maputo to decisively alter the course of the war.

Machel and Frelimo, for their part, knew how close they came to collapsing in 1985. Harare's direct military intervention undoubtedly was instrumental in ensuring Frelimo's survival. The Zimbabwean (and later Tanzanian) involvement would shift an enormous part of the military burden off Maputo's shoulders—especially north of the Save River—and allowed the FAM to concentrate on the defense of the critically economic and politically important south. Moreover, it would buy time for Frelimo. Time not only to regroup and re-equip its military, but time for its rapprochement with the West to bear fruit in terms of greater economic and military assistance. It would also allow Frelimo to pre-empt once and for all any chance of Western support to the insurgents by solidifying Renamo's international pariah status as 'the Khmer Rouge of Africa.'

Given the geo-political reality of the times, Zimbabwe's entry into the war was probably inevitable. Mugabe had little real choice given the economic squeeze by Renamo's disruption of the Mozambican transportation infrastructure and by ongoing South African destabilization. Mugabe's personal history with Machel and ZANU's indebtedness to Frelimo, however, ultimately heightened the level and intensity of Zimbabwe's military role. The Zimbabweans could easily have continued their defensive role rather than move to aggressive offensive operations after mid-1985, for instance. Harare's initial military successes no doubt also led it to believe that its engagement would be short term, and the 'Renamo bandits' quickly quelled. Of course this would turn out to be a terrible strategic miscalculation. It seems too many of Zimbabwe's post-independence commanders forgot their own hard-earned lessons of the Rhodesian bush war, and of the resilience of guerrilla armies. Ultimately, the cost of Harare's nearly ten-year involvement would be substantial: at least $300 million in military expenditures,[355] as many as 1,000 casualties,[356] and the loss of large quantities of military equipment and irreplaceable aircraft.[357]

CHAPTER SEVEN
THE SLUGFEST CONTINUES

The body blow struck by Renamo's October offensive at the end of 1986 sent Frelimo reeling and would seriously test the mettle of the new Chissano regime. It also backed Chissano into a corner. As a CIA analysis of the time noted, "the new government will probably take a hard line at first toward the rebels and pursue a military solution" to allow it time to consolidate its hold on power.[358] Not only would the scope of fighting and level of violence continue to rise over the next several years, but the ferocity of the conflict would pull increasingly more regional and international actors into the fray.

None of these developments, however, would prove to be decisive in turning the tide of war in favor of either Frelimo or Renamo. A military stalemate was emerging, but neither side was willing to call it quits. Even as the spoils of war were growing ever sparser, the two exhausted sides fought on.

In the face of Renamo gains, Frelimo was far from ready to throw in the towel, despite some rumbling of discontent within its military. And while the most intense fighting had grown to include a vast stretch of central and northern Mozambique—from north of the Beira corridor across the Zambezi River valley and into Tete, Zambezia, Niassa and Nampula provinces—fighting was also escalating in the south, especially in the tri-provincial area of southern Gaza and Inhambane and northern Maputo Province. Nonetheless, Frelimo had weathered the worst of the Renamo onslaught. Its army was battered but intact, and its military alliance with Zimbabwe was now reaping huge operational and strategic benefits. Moreover, the political transition following Machel's death had gone rather smoothly and freed Chissano to chart his own course unburdened by past obligations or unworkable military strategies. His first order of business would be to send Dhlakama a clear and powerful message.

In an effort to regain the military initiative, Frelimo and Zimbabwean forces launched a major counter-offensive in December 1986 to rollback Renamo gains.[359] A central objective of this offensive was the retaking of a number of key towns along the Zambezi River. A forward command post

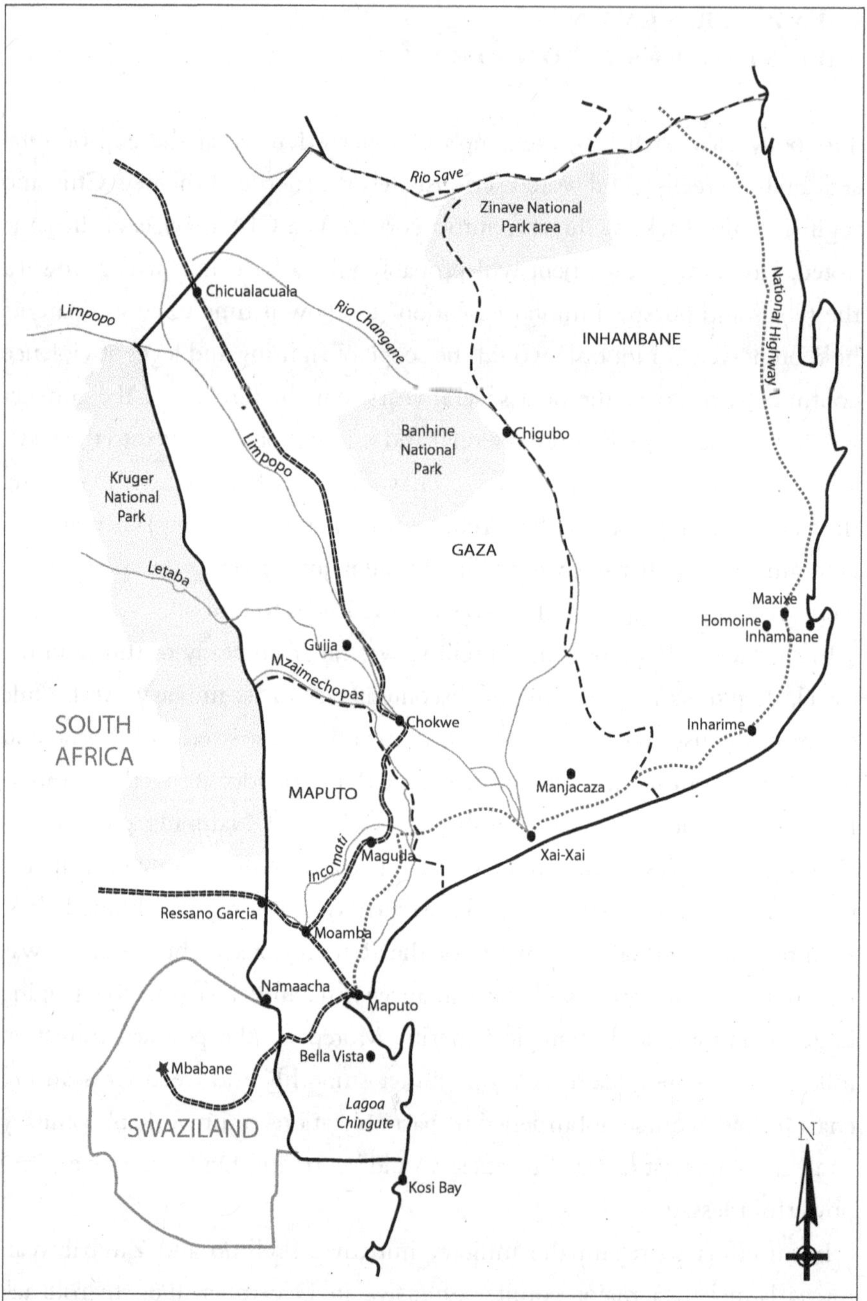

Map 7: Southern Region

was established at Quelimane to support the offensive, which came under the direct command of Lieutenant-General António Hama Thai. By mid-February the joint ZNA–FAM operation had recaptured the insurgent-held towns of Mutarara, Sena, Vila Nova, Mopeia, and Caia. The important lower Zambezi River crossing at Luabo and the nearby sugar plantations would once again come under government control by early March 1987. By April, Frelimo forces had once more retaken control of the district capital of Morrumbala in western Zambezia as well.

With critical help from elements of the ZNA's 2 Para, Renamo forces were finally pushed out of towns across Tete Province and back into the countryside; the heavily looted Angonia District capital in the northeast was retaken in early 1987. "If not for the ZNA the whole of Tete could have been taken by Renamo," the FAM commanding general acknowledged.[360] Nonetheless, Frelimo barely maintained a tentative hold on the province with the FAM's control rarely extending beyond the edges of towns and major transportation routes. Other smaller-scale operations in the Gorongosa and Maringue districts of Sofala Province, however, were less successful at dislodging the insurgents. Still, Frelimo would claim its operations across central Mozambique had killed up to 2,000 insurgents in the first quarter of the year.

Even as Frelimo moved to regain control over the core central provinces along the Zambezi River, Renamo activity continued unabated as the insurgents shifted their attention ever northward in the early months of 1987. Advancing up the Licungo River into the tea growing region of northern Zambezia, insurgent attacks there left some 50 workers dead, tons of tea destroyed, and processing facilities seriously damaged in early February. Previously, Renamo forces in Nampula raided the rail town of Monapo, just 75 kilometers southwest of Ncala, killing civilians and destroying tons of the cashew harvest. Renamo was also claiming major victories in Cabo Delgado Province in the far north, including overpowering the FAM garrison at Meluco and capturing large amounts of military equipment. Ambushes of FAM convoys between Pemba and the district capital of Montepuez intensified too.[361] And in Tete Province the insurgents were now active south of Lake Cahora Bassa and reportedly shelled Tete with mortars and rockets.

Overall however, the young Chissano government had to be pleased with its military recovery and successes. Not only were FAM units now actively taking the fight to Renamo—albeit with extensive Zimbabwean support—but recent reforms appeared to be returning positive results. Machel's loyal warhorse, Colonel-General Sebastião Mabote was replaced by the air force commander, Lieutenant-General Hama Thai, and all three service chiefs, all the provincial commanders, and the heads of the FAM headquarters directorates were similarly replaced in early 1987. Thus signaling Chissano's move away from the Frelimo old guard, to developing a lighter, more specialized force structure specifically designed and equipped for counter-insurgency warfare.

The creation and training of specialized counter-insurgency units, such as the "Red Beret" commandos, were an example of this new approach in action. Although Mozambique's original Soviet-style special forces structure and training had been undergoing an overhaul since at least 1983,[362] the FAM high command's resistance to employing them in unconventional warfare prevented elite units from being much of a factor in the war until 1987. The newly created 500-man Red Beret commando unit, headquartered at Boane just outside the capital, would first see action in Zambezia during the March recapture of Luabo on the lower Zambezi. These troops would continue to operate there during the course of the year, but their primary mission became one of relieving pressure on Maputo by disrupting Renamo operations and dismantling insurgent infrastructure in the south of the country during the latter half of 1987, according to a former commando officer.[363]

One of these early operations involved infiltrating a large Renamo base in southern Gaza Province that was ringed by advanced outposts and a network of lookouts. The operation was led by a 28-year-old major with the rest of the unit averaging only 25 years of age. As one commando remembers:

> This operation would be a test of our abilities. Not only of silently infiltrating the base undetected, but also of our 'shoot to kill' training after clearly identifying our targets. We learned through a network of spies that the Renamo commander was getting married so we planned to surprise

> them. We were successful. After a short ten minute fire fight, they broke and ran. The next day, we captured five Renamo spies sent back to check on the status of the camp. We released one to let Renamo know that we were still in control of the base. Later on, we handed over the base to regular FAM troops and withdrew back to our base.[364]

While the Red Berets normally liked to operate in small ten-man squads, they would frequently operate in larger formations of 150 men or more, or in conjunction with other FAM units, to attack large Renamo contingents or heavily defended enemy bases. Against well-entrenched Renamo positions these operations would often entail the use of heavy artillery or air bombardment prior to the ground assault. In one such operation in July 1987 a company-sized Red Beret unit linked up with elements of the FAM 1st Brigade to assault an estimated 2,000 insurgents defending their mountainous base in the Namaacha area near the South African-Swazi border.[365] Given the difficult terrain and Renamo's extensive use of caves in the area, the FAM had failed in previous attempts to dislodge the insurgents. This time, however, following BM-21 bombardment of the position, the joint Frelimo force broke into dozens of small groups and clawed their way up the mountain and into the base successfully. The Renamo defenders then broke and fled. The attacking Frelimo force suffered only light casualties in the assault; insurgent losses were unknown. Unfortunately, one week later the commandos were back at it again following Renamo's return to the area.

A Mozambican mêlée

The latter half of 1987 and into 1988 gave rise to heavy fighting in southern Gaza and Inhambane provinces, as well as the expansion of the war to all reaches of Maputo Province. And despite government forces successfully over-running numerous Renamo bases, and the seizing of large quantities of supplies, few insurgents were killed or captured. Instead the guerrillas continued their deadly strikes on vital transportation links in and out of the capital with seeming impunity. Likewise, the constant presence of 3,000–4,000 ZNA troops along the Beira corridor still did not put an end to insurgent attacks on the corridor's road and rail network. Meanwhile, north of the Zambezi River, both Frelimo and Renamo were engaged in an ongoing slugfest over control of key towns and transportation links across Zambezia, Tete, Nampula and Niassa provinces with neither side gaining the upper hand for long. During a single week alone in late August 1987, Renamo reported engaging in 56 infantry attacks nationwide that destroyed a dozen communal villages and eight military vehicles, while killing 168 FAM and 4 ZNA soldiers. It claimed to have suffered 31 infantry and six air attacks by Frelimo forces that resulted in 29 Renamo dead and 119 wounded during the same period.[366] Moreover, rather than each side mounting the traditional large-scale rainy/dry season offensives of the past, the combat would now span longer periods, over wider areas, and spawn rising civilian deaths as a direct or indirect consequence of the constant fighting. Also spinning out of control was the unprecedented level of brutality.

Free for all in the south

Renamo moved to raise the pressure on Frelimo by shifting its focus southward after April 1987. Unsubstantiated claims of "large numbers of well-armed units" crossing the South African frontier into Gaza and Maputo provinces were used by Frelimo to rationalize this increase in activity.[367] It was easier to blame Pretoria than acknowledge Renamo's formidable ability to effectively and rapidly redeploy its forces nationwide as the situation warranted. The next nine months would see Renamo unleash its most intense assaults to date on Frelimo's lines of communication, transportation links, and district capitals in the south.

By August 1987, Renamo General Vareia Manje was reporting numerous Renamo attacks on Frelimo positions in north and western Maputo Province as part of *Ofensiva Relâmpago* (Operation Lightning).[368] Important rail and road hub towns were not only raided, but often completely leveled; this fate befell Manjacaza in southern Gaza in early August. Repeated ambushes of civilian-military convoys from October to December killed hundreds of civilians and soldiers, and left the roads leading north and west of the capital littered with dozens of burnt out vehicles. One particularly violent ambush on 28 October at Taninga (80 kilometers north of Maputo) left 278 dead. Rail traffic from South Africa along the Ressano Garcia line and from Swaziland came under heavy attack too. Rail bridges were repeatedly sabotaged. Trains were derailed and looted, while passengers were robbed, killed or taken prisoner. Police stations in and around Maputo came under regular Renamo assault, as did Frelimo party offices during the last half of the year. Dozens of policemen and militia were killed in these attacks.

As far back as 1985, Renamo unit commanders were given more "freedom to attack military targets," especially to acquire heavy weapons and munitions from Frelimo stockpiles, according to a senior Renamo commander.[369] This operational task primarily fell to one of Renamo's 12 semi-conventional battalions,[370] but all insurgent units had some degree of capability to harass FAM garrisons and capture supplies. By 1987–88, there were probably at least three Renamo semi-conventional battalions, or upward of 3,000 men with heavy weapons, operating south of the Save River. Most of these troops were active within a 150-kilometer radius of the capital, and were further supplemented by hundreds of additional guerrilla fighters and small sabotage teams. In the last few months of 1987, Renamo would claim to have captured nearly 1,800 small arms; dozens of heavy weapons, including 14.5mm heavy machine guns, B-10 recoilless rifles, SAM-7 rocket launchers, and over 43 tons of ammunition to replenish its stockpiles, while destroying ten T-54 tanks and several armored personnel carriers.[371]

Frelimo officers operating in the south at this time also noted a more aggressive attitude on the part of the Renamo soldiers; it seemed like "no day would go by without us having to fight two to three times a day."[372] For instance, after pushing the insurgents out of their Inharrime District base in southern Inhambane Province in 1987 a small FAM stay-behind force suddenly found that guerrillas had re-infiltrated its defensive perimeter in the middle of the night. A former Frelimo officer recalls: "There was shooting from all directions. I thought my own men were shooting at me."[373] There was confusion everywhere, as it was difficult to determine friend from foe. In the end the defending FAM force was forced to abandon the position once again to Renamo.

Not only was Renamo becoming more aggressive and destructive on the offensive, but it was increasingly tenacious in defense. Rather than fleeing FAM attacks on its major bases as in the past, "they tended to resist now when attacked unless there was an overwhelming FAM force" and "sometimes we even had to pull back if not in strength," remembers a Frelimo officer.[374] During one FAM brigade-size attack in March 1987 on an important Renamo regional supply base near Lagoa Chingute in the Matutuíne District of Maputo Province, it took three assaults and nearly ten hours to finally capture the base. The FAM force lost 27 men, including two officers, while Renamo lost 87 men in the bitter fighting. The seized supplies included over 1,000 small arms, mortars, and RPG-7s, plus dozens of boxes of ammunition, "enough to fill two truckloads," according to a FAM officer present.[375] The Frelimo force also captured over 2,000 head of cattle and freed 800 civilians. The huge stockpile probably accounted for Renamo's fierce resistance, and the withdrawing FAM column came under nearly constant harassing attacks by small guerrilla groups, which apparently were trying to recover at least some of the lost cattle and arms.

Late 1987 and early 1988 witnessed a spate of Renamo strikes against district capitals and garrisons across Gaza to Maputo provinces. Namaacha was hit on 19 January, Guija four days later, and Moamba on 6 February. Even the southernmost district capital of Bella Vista on the Maputo River was raided in mid-February 1988. Road and rail links from Maputo to South Africa and Swaziland continued to come under intensive attacks, "tightening the siege" around the capital, according to the international press reporting.[376] One mine blast alone, on New Year's Eve 1987, derailed a train packed with migrant workers, killing at least 22 and injuring 71. Meanwhile, nine Zimbabwe railway workers were killed inside Zimbabwe during an insurgent attack on the Chicualacuala to Maputo rail line in mid-March; the rail link would become an increasing center of attention, and test of will, for both sides in the years ahead. Alarmist reports claimed that "up to 5,000" insurgents were massing in southern Inhambane and Maputo provinces to choke off the capital from the outside world.[377] And in late March, Dhlakama publicly called on Frelimo: "To begin direct negotiations" with Renamo. "It is time to stop talking with guns, we must now sit down and seriously talk about peace in our war-ravaged land," said Dhlakama.[378]

To contest its increasingly beleaguered image, Frelimo touted major battlefield victories over Renamo. It announced the overrunning of several key insurgent bases in southern Gaza, and also near the South African border, that left hundreds of insurgents dead. In an apparent effort to boost flagging morale, President Chissano made a tour, in March 1988, of the three war-torn provinces in the south, as well as Sofala, Manica, and Zambezia in the north. He reiterated Frelimo's long-standing position that there would be no negotiations with Renamo. In April 1988, the FAM would report it captured 18 insurgent bases and large quantities of supplies while killing about 200 during the first part of the year. Major success in undermining Renamo morale was touted as well; Frelimo announced in July that 1,000 guerrillas had surrendered—including several high-profile defections—under its latest amnesty program. This number would rise to over 3,000 by the end of 1988. The year ended, however, with high-profile insurgent attacks on President Chissano's home district and the FAM provincial headquarters in southern Gaza Province.

Regardless of the opposing claims as to who was actually winning the war, the fighting during this two-year period proved to be some of the fiercest of the war in the south. For example, after pinpointing the location of Renamo's Gaza provincial base, and headquarters of General Francisco Paulo Gomes in December 1987, the FAM put together an elaborate attack plan utilizing 8th Brigade elements out of Chokwe, Red Beret commandos, and the air force, to take the base and hopefully capture or kill Gomes and his staff. The original plan called for commandos to be uplifted to form stop lines south of the base, while an infantry and heavy weapons assault from the north drove the insurgents out of the base into the awaiting arms of the commandos, according to a FAM officer involved in the operation.[379] Difficult terrain and delays, however, prevented the 8th Brigade ground force from taking up their positions in time. Fearful of losing the element of surprise, the 300-man commando unit repositioned itself and commenced the attack from the north in the early dawn hours. In the confusion, some of the pre-attack air strikes ended up hitting the advancing commandos. The air attack was then aborted. Attempting to protect their large quantities of supplies, the insurgents put up stiff resistance and it was only after several hours of fighting, and the assistance of the arriving 8th Brigade armored personnel carriers and artillery, that the commandos broke through the perimeter defenses and into the base.[380] Renamo pulled back, but did not abandon the area completely, as was evidenced later when Mozambican journalists were flown in by helicopter to view the captured base only to come under heavy insurgent fire.

The view from the Renamo perspective of these battles was remarkably similar. A female Renamo soldier remembers a "large battle" in late 1988 that left 42 insurgents dead when the FAM caught them by surprise in the middle of the night:

> A defector, who had a falling out with the camp's commander, led the Frelimo force to our base. We were caught sleeping. The next thing we knew, enemy infantry was attacking. Then came the tanks and helicopters. It was very fierce. There was confusion everywhere. I was wounded but managed to escape. I thank God for saving me.[381]

The struggle in the north

Even as the heaviest fighting raged across the south, both sides continued to exchange body blows during the second half of 1987 and throughout 1988 in their struggle to control key districts in central Mozambique and the Zambezi River crossing points. Territory and towns were won and lost. Gains in one region by Renamo would be quickly countered by gains in another by Frelimo. And so it went.

In response to Frelimo's earlier successes in the north, Renamo launched its *Offensiva Vento* (Operation Wind) in May 1987. In short order the insurgents were claiming the seizure of numerous small towns in Zambezia and Niassa provinces and the killing of hundreds of FAM soldiers.[382] Likewise, Renamo battlefield reports would also show heightened activity, including assaults and shelling of Frelimo towns and garrisons across much of Tete Province from south of Lake Cahora Bassa to Zobue on the Malawian frontier during August and September 1987.[383] Much of Renamo's success was due to the Northern Front commander, Calisto Meque, a hardened veteran fighter reputed by his men and locals to have magical powers, but also known for his heavy-handed authoritarian leadership style.

Personality and ethnic tensions between Meque and Renamo commander Jimo Phiri, however, would result in Phiri's breaking away from the insurgents with 500 of his men in late 1987 and forming the National Union of Mozambique (UNAMO).[384] UNAMO would begin to operate independently of Renamo in the Milange and Gurue districts of western Zambezia. Adding to the anarchy in the region, UNAMO forces attacked both its former Renamo partners as well as Frelimo troops. Even after Meque's death on 11 September 1988, at the hands of FAM forces during an attack on Gile in Zambezia,[385] tensions would remain strained between UNAMO and Renamo. And by 1988, Phiri and his men would defect completely to Frelimo and fight alongside the FAM against Renamo for the remainder of the war.[386]

This pattern of conflict—with each side unable to secure long-lasting gains—would continue well into 1988. In January insurgent forces destroyed the town of Namacata, just outside of Quelimane and later cut the Nampula to Alto Molocue road by occupying Marrapula, 75 kilometers southwest of the city of Nampula. Meanwhile, FAM forces retook Milange on the Malawi border (again) in June and recaptured the district capital of Gile in early July with the assistance of Tanzanian troops. This constant upheaval north of the Zambezi fueled refugee flows, the United Nations estimating 570,000 refugees in Malawi by July and growing at the rate of 20,000–40,000 per month.

Frelimo forces, along with their Zimbabwean and Tanzanian allies, also undertook several simultaneous large-scale operations in August to secure major lines of communications across central Mozambique, including the Beira corridor.[387] As part of this effort, the ZNA apparently increased its use of chemical defoliants along roadsides, and forcefully relocated large numbers of civilians away from the Beira and Tete corridors. The Chimoio to Nhamatanda stretch of the Beira corridor, for example, was cleared to 500 meters on each side and the Amatongas forest and "was literally wiped out," according to a senior Renamo general.[388] Nonetheless, the insurgents still were able to strike the rail, road, and pipeline seemingly at will throughout the remainder of the year.

The fighting heated up once again in Sofala Province too. Renamo embarrassed Frelimo by retaking the important rail town of Inhaminga that linked Beira to the embattled Zambezi River valley garrisons in October. To the south of the Beira corridor the insurgents launched a major raid on Chibabara in November that inflicted heavy losses on the FAM garrison. However, at the close of 1988 Zimbabwean forces were claiming to have achieved significant successes in Manica Province by destroying four large Renamo bases along the border.

Caught in the crossfire: violence and brutality against civilians

The war was becoming especially traumatic—and deadly—for those civilians caught up in the conflict. According to best estimates, the overwhelming majority of the nearly one million people that died either directly or indirectly as a result of the war were civilians—men, women, and children.[389] Another nearly four million Mozambicans were internally displaced or made refugees. And while it is certainly not unusual for civilians to bear much of the suffering in a civil war, the level of violence and extreme brutality in the latter years of the Mozambican conflict was anything but typical. What was very typical, however, was the finger pointing from both sides as Frelimo and Renamo each blamed the other for the most egregious acts of violence against civilians.

As with a number of highly contentious issues surrounding the war, the truth behind a number of high profile incidents will likely never be known. There is, however, more than enough blame to go around. And neither Frelimo nor Renamo has clean hands. Nonetheless, it is reasonable to make a number of inferences as to culpability of each side and, more important, as to the impact of this type of violence on the course of the war. This was particularly salient with regard to the international community's perception of the war. This was a perception shaped by several high profile incidents that took place over the course of less than a year and of the much publicized report on the violence by U.S.-funded researcher Robert Gersony.[390]

Terror as a weapon of war

Renamo insurgents have been blamed for much of the brutality unleashed against civilians during the war. And rightly so. The insurgents' use of terror to intimidate their enemies and ensure support among wavering peasant populations is well-documented in anecdotal accounts, refugee interviews, and multiple post-war studies on the use of violence during the conflict. Although not by any means flawless in methodology, sampling, or pro-Frelimo bias, these collective works clearly show a calculated pattern of terror tactics used as an asymmetrical weapon of war by Renamo. As Jeremy Weinstein's post-war analysis shows, Renamo was "responsible for the vast majority of incidents of violence."[391] While high levels of violence against civilians—and even the use of terrorism—have been an integral part of African insurgencies, the central issue has always been one of the combatants justifying some level of this violence to achieve a greater good.

What appears to be less clear, however, is the driving force behind Renamo's specific use of terror. In fact, much of the senseless brutality against civilians during the war contradicts long-established guerrilla warfare principles and Renamo's very own attempts to groom its international image as a true Mozambican populist movement. According to Weinstein's findings, "Renamo rarely showed restraint" and its victims were just as likely Renamo supporters living in insurgent-controlled zones as Frelimo supporters or those in government-controlled areas.[392] This is even more puzzling, given the insurgent's highly central leadership and strong command and control structure. Several senior Renamo commanders emphasized the strategic requirement to obtain and maintain popular support "because we realized guerrilla forces can only survive if people can render support."[393]

The issue of ethnicity and geography—particularly of ethno-regional conflict between the Shangaan people in the south and the rest of the population north of the Save River—was frequently cited during the war as the key factor driving the violence.[394] According to this argument, Frelimo's strong support among the Shangaan people fueled ethnic and regional rivalries with the Shona-speaking people of central Mozambique that Renamo relied on for support. Thus, the large-scale massacres in the south by the insurgents during the war were the result of ethnic bloodletting and Renamo's deliberate targeting of Frelimo's support base. In the taxonomy of the Gersony Report, most of Renamo's "Destruction areas" naturally tended to be found in the southern provinces and hence the higher level of brutality against civilians. Moreover, international press reporting of the time would appear to validate this belief too. A number of high profile, large-scale atrocities against civilians did in fact take place in Gaza, Inhambane and Maputo provinces following the increase in Renamo activity from 1986 onward.

Nonetheless, more recent post-war studies cast serious doubts on this widely-held perception of southern-centric violence. As Weinstein notes:

> In spite of ready-made national divisions, patterns of Renamo violence exhibit surprising consistency both geographically and temporally [and this] violence also appears fairly indiscriminate when broken down geographically: while a greater number of massacres took place in the southern provinces—regions of Frelimo support—the Center and North were not immune from Renamo's brutality.[395]

He goes on to point out that importantly this pattern is "consistent over time and across geographic regions, even as the level of violence varies," which is in marked contrast to Gersony's earlier findings.[396]

It is more likely that Renamo's operational requirements were a critical factor in its attack patterns and the resultant high civilian death toll. From the outset, as we have repeatedly seen, the insurgents focused their operations on interdicting Frelimo's lines of communications, disrupting the country's transportation network, and conducting economic warfare by targeting important infrastructure and production centers. Thus Renamo's extensive use of ambushes against road and rail traffic, its sabotage of pipelines, electrical pylons, and bridges and the deliberate destruction of communal villages, cooperatives, and commercial agricultural facilities. This strategy also had the added benefit of tying down large numbers of Frelimo forces in a defensive role. Likewise, the destruction of symbols of government power and presence, such as schools, health clinics, police stations, and Frelimo party offices was viewed as instrumental in undermining confidence in the government and demoralizing Frelimo supporters. In the eyes of Renamo commanders and soldiers, all of the above were valid military targets in guerilla warfare. This helps explain how civilians easily got caught up in the fighting, especially ambushes of road convoys with military escorts, although it does not account for the level of extreme brutality that sometimes occurred during or immediately after these attacks.

A good deal of the violence during these operations has been blamed on specialized Renamo units, most infamously *Grupo Limpa*. The widely-held myth is that *Grupo Limpa* soldiers were primarily responsible for conducting large-scale massacres in the south.[397] Much of the confusion surrounding this unit resides in its unique composition and specialized role. It was first and foremost an infantry unit, but one manned with specially-trained personnel, to include special forces operators, mortars and heavy weapons specialists, those trained in sabotage and explosives or in intelligence collection.[398] Although it was Renamo's largest semi-conventional battalion at nearly 1,500 strong, it rarely if ever deployed and operated as a full battalion. Rather, *Grupo Limpa* provided specialized personnel, or even company-strength elements, to other insurgent units during ongoing operations. More commonly, very small teams (sometimes only one or two people) "operated in very difficult places" behind enemy lines for high-value operations such as sabotage or intelligence collection, according to Dhlakama. *Grupo Limpa* was not, as has been portrayed, a "purely N'dau battalion" nor did it function "as a praetorian guard" for Dhlakama.[399] It certainly was not 'an assassination unit' as many have labeled it, nor was it charged with meting out punishment against civilians or Frelimo officials. "No, no. Absolutely not," said Dhlakama when confronted with this charge.[400]

Frequently overlooked (or at best given minimal coverage) when discussing attacks on civilians is Frelimo's—and Zimbabwe's—parallel use of terror as a weapon of war. While the majority of violence against civilians in the south can reasonably be attributed to Renamo, Frelimo and its Zimbabwean allies appeared equally willing to employ heavy-handed tactics in areas under insurgent control or against suspected Renamo sympathizers in central and northern Mozambique. Frelimo's major offensives in Manica and Sofala provinces in the early 1980s, for example, were characterized by the indiscriminate use of artillery fire and air bombardment against suspected Renamo bases. This was often done without any consideration for civilian casualties, much to the shock of some FPLM officers at the time.[401] As former Frelimo cabinet minister José Luis Cabaço candidly acknowledged years later, "sometimes we [Frelimo] responded too readily with force and the army often roughed up the civilian population."[402]

As the war intensified, so did Frelimo's harsh tactics against civilian populations suspected of supporting or sympathizing with the insurgents. For instance, the FAM counter-offensive at the end of 1986 and into early 1987 to rollback Renamo gains in Zambezia Province was done "with a lot violence," according to Cabaço.[403] The appointment of the former Mozambican counter-intelligence chief, Lagos Lidimo, as provincial military commander in June 1987 provided tacit endorsement of these harsh measures. Lidimo was seen as ruthless in implementing a scorched-earth policy across the province, and willing to personally execute even his own officers who failed to comply with his orders.[404] He was "no soldier, but a security man."[405]

Even Frelimo's allies were aghast at the indiscriminate use of air power by Maputo in some of these operations. According to the senior Tanzanian commander in Zambezia, it was the Mozambican people who "were being killed in these bombings in a manner amounting to genocide."[406] In one instance Tanzanian troops reportedly discovered some 300 civilians who had been killed in bombings or were shot by FAM forces near one village in eastern Zambezia. Not surprisingly, the Tanzanian commander noted his troops "were more popular amongst the masses than FAM forces," because the latter not only killed civilians but also pilfered relief supplies to make ends meet since they were not adequately fed, paid or clothed.[407]

Renamo was far from blameless too. The populations in war-torn Zambezia and Nampula provinces were all too often caught in the middle. Many ended up becoming victims of killings, rapes and looting by both sides. Civilians were often simply killed on the pretext of being "agents of the enemy" by Frelimo and Renamo. The practice became so widespread and common that such killings were ordered with the phrase to "go get firewood."[408] Not surprising this rising, indiscriminate violence produced huge refugee flows into Malawi and displaced hundreds of thousands across the north.

Perception as reality

Although Mozambican non-combatants found themselves caught up in the crossfire of the war for years, the period from mid-1987 to early 1988 would become a new defining point. It would bear witness to heretofore unseen levels of public brutality and to several large-scale massacres in southern Mozambique that left hundreds dead that would gain international attention. Charges and counter-charges of complicity would fly back and forth between Frelimo and Renamo fueling the propaganda machines of both sides. Ultimately, the damning indictment of Renamo's predominant role in civilian mistreatment and deaths revealed in the April 1988 Gersony Report would effectively end any realistic hope of the insurgency garnering Western support. Moreover, these events would burden Renamo with the moniker of a terrorist organization and undermine its future efforts to be recognized a legitimate political party.

The most notable of these events was the Homoíne massacre. On 18 July 1987 in the town of Homoíne, a mere 25 kilometers southwest of the provincial capital of Inhambane Province, one of the worst—and undoubtedly the most widely publicized—massacres of the war took place. That much is for certain. Nearly everything else surrounding the incident, however, is open to debate, and multiple competing versions of the events that day continued to surface long afterward. Not surprisingly, both Frelimo and Renamo accused the other of culpability. Follow up visits to Homoíne by Western journalists and diplomats in the weeks following the massacre were unable to resolve definitively the competing claims, but a developing consensus from late 1987 onward held Renamo forces responsible for the massacre.

According to the official government version,[409] a large group of well-armed Renamo insurgents (the numbers vary from "several hundred" to "40 to 50") entered the town in the early morning hours of the 18th and began systematically shooting people, looting shops, and pilfering the hospital of medical supplies. A number of those killed apparently were patients at the hospital. A large group of children were kidnapped and later found murdered outside of the town. A reacting FAM unit eventually pushed the remnants of the attackers out of town and discovered several hundred dead civilians and many seriously injured, according to the government account. The official death toll was initially listed at 380 including many women and children, but would later rise to 424 as additional bodies were discovered and those injured died of their wounds.

A FAM officer in the hastily assembled 150-man responding force from the nearby town of Maxixe recalls his unit facing strong resistance from Renamo forces still in Homoíne at the time of the relief force's arrival at midday.[410] Their initial attack failed, but a flanking maneuver enabled the FAM force to dislodge the insurgents. By 1600 the town was back in Frelimo hands. It was only then that the scope of the tragedy began to unfold, recalls the officer. Although the situation was far from clear, higher command demanded a detailed death toll, so the FAM commander on the scene reported "388 dead." The FAM officer believed that the actually number was closer to 600.[411]

Renamo sources, however, claimed that after raiding Homoíne and forcing the FAM garrison to flee, a concerted Frelimo ground and air counterattack from the north pushed Renamo out of the town. Then another arriving FAM unit from the south, unaware of the situation, mistook the Frelimo force in the town for Renamo insurgents and "acted accordingly."[412]—hence the resulting carnage and the government cover up blaming Renamo. Other sympathetic Renamo supporters likewise have raised the specter of rogue FAM elements or Frelimo pseudo-guerrilla operations involvement at Homoíne and other similar incidents in the south,[413] believing that this aspect of the war "has still to be written."[414] Frelimo soldiers familiar with the incident, however, bristle with anger at the suggestion of any Mozambican military involvement in the massacre.[415]

Implications for the war

As is true for many conflicts, perceptions of violence often drive the response, whether these perceptions are grounded in fact or not. In this case the Homoíne massacre, subsequent large-scale killings of civilians in the south, and the release of the Gersony Report, clearly turned the tide of world opinion against Renamo. Thus by the end of 1988 Renamo came to be perceived internationally as evil incarnate, "the Khmer Rouge of Africa," and effectively labeled a terrorist organization by many observers and foreign governments. A senior U.S. Department of State official, for example, publicly declared in April 1998 that "Renamo is waging a war of terror against innocent Mozambican civilians through forced labor, starvation, physical abuse and wanton killing."[416] Vines's portrayal is also typical, writing that "although Renamo obtains some support from the Mozambican peasantry, most of this is obtained through terror and coercion. This is why politicians such as Mrs. Thatcher have described Renamo as one of the 'most brutal terrorist movements that there is'."[417]

This overwhelmingly negative characterization of the Renamo insurgency (along with its tainted Rhodesian and South African historical roots) and Renamo's political inability to alter its negative global persona, made it an international pariah. More important to the war itself, it effectively extinguished any last hope of gaining external support for its cause beyond some fringe rightwing elements in Europe and the United States. The fall of the Berlin Wall, and the resulting collapse of the Soviet Union in 1989, would prove the final death knell as the Cold War came to an end. This international ostracizing, however, forced Dhlakama and Renamo to be self-sufficient and adopt a survival strategy, whereby military victories on the battlefield were less important than the continued existence of the insurgency itself after 1988.

Diplomacy bears fruit for Maputo

Even as Frelimo and Renamo pummeled each other across the length and breadth of the country, Chissano's diplomatic offensive was gaining momentum. This effort ultimately would prove successful in shoring up the embattled regime with desperately needed military and economic assistance, as well as solidify its political support. So much so, that by the end of 1988 Frelimo had not only established strong security alliances with a number of its regional neighbors, but it also successfully wooed key Western governments to its side. Thus, Renamo found itself more politically isolated than ever before. Ironically, this network of support would be a mixed blessing for Frelimo, because several of these new allies would later leverage their influence to strong arm Chissano into direct peace talks with Renamo.

Regional developments

As the war intensified north of the Zambezi from late 1986 onward, Chissano stepped up his diplomatic efforts to build or enhance regional security cooperation and over the next several years Mozambique would successfully cultivate new ties with Malawi and Zambia, while simultaneously strengthening its existing security relationships with Zimbabwe and Tanzania.

A legacy of Malawi's granting sanctuary to Frelimo dissidents and northern Mozambican separatist groups, as well as long-running ideological differences between Blantyre and Maputo had complicated bilateral relations and fueled mutual distrust.[418] Renamo's expansion north of the Zambezi into Tete, Zambezia, and Niassa provinces bordering Malawi simply exacerbated these tensions, which nearly exploded just prior to Machel's death in October 1986.[419] However, in a sharp reversal of Machel's confrontational approach, Chissano was able to win President Banda to his side by tactfully aligning Mozambican and Malawian security and economic interests against the destabilizing impact of the war. The mutual need of both men to secure vital transportation and trade routes through Mozambique and address the rising tide of refugees fleeing the fighting, led to the signing of a joint Mozambique–Malawi security pact in December 1986. This agreement would lay the foundation for Malawi's initial deployment of 300 troops in April 1987 to help safeguard the western segment of the Ncala to Malawi rail line.[420] FAM troops were also granted the right of transit through Malawian territory as well as the right of hot pursuit into Malawi. In mid-1988 both countries issued a joint statement reiterating their cooperative efforts to ensure the continued functioning of the Ncala rail line.

Despite Blantyre's official alignment with Maputo, some elements within the Banda government and security forces remained nonetheless sympathetic to Renamo. Moreover, Malawi would continue to function quietly as an essential transit point for Renamo officials, serve as a base of operations for some private supporters, and provide a critical communication link to the outside world until the end of the war. The country's porous borders also continued to make it a convenient source of supplies for the insurgents. Renamo soldiers frequently recalled making trips into Malawi from southern Tete Province up to the end of the war "to collect weapons and food."[421] However, this level of lingering involvement appeared to be highly localized and ad hoc, with Vines assessing by 1991 that "there does not seem now to be any official support for Renamo" by the government of Malawi.[422]

Early on Chissano also made it a priority to obtain expanded military assistance from Tanzania, a historically strong supporter of Frelimo going back to the liberation struggle. During a December 1986 visit to Dar es Salaam, Chissano was able to secure President Nyerere's commitment to send 1,000 Tanzania People's Defence Force (TPDF) combat troops (instead of trainers) to embattled Zambezia Province. The TPDF initially established its main headquarters at Quelemine and later on at Nicuadala along with a forward command post at Mocuba to coordinate counter-insurgency operations. The advanced elements of what would eventually grow to a 3,000-man force began arriving in Zambezia Province in early March 1987.[423] This new force was quickly able to stem and later reverse Renamo gains in the province by retaking numerous towns previously lost to the insurgents.

The Tanzanian troops were generally viewed as excellent trainers and "good fighters with high morale" by FAM soldiers who worked with them.[424] As part of their mission the TPDF also agreed to train six FAM battalions and militia forces to secure Zambezia.[425] Renamo forces initially tended not to directly confront the well-trained and equipped TPDF troops, preferring instead to strike at weaker FAM units charged with garrisoning the recaptured towns and territory.[426] Despite the TPDF's success, the burden of the military deployment on the fragile Tanzanian economy forced Nyerere to begin withdrawing the contingent from Zambezia and Nampula provinces in late 1988. By December all Tanzanian combat troops had been pulled out.

Zambia, sharing an extensive border with northern Tete Province, also found itself reluctantly dragged into the war by 1988. Although insurgents had been active in the Zumbo, Maravia, and Chifunde border districts north of Lake Cahora Bassa for several years, it was only in 1987 that regular Renamo incursions into Zambia began to create a problem for Lusaka. Between March 1987 and May 1989, 75 Zambian civilians were reported killed, 171 others abducted, nine stores were looted, and dozens of clinics, schools, and villages attacked by Renamo, according to Zambian officials.[427] In response, the Zambian army began conducting aggressive hot-pursuit operations into Tete Province with some reported success. By May 1988 the army claimed to have killed 73 insurgents and destroyed two large Renamo bases.[428] These offensive operations would later be officially sanctioned with the creation of a joint Mozambican–Zambian security commission in November 1989. Nonetheless, Lusaka's thinly-stretched forces found themselves hard pressed to do little more than react to Renamo incursions across more than 400 kilometers of frontier. Zambian military involvement was important, however, not only in providing another check on Renamo expansion in this remote region and in denying the insurgents use of Zambian territory to facilitate resupply, but also in underscoring Lusaka political commitment to Frelimo and furthering Renamo's regional isolation.

In Harare, Frelimo had found its strongest and most steadfast ally. And it was to Mugabe that Chissano once again turned to for help. Despite growing frustration within the Zimbabwean military hierarchy over its failure to deliver a decisive blow to Renamo, the continuing inability of FAM forces to hold on to ZNA hard-won territory, and the small but growing public dissatisfaction with the war at home, Mugabe showed no sign of faltering in his support. He even upped the ante. Training assistance would be expanded, another joint military cooperation agreement was signed in June 1988, and troops would be deployed permanently south of the Save River for the first time. Moreover, Mugabe publicly resolved to keep Zimbabwean forces in Mozambique until Renamo was 'neutralized.' Like it or not, Zimbabwean military commanders needed to gird themselves for the long haul, because Mugabe was not backing down.

Since the mid-1980s, the ZNA sought to upgrade the capabilities and professionalize the FAM through increased training both in Mozambique and in Zimbabwe. Much of this training, however, was haphazard and cursory, as the requirement to push raw FAM recruits into the field as quickly as possible took precedence. However, with the 1986 arrival of the British Military Advisery Training Team (BMATT) and the establishment of a joint UK–Zimbabwe training program at the ZNA's infantry battalion training camp at Nyanga in the eastern highlands, just north of Mutare, the effort became more professional and the quality of instruction vastly improved. Nonetheless, given the limited capacity at the Nyanga camp, the majority of Zimbabwean training assistance continued to be conducted in the field at venues inside Mozambique and remained rudimentary at best.

Although Zimbabwean troops had on occasion conducted joint operations with the FAM south of the Save River prior to 1987, these were limited in scope and concentrated along the border. Ultimately the primary military burden in the south fell on the FAM's shoulders. The escalating war in the south and nearly constant Renamo pressure on the capital and its lines of communication, however, pushed Chissano to seek more direct help.

Of particular concern was the need to secure and reopen the 520 kilometer rail and road network connecting the Mozambican capital to southeastern Zimbabwe, which held the potential to annually handle three million tons of freight traffic.[429] The Limpopo corridor ran north from the capital to Chokwe in Gaza Province and then paralleled the Limpopo River northwest to the frontier town of Chicualacuala where it entered Zimbabwe. Reopening and controlling this strategic economic and communication corridor became a priority for both governments. Not only would its revitalization provide the Front Line States with an alternative non-South African export route, while filling the coffers of the Mozambican treasury, it would also facilitate military operations in Gaza Province, and serve as a significant obstacle to Renamo troop movements and resupply.

Planning to rehabilitate the rail line had been underway for some time, but actual work only really began in late 1987 following a joint ZNA–FAM effort to clear Renamo forces from the northern segment of the line. Hampered by funding problems and continually harassed by insurgent raids, the National Railways of Zimbabwe (NRZ) work crews made little progress in advancing southward from Chicualacuala. These problems were even more pronounced for the Mozambican railway crews attempting to rebuild the southern Maputo to Chokwe segment of the line. To improve protection for the NRZ workers, elements of the ZNA's 4 Brigade began regular deployments along the northern part of the corridor. Code-named Operation Open Way, several thousand Zimbabwean troops would eventually be tasked with providing a permanent security presence from Chicualacuala to Chokwe. By August 1988, additional funding from the United Kingdom and Mugabe's pledge to commit 10,000 troops to the effort, provided a badly-needed stimulus to the line's rehabilitation. In reality, however, the ZNA was never able to commit at any one time more than 2,500–3,000 men and establish a small forward headquarters detachment at Chokwe as part of Operation Open Way.

Over the coming years a series of fixed defensive positions were built, along with protective minefields,[430] to fortify the corridor against Renamo attacks and sabotage. Despite these efforts, most positions "were in pretty poor shape ... with unprotected slit trenches, haphazard barb wire perimeters and badly dressed soldiers," according to a former foreign military adviser.[431] Zimbabwean officers also were frequently disengaged and often their command posts lacked even basic operational maps of their area of responsibility. While security for the NRZ work crews improved, the insurgents, not surprisingly, continued to strike the corridor at will.

In addition to the defensive mission of Operation Open Way, the ZNA also began conducting counter-insurgency operations in Gaza Province. Relying on ad hoc Strike Force units or small mobile teams from 1 Para, the Zimbabweans began aggressively seeking out and attacking Renamo bases or launching harassing raids into insurgent-held territory. Unlike the large-scale offensives north of the Save and along the Zambezi, these operations tended to be very limited in scope and duration, frequently characterized as "in and out operations," by Lieutenant-Colonel Dyck.[432] A small 1 Para camp just north of Chokwe housed some 40 to 50 troopers, but as there was no forward air facility in southern Mozambique, limited air support was provided by the AFZ out of Buffalo Range forward airfield in southeastern Zimbabwe. While these combat operations apparently inflicted few insurgent casualties, their primary purpose was to keep Renamo forces in the area off balance and away from the corridor.

Most of all, Operation Open Way and the introduction of a limited ZNA offensive capability in the south after 1987 provided a huge psychological boost to the Chissano government. Mugabe's unwavering commitment to the Frelimo war effort also signaled the strategic failure of Renamo's attempt to foment anti-war sentiment in Zimbabwe and force Harare to withdrawal all its forces. The Zimbabwean troop presence along the Limpopo corridor would become a permanent fixture in the south, just as it had become along the Beira and Tete corridors to the north. A presence that would last—as Mugabe promised—until the end of the war.

Growing Western assistance

Unlike his predecessor Samora Machel, who only reluctantly began a rapprochement with the West prior to his death, Chissano fully embraced and actively courted the support of key Western countries. And while garnering increased economic and military assistance was important, the overriding objective of this effort was to isolate Renamo internationally. If Chissano was successful, he would eliminate once and for all any chance of Western assistance to the insurgents. His timing could not have been better, given the impending collapse of the Soviet Union and the winding down of the Cold War in Africa. Although unintended, improved relations with the West would be a critical factor in overcoming major obstacles during future peace talks. But for now Chissano had to go on the diplomatic offensive.

In Washington, Chissano found a very receptive audience. The long-held U.S. diplomatic goal of luring Mozambique away from the Soviet orbit and promoting democratic and economic reform, appeared to mesh well with Chissano's move to become more non-aligned and abandon hardline socialist policies. Despite skepticism within some elements of the U.S. government as to his sincerity, the Reagan administration took steps to encourage Frelimo's turn to the West. In a dramatic policy reversal, President Reagan played host to a state visit by Chissano in early October 1987 and became supportive of Mozambican economic reforms and increased international aid. Although no direct U.S. military assistance was forthcoming, Washington encouraged other Western efforts to provide training and non-lethal assistance to Frelimo.

Unfortunately for Maputo, U.S. foreign policy toward Mozambique—like much of southern African policy during the 1980s—was heavily buffeted by the competing and conflicting cross-currents of the Cold War, the regional politics of the anti-apartheid struggle, and of domestic American politics. These factors would greatly hamper Washington's response to Chissano's overtures, and also limit the degree of American leverage over either Frelimo or Renamo. Although beyond the scope of this book, the behind-the-scenes struggle over Mozambican policy within the U.S. government during the second half of the 1980s was one that both proponents and opponents of Frelimo and Renamo alike sought to influence and shape to fit their own beliefs and political agendas. That factions advocating support for Chissano's reforms, and distancing the United States from Renamo won out in the end is important, but so too is the "noise" and mixed messages that this internal U.S. government policy debate generated. These mixed messages undoubtedly confused both Chissano and Dhlakama at times, and complicated the peace process as each leader held out hope of swinging the Americans to his side. This circumscribed American role, however, would open the door for other Western governments—notably the United Kingdom, Portugal, and Italy—along with non-government organizations, to play a more active and direct role in influencing the course of the war and its resolution.

It was the British Conservative government of Margaret Thatcher, however, that spearheaded Western military and economic assistance to Frelimo from the mid-1980s onward. In a strange Cold War twist in Africa, opposing political ideologies were overcome by a shared personal history and level of individual trust between Prime Minister Thatcher and President Machel going back to the Lancaster House talks over Zimbabwean independence in 1979, according to Vines.[433] And following Machel's 1983 visit to London, British aid to Mozambique grew steadily. Although much of this aid was directed at improving transportation corridors running through Mozambique, the indispensable need to protect and secure these corridors against Renamo attacks quickly became a priority for London as well. First, through the use of private security companies funded by Her Majesty's Government in 1983, and then through direct British training of Mozambican soldiers in 1986, the level and scope of Whitehall's direct military assistance expanded.[434]

The burden of training from February 1986 onward fell upon the small British training contingent under the command of then Lieutenant-Colonel Rupert Smith located at Zimbabwe's Nyanga camp. The initial British goal was to train up two full battalions of FAM troops and provide leadership training for the Mozambican officer corps.[435] Despite more than a decade of Soviet, Cuban, and East European military assistance to the Mozambican armed forces, the BMATT advisers found the existing FAM training regimen of poor quality, haphazard and poorly suited to current counter-insurgency requirements. The British plan called for developing a small core of well-trained, motivated, and professionally-led units from scratch that would raise the overall quality of the FAM over time.

After overcoming numerous logistical and coordination obstacles, the training effort would steadily grow. By April 1987 BMATT and ZNA instructors were providing basic infantry training to some 300 recruits every three months. FAM officers would be brought in during the final month of training to marry up with their new commands and conduct field training exercises with their units, according to a former BMATT officer.[436] Much of the initial training period was focused on physical conditioning, especially as most recruits arrived in rags, undernourished and suffering from one or more diseases. Then Brigadier-General Tim Toyne Sewell (Commanding officer of BMATT from February 1989 to February 1991) recalls that Mozambican recruits "made excellent soldiers when [they were] well motivated" and "took great pride in their new clothes and equipment and bonded very quickly with their instructors." [437] Later when Brigadier Toyne Sewell visited these soldiers back in Mozambique, he would frequently see them wearing British cap badges alongside their own FAM insignia with the pride of belonging to the 'British Brigade.' By late 1989, the Nyanga facility was training 1,000 new recruits every three months.

Unfortunately once back in Mozambique, the abysmal condition of the FAM—lack of pay, little to no logistics support, and poor leadership—tended to undermine BMATT training and professional standards quickly deteriorated. It was also not uncommon, according to a former BMATT officer, for British-provided kit and non-offensive equipment to show up in Zimbabwean street markets after having been sold or traded by the newly-trained troops for food in Mozambique.[438] While a number of FAM officers earned the respect of their British advisers, Frelimo's officer corps as a whole was considered sub-standard. Too many officers were "corrupt, selfish and not interested in the welfare of their soldiers" and "it was not unusual to find entire company-sized units in the field without a single officer present," because the officers had all gone back to Maputo and their families, or to live in nearby towns, leaving troops to fend for themselves.[439] The more senior ranks of the FAM were even worse—seen by both external observers and within the FAM ranks as being the most corrupt and ambivalent to chronic supply and equipment problems facing troops in the field. As we shall see, poor morale of FAM units engaged in long and isolated deployments would become an increasingly serious problem which was reflected in rising desertion rates in the later years of the war.

Economic aid to the embattled Frelimo government was another important component of British engagement, and by 1989 London had committed at least $85 million in financial aid. And while not huge in monetary terms, this financial assistance was well-timed and directed at critical infrastructure projects (such as the Ncala and Limpopo rail corridors) providing Maputo with not only economic benefits, but also an important political and psychological boost. This financial assistance, in combination with a steady stream of high-level visits of British government officials cumulating in the April 1989 meeting between Thatcher and Chissano in Nyanga, would solidify British support for the Frelimo government, and vastly increase Whitehall's diplomatic influence with Maputo.

Chissano's diplomatic outreach also proved highly effective in transforming an extremely complicated post-independence, love-hate relationship with Portugal. Portugal had long played host to rightist anti-Frelimo elements and was home to Renamo's chief political representative, Evo Fernandes, from March 1984 until Fernandes's death in April 1988.[440] Moreover, elements within the Portuguese intelligence community appeared to be actively in contact with, if were not outright sympathetic, to Renamo throughout the war. Nonetheless, longstanding Portuguese economic interests in Mozambique—most notably the high profile Cahora Bassa hydroelectric dam project in Tete Province—required a degree of pragmatic cooperation between the two governments, which Chissano used to normalize relations. From the beginning of 1988 official policy in Lisbon began shifting clearly in favor of actively supporting Maputo. The signing of fourteen major protocols on economic, financial and social matters during the September 1989 state visit of Prime Minister A. C. Silva left little doubt as to where Lisbon now stood.

The relationship between numerous Italian political parties and individuals within Frelimo actually predated Mozambican independence, which made reaching out politically to Italy a logical extension of Chissano's turn to the West. In point of fact, Italian investment and development aid continued throughout the worst years of the war; Mozambique was the single largest recipient of Italian foreign aid by 1987. Rome was also the biggest contributor to the Beira corridor rehabilitation, funding rail, road, pipeline, and port improvement projects.[441] It was, however, the increasing humanitarian engagement of the Italian government in Mozambique, via its support for the work of the Italian-based *Sant'Egidio* Catholic lay community (whose critical role will be discussed in the next chapter) in delivering aid relief from the mid-1980s, that would steadily draw Rome into an important behind-the-scenes role in facilitating future peace talks, and in implementing the eventual ceasefire protocols.

Assessment

As the war was entering its thirteenth year at the start of 1989, both Frelimo and Renamo had been severely tested. Both armies were battered and bleeding. A seemingly non-stop series of offensives and counter-offensives by both sides over the past two years had achieved little to alter the strategic situation on the battlefield. Renamo forces continued to operate and strike at will all across the country, overrunning towns and government garrisons to capture supplies and destroying economic infrastructure and cutting lines of communication. Yet the insurgents were incapable of cementing their battlefield gains in the face of concerted FAM and allied counterattacks.

Fierce fighting in the south had forced Frelimo to concentrate its forces and request additional Zimbabwean intervention, but Renamo still lacked the capability to completely isolate Maputo despite its best efforts. Likewise, FAM efforts to sweep Renamo forces permanently away from the capital were usually short-lived as the insurgents simply scattered and returned later. Despite war weariness setting in, each side still clung to the hope of achieving a military victory.

With the escalation in the severity of the fighting, and its spread to every corner of the country the plight of the average Mozambican worsened too. The further destruction of the country's already shattered economy, combined with repeated droughts and accompanying famines, unleashed growing waves of Mozambican refugees and internally displaced people, which the international community could no longer ignore. Direct civilian deaths rose markedly too, as non-combatants found themselves increasingly caught up in the crossfire of the war. Frelimo blamed Renamo. Renamo blamed Frelimo. But the atrocities and the war continued anyway.

The withdrawal of Tanzanian combat troops from north of the Zambezi River at the end of 1988 was a setback for the Chissano regime, but it was more than offset by the introduction of Zimbabwean combat forces along the Limpopo corridor to the south. This new Zimbabwean intervention, the failure of Renamo to foment large-scale unrest in eastern Zimbabwe, and Mugabe's public pledge to remain in Mozambique to the end, gave Chissano a huge political and moral victory. Improved security cooperation between Maputo and its other regional neighbors not only kept the insurgents on the defensive, but isolated Renamo politically within the region. Frelimo now had hope that it could outlast Renamo.

While Chissano's rapprochement with the West would force him to moderate Frelimo's hardline socialist policies and would vastly increase the leverage and influence of Western governments, it brought with it not only badly needed Western assistance but, more importantly, dashed any remaining Renamo hope of creating an ideological alliance with Western governments. Both these factors would lend great impetus in pushing the warring parties toward peace talks in the years ahead.

CHAPTER EIGHT
THE HARDEST BATTLE OF ALL

The start of another year held out little hope of change. Bitter fighting continued to rage across central Mozambique and around the capital in the opening months of 1989. Both sides still struggled to control important towns, and crossings along the Zambezi River, even as the center of war in the north shifted deeper into Zambezia, Nampula, and southern Niassa provinces. Repeated Frelimo and allied efforts to relieve insurgent pressure on the capital and its lines of communication provided only brief respite at best. Renamo battlefield gains were typically offset by government counter-offensives, but the insurgents were still able to strike at will, and maintain the strategic initiative. Frelimo found itself increasingly confined to major cities, isolated garrisons, and Zimbabwean-protected transportation corridors, while Renamo maintained a tenuous hold on an increasingly sparse and depopulated countryside. Despite the growing war weariness, the country continued its downward spiral as neither Dhlakama nor Chissano were willing to call it quits. With no apparent end in sight, the war—and the accompanying suffering—would continue.

Although unclear at the time, the next two years would prove, in hindsight, to be a significant turning point in the conflict, because of diplomatic developments from some of the most unexpected quarters. Like the war itself, however, this newly energized peace process would be ploddingly slow and deliberate. It would be beset by many missteps, competing against external agendas in an uncertain post-Cold War environment, and take place amid enduring mistrust and mutual suspicion. Multiple regional and international actors, as well as non-governmental organizations would become heavily involved—for better or worse. The chain of events set in motion in mid-1989, however, would ultimately prove successful in driving Frelimo and Renamo toward peace.

Even as calls for some type of ceasefire gained momentum in 1990, the fighting continued unabated across Mozambique, albeit on a much-reduced scale as growing problems for Frelimo and Renamo began to take their toll.

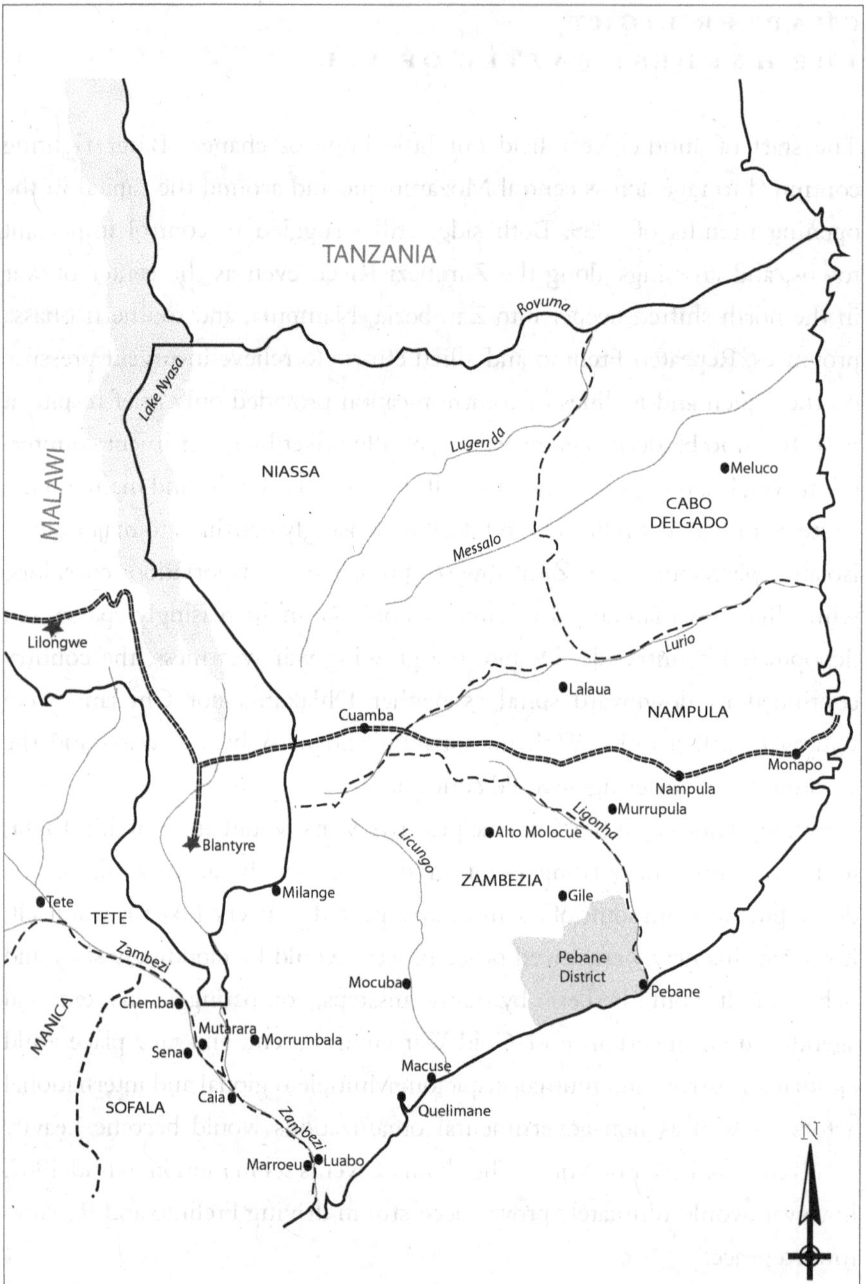

Map 8: Northern Region

The war was also becoming increasingly decentralized and localized. Despite military exhaustion and declining capabilities neither party was yet ready to completely abandon the use of force. Even an increasingly weak bargaining chip in peace negotiations was better than none at all, especially when both sides had few chips at all to play.

Military stalemate sets in

None of this would matter much to Frelimo and Renamo soldiers in the field. The self-perpetuating cycle of the war—attacks followed by counterattacks, followed by retreats and regrouping only to attack again—showed little sign of changing. But with the once plentiful South African supply pipeline now slowed to a mere trickle, Renamo operational requirements and tactics were forced to change. Ammunition and weapon shortages became acute. Renamo's aging military communications network broke down, and with it, its once superior command and control advantage. Likewise, Frelimo forces outside the capital environs and major cities to the north were increasingly on their own, or dependent on Zimbabwean military largess, given the FAM's near complete inability to supply its troops in the field. Food, clothing and ammunition shortages in FAM units were now chronic. The depleted ranks of hardened battle veterans on both sides were now being filled with raw, young and marginally trained recruits as desertion rates (despite the penalty of death) soared. Moreover, surviving combat often took a backseat to basic survival as malnutrition and disease depleted the ranks and capabilities of both armies.

This increasing anarchical situation on the battlefield in the waning years of the war also gave rise to a new type of military actor—independent militia forces led by charismatic leaders with mystical powers. Tired of being preyed on repeatedly by both sides, these leaders sought to protect their local communities and free their people from the ravages of war. In forming homegrown militaries they created a powerful deterrent to any and all who would seek to victimize them. While these types of non-government, self-defense forces sprung up all across war-torn regions of the country, the most prominent and influential were found north of the Zambezi. One in particular, Naprama, would end up playing a major role in the closing years of the war. Widespread banditry too was on the rise across the country. "Probably 70 percent of the war isn't controlled by anybody," claimed one government official in the late 1980s.[442]

Keeping the pressure on in the south

Despite the past lack of success in isolating the capital and keeping Frelimo forces on the defensive, Renamo strategy in the south remained largely unchanged. The only real chance the insurgents had to bring Frelimo to its knees, was to maintain pressure on Maputo's vulnerable lines of communication and demoralize the FAM to bring about its collapse. Difficult operating conditions—most notably ammunition and supplies shortages—prevented Dhlakama from deploying sizeable numbers of troops as in the past, but the insurgents still tried to maintain the battlefield initiative. Unable to attack the capital directly, General Gomes' forces did the next best thing. They created a climate of insecurity and fear throughout the region by repeatedly striking economic and infrastructure targets, raiding garrisons and towns in search of supplies, and constantly ambushed vehicular and rail traffic to and from Maputo.

The areas to the west and north of Maputo along with the southern districts of Gaza Province continued to experience the heaviest fighting throughout 1989 and 1990. Reoccurring Renamo attacks on large sugar plantations, commercial farms, and agricultural processing facilities in early 1989 led to the increased hiring of private security firms to provide protection, train or even lead local militias and paramilitary forces.[443] FAM troops were simply stretched too thin. Likewise, Frelimo forces were unable to halt the spate of deadly attacks on trains and vehicular traffic across Maputo Province. In February 1990 a major Renamo attack on the Ressano Garcia rail line to South Africa left 66 people dead and destroyed a large segment of the track. In May the line was hit again and the train looted.

Frelimo force did have some successes. They overran and destroyed a large Renamo supply base near the South African border in May 1989. More important, by mid-year FAM troops were successful in retaking control of the central Gaza town of Chigubo, the last remaining district capital held by the insurgents in the province. For the first time since the mid-1980s Renamo did not hold a single district capital in the south. Nonetheless, the insurgents were still able to mount well-timed, symbolic attacks as a reminder of their staying power. On 16 September 1990 they sabotaged Maputo's power lines again, plunging the city into darkest just prior to an upcoming round of peace talks.

The war grinds on in the north

Renamo's hold on the territory north of the Save River was much stronger than in the south. The combination of strategic considerations, declining military effectiveness, and growing logistical problems, forced Dhlakama to concentrate most of his efforts on northern Sofala, Tete, Zambezia, Nampula, and the southern Niassa provinces. The Beira and Tete corridors continued to be the target of ongoing Renamo raids, ambushes, and sabotage despite the continuing presence of several thousand ZNA troops protecting these routes. Outside this core area of activity, smaller guerilla units opportunistically engaged in harassing FAM positions, raiding and looting villages, attacking agricultural cooperatives and commercial farms, and ambushing road traffic. As for Frelimo and its Zimbabwean allies, maintaining control of important lower Zambezi River towns from Tambara to Marromeu and key districts of Zambezia Province, as well as ensuring the functioning of the Beira, Tete and Ncala corridors, was the overriding priority. It is here that they would commit the bulk of their efforts. As a result, these areas of central and northern Mozambique would bear the brunt of a grinding war of attrition.

Not surprisingly, the bitterest fighting centered on the Zambezi valley and northward into Zambezia and southern Nampula. The situation became so bad in parts of Zambezia Province in 1989 that Frelimo redeployed some of its more experienced field commanders there from the south. Their mission was not only to provide desperately needed leadership in the field, but to implement more aggressive tactics that they had developed in the south.[444] Success came quickly for many of these new commanders. In one mid-1989 operation a brigade-size FAM force under new leadership overran a major insurgent base in the strategic Alto Ligohna area of Gile District and freed over 1,000 civilians from Renamo control.[445] Large quantities of supplies were also captured in the operation.

Other experienced soldiers were sent to stiffen the defenses of strategic Zambezi River towns to keep them from falling into Renamo hands again. Many, however, quickly found themselves and their men fighting for their lives. Recalls one FAM commander:

> I was sent to Sena with some 220 men to reinforce a company that was holding the town and protecting the bridge from further damage [the bridge was heavily damaged in 1986 when Renamo blew two spans on either side]. The garrison was badly beaten up by a series of recent attacks. Shortly after my arrival, the besieging Renamo massed a large force and began what was to be a week long attack against our position; attacking at least twice a day. We were very isolated and supplies arrived late or not at all. With supplies running low on the sixth day, I ordered my officers to the trenches to face the next attack. Then I saw a column of enemy soldiers marching out in the open, only 100–150 meters away. In broad daylight! Out in the open! We opened fire on them, but they kept on marching as we picked them off one by one. They were mostly kids of 14 to 16 years old; something was wrong in their minds, as they were not fearful. It was an unreal experience, like a movie, and I couldn't understand why the enemy was acting this way.[446]

This officer would later learn that it was not uncommon for young Renamo soldiers to consume a fermented mixture of cannabis and alcohol before battle "to numb them" and "become a machine that does not fear anything."[447] The Sena garrison held out, but desertions took their toll and the unit became increasingly reliant on resupply from across the border in Malawi (as too did Renamo forces). Other besieged garrisons along the Zambezi would not be so fortunate. Many simply imploded and melted away under the weight of constant insurgent harassing attacks, lack of supplies, and morale problems. "Our mission was not so much to overrun Frelimo forces, but to force them to abandon their posts through persistent ambushes of their lines of communication and by shelling with mortars and B-10s," recalls a former Renamo soldier operating with a 100-man company in the Mutarara District of southern Tete Province in late 1989.[448] From Chemba down to Sena and up to Vila Nova da Fronteira on the Malawi border, "We attacked everything," he said.[449]

Farther south of the Zambezi valley, old battlefields and ravaged towns across northern Sofala and Manica provinces continued to be the scene of unremitting assaults, skirmishes, and raids by both sides throughout 1989. The ZNA still maintained a firm grip over the Beira corridor and its symbolic hold on the Gorongosa area by committing a battalion to the permanent defense of the old Casa Banana airfield (now known as Delta Base). And while the Zimbabweans persisted in making life difficult for the insurgents by launching periodic air and ground strikes deep into the Renamo-held territory, the insurgents continued to enjoy freedom of movement throughout the countryside and to strike roads, rail, and economic targets at will. With declining operational capability and sagging morale, beleaguered FAM units south of the Zambezi became largely confined to static defense and small reactive strikes. By the end of 1989, the FAM was viewed as combat ineffective by its Zimbabwean counterparts.

A major assault by the ZNA, along with Mozambican air support, on Renamo's main Massala base and airfield in Maringue District of northern Sofala in early July 1989, however, nearly tipped the military balance in Frelimo's favor when it just missed killing or capturing Dhlakama.[450] It also nearly turned into a political disaster by threating to scuttle nascent peace talks. The attack came just as Dhlakama and his staff were preparing to leave for Nairobi for discussions with Mozambican Catholic church leaders about the possibility of ending the war. Renamo publicly claimed the attack was specifically designed to disrupt the talks and said it clearly showed the insincerity of the Chissano government and of "Frelimo radicals trying to sabotage" any negotiated settlement with Renamo.[451]

By 1990 both Frelimo and Renamo forces were spent. They lacked the capability to launch and support large-scale dry or rainy season offensives as in the past and prosecution of the war increasingly devolve to local commanders. Most operations from 1990 onward were directed at maintaining existing positions and consolidating control over the territory they already held.

Many units on both sides found themselves simply struggling to survive. In more remote parts of the country looting and robbing became their primary activity.

Zimbabwean forces would continue to shoulder the offensive burden, launching yet another campaign in February 1990 to root Renamo out of its central Mozambican strongholds. The results were much the same as in the past—few enemy killed, insurgent operations briefly disrupted, and an eventual return of Renamo to areas it vacated. And while the ZNA still possessed the capability to conduct operations after this period, the growing disillusionment with the war and the FAM's fecklessness pushed Zimbabwean forces to assume a more defensive role from hereon. By late 1990 few Zimbabwean soldiers, it would appear, were willing to die to keep Frelimo in power.

The rise of Naprama[452]

The notable exception to this new pattern of the war could be found in Zambezia and southern Nampula provinces. For here, in late 1989, a new military force would arise that sought to alter the course of the war in this heavily contested region. And it nearly did. The story of Manuel Antonio and the rise of Naprama are fairly well documented now,[453] but at the time of its creation and its rise to prominence it was a mysterious force that caused great consternation within both Renamo and Frelimo ranks. While certainly the most well-known of the charismatic, messianic movements to arise in the latter years of war, it was also demonstrative of a more widespread national frustration with the excesses of the warring combatants, and reflected a desperate search for alternative sources of security. Or, as the governor of Nampula Province in 1991 simply put it: "The people are tired of war, are embracing superstitious beliefs, in an attempt to find a way out of the war."[454]

The Naprama movement traces its roots to Manuel Antonio in late 1989. He was then a 27-year-old traditional healer from the Pebane District of eastern Zambezia Province, who claimed to have died of measles, but after six days in the grave "was revived and told by God to free people" from the ravages of war.[455] Using large ritual ceremonial gatherings, Manuel Antonio "vaccinated" his followers using special medicinal plants and symbolic razor cuts, making them immune to enemy bullets. "We are bulletproof" and "cannot be hurt," said one warrior, because "the bullet comes straight at me, it doesn't reach me."[456] Manuel Antonio soon gained a loyal following in northern and eastern Zambezia.

In March 1990 Naprama went on the offensive against Renamo in the Alto Molocue District. Wearing red head bands and armed only with spears and belief in their invulnerability, hundreds of barefoot Naprama warriors marched on Renamo-held towns and bases, singing songs and blowing whistles as they approached. More often than not, the insurgents simply fled at the sight of this mystic army without putting up a fight. By December, Naprama soldiers had overrun some two dozen Renamo strongholds in northern and eastern Zambezia, freeing as many as 200,000 civilians in the process, according to press reports.[457] Even more remarkable, many of these Renamo positions were considered impregnable and the FAM had repeatedly failed to take them in past attempts.

At the height of its power in 1991, Naprama could field some 3,000 core warriors plus tens of thousands of local Naprama militiamen that operated in conjunction with FAM troops from northern Zambezia, across Nampula and into southern Cabo Delgado Province. The people of this region also "developed a faith in Naprama they had lost with FAM troops" and in Manuel Antonio's mystical power to protect them.[458] Naprama, said one villager, is "allowing us a life like before," because "the life of war is a spoiled life, and Naprama is saving us from this."[459] Nonetheless, by 1991 the movement started to move away from its people's army roots. Some elite Naprama troops began wearing uniforms and even arming themselves with captured AK-47s. The role of women became increasingly marginalized too, and many followers abandoned the movement's non-violent tenets. Looting, kidnapping for ransom, and abuses against civilians became increasingly common. And in some instances local commanders, such as 'Commander Cinco' in northern Nampula Province, would eventually break away to lead roving bands of brigands preying on the civilian populace.[460]

The rapid rise and success of Naprama appeared to surprise and stun

Renamo's senior leadership. The poor showing of its troops and the failure of local commanders to stem the rising Naprama tide, threatened to seriously undermine Renamo's strategic position in this critical part of the country. Moreover, it came at a time when Dhlakama desperately needed to leverage his military position to gain future concessions at the negotiating table. An indication of the seriousness of the situation was the decision by Dhlakama to take to the field personally to lead a counter-offensive against Naprama forces in late 1991.[461] Renamo's semi-conventional battalions spearheaded the operation against Naprama over the course of the next year, and other war veterans were used to stiffen the defensive resolve of existing irregular guerrilla forces in the combat zone as well.

To counteract Manuel Antonio's mystical power and Naprama's image of invulnerability to bullets, Renamo created its own powerful medicine to make it soldiers "immune to the attacks of Naprama warriors."[462] The insurgents also unleashed a new wave of brutality against Naprama and its supporters. For example, following Renamo's capture of the Naprama-controlled town of Lalaua in Ribáuè District of western Nampula in September 1991, the town was looted and 49 people killed. Many of the dead had their severed heads placed on empty shop shelves by Renamo as a warning to all of the cost of resistance.[463] The fierce fighting continued throughout the remainder of the year with the reinforced insurgent forces steadily gaining the upper hand.

Then the unthinkable happened in early December 1991. Manuel Antonio was killed during a clash with Renamo forces near Macuse in eastern Zambezia and his body later taken to Quelimane for burial.[464] Following Manuel Antonio's death, the movement fragmented and ended its effectiveness as a military force. Most of his followers simply returned to their villages, but some former Naprama soldiers joined Frelimo ranks, while still others turned to banditry.

The death of Manuel Antonio and the resulting collapse of Naprama were not entirely unwelcomed by Frelimo as the movement had always been viewed as a mixed blessing. Yes, the movement had provided a huge boost in rolling back the Renamo presence in key areas, but it had done so at the expense of the government's credibility. And many civilians "developed a faith in Naprama they had lost with FAM troops" as the populace increasingly came to view Naprama, not government troops, as their savior.[465] Moreover, the movement had empowered local communities and their sense of independence, thus laying the groundwork for an alternative system of political power outside of Frelimo control.

Declining capabilities, growing problems

As the war entered what would be its final years, the operational effectiveness of Frelimo and Renamo forces declined sharply. More than a decade of endless combat had clearly eroded the military capabilities of each and much of the country was devastated by drought and lying in ruins.[466] Mounting problems for Renamo were beginning to seriously hamper its prosecution of the insurgency. And Frelimo's continuing inability—even with critical foreign assistance—to resolve its long-standing problems made its military increasingly ineffectual. The only real question remaining was which side would collapse first. But much to the surprise of nearly all observers Frelimo and Renamo would continue to fight on even as the prospect of victory on the battlefield grew ever more elusive.

Renamo

Renamo's military effectiveness for much of its existence was largely rooted in its Rhodesian and South African patrimony, adherence to a guerilla warfare strategy, strong command and control, and a steady, secure source of war material. As the war entered a new decade, however, nearly all of these heretofore advantages had seriously eroded.

The formidable years of the insurgency in the late 1970s and early 1980s were powered by the formation of a professional cadre of leadership and well-trained guerrilla fighters. While the senior ranks of the insurgents had remained largely intact throughout the war, Renamo was only able to swell its ranks to over 20,000 and expand operations countrywide through massive forced recruitment. Training of new recruits later in the war suffered too, many soldiers calling their military indoctrination limited to basic weapon's handling and learning simple guerilla tactics.[467] Renamo was, however, able to maintain a degree of specialist training at its main headquarters throughout the course of the conflict. Thus, despite retaining a core of 10,000–12,000 well-trained troops and other specialists, by the early 1990s the insurgent rank and file was notably much younger, more poorly trained, and less disciplined than in the past.

Thanks to Rhodesian and later South African technical support, Renamo had long enjoyed an extensive command, control and communication advantage over Frelimo forces. The provision of powerful, frequency-hopping field radios, central transmitters, and even solar-powered laptop computers along with a code book system allowed Dhlakama and his headquarters staff to maintain secure and constant contact with Renamo commanders in the field. "Our strong point was our communications system" that linked all units down to company level with radios, boasted a former senior general.[468] This gave the insurgents the ability to mass or reposition attacking forces as the changing tactical situation warranted, or to redeploy entire units and specialized personnel quickly across regions. Likewise, poor FAM communications security throughout the war allowed the insurgents to regularly intercept military transmissions and target vulnerable Frelimo garrisons, supply convoys or avoid numerically superior attacking forces. Raúl Domingos remembers how Renamo was able to effectively monitor Frelimo radio and signal communications and "knew all the FAM deployments" and details of their operational status.[469] This information up to March 1984 was also provided to the South Africans who routinely shared their Mozambican signals intercepts with Renamo as well.

By 1989, however, Renamo's communication network was beginning to show its age and encounter growing technical problems.[470] Spare parts were hard to come by. Lack of maintenance and technical ability pushed the equipment to the brink. Handwritten messages and orders became more commonplace as problems grew. And while Renamo headquarters never suffered a complete communications breakdown with its forces in the field, smaller and more far-flung units likely found it increasingly difficult to communicate between themselves, as well as with Renamo high command. According to Western diplomatic sources, rising concerns over Dhlakama's ability to maintain control over all Renamo field commanders was especially troublesome during peace talks.[471] However, the concentration of insurgent forces north of the Beira corridor into southern Tete, Zambezia, and Nampula provinces late in the war had the indirect benefit of negating many of these growing command and control problems. By 1990 more than half Renamo's combat strength was probably concentrated in these areas.

Throughout most of the war Renamo was able to provide a relatively steady flow of arms, ammunition and supplies to its troops in the field because of a highly effective logistics network. Although primitive by modern standards and reliant on back-breaking labor, Renamo was able to distribute weapons and ammunition across the length and breadth of the country. And thanks largely to South African assistance, insurgent operations early in the war were rarely constrained by lack of these war matériel. This advantage began to steadily diminish from 1985 onward as we have seen, and by 1989 the once plentiful foreign assistance pipeline had all but dried up. Several insurgents operating in the south of the country reported that resupply from Gorongosa (and later Renamo's Maringue headquarters)—including AK-47s, heavy machine guns, mortar rounds and ammunition "new from boxes with packing material still intact"—declined from multiple deliveries per year to only once a year by 1985 and none after 1990.[472]

This growing strain on the logistics network is reflected in Renamo field reports of the late 1980s. These reports tend to be highly detailed, listing the number of weapons (down to ones and twos) and boxes of ammunition expended or captured during clashes.[473] Heavy emphasis was placed on conserving ammunition whenever possible and capturing Frelimo supplies and equipment. The resupply problem apparently was less acute for those insurgents operating in central Mozambique: "we never had any weapon or ammunition shortages, only food shortages," recalls one guerrilla active in southern Tete Province in 1989–1990.[474] Some medicines and other small supplies were flown into central Mozambique by small private aircraft from Malawi or transported overland until the end of the war, but many units in more remote regions of the country were on their own.

A series of devastating droughts in the late 1980s and resulting population displacements also constrained Renamo's ability to subsist off the local population, which itself was often on the brink of starvation. Parts of the countryside became depopulated as the people fled to the cities or congregated at international relief centers in search of emergency assistance. Simply finding food to survive became a daily struggle for many Renamo units. "We were really suffering," remembers a Renamo soldier fighting in Gaza Province in 1989, as it was "hard to find food and sometimes all we had was hot water and wild fruit and nuts to eat." [475] It also appears that this situation may have contributed to a rise in insubordination and a lack of discipline within some Renamo ranks.[476]

Frelimo

Even as Renamo's problems were mounting, the situation was even worse for Frelimo. Repeated reorganizations, the creation of new specialized units, extensive foreign training assistance, and multiple leadership changes at the top, had still failed to turn the FAM into an effective counter-insurgency force. Any progress over the years became completely overshadowed by Frelimo's inability to overcome massive logistics problems, lack of operational coordination across its forces and allies, and a corrupt and indifferent command structure that failed to reward success on the battlefield. The result, not surprisingly, was a demoralized and ineffectual fighting force barely holding on.

One of the central failures of the war was Frelimo's habitual inability to support its troops in the field for any length of time. Large-scale government offensives repeatedly fell victim to logistical problems. Resupplying food, clothing, and ammunition to FAM garrisons was a perennial challenge. Constant petrol shortages hindered operations, and maintenance on equipment, especially aircraft, was problematic. "It became very difficult to survive," recalls one soldier fighting in southern Sofala Province in 1989. "There was no rice, no meat or fish. We came back hungry from patrol, but there was no food." [477] This situation often meant that units in the field were left to their own devices, and to forage off the already impoverished local population. Emergency humanitarian food shipments were regularly pilfered by Frelimo troops, and it was not uncommon for individual soldiers or small groups to engage in part-time banditry as a survival mechanism.

As the war entered its final years, this long-broken logistics system effectively collapsed for Frelimo forces deployed outside major cities, towns or the country's main transportation corridors. This became especially critical for those units defending the strategic towns of the lower Zambezi River valley. In the Caia District of northern Sofala Province one FAM officer recalls "there was no life" and "not even a cat could be found" after years of war and drought.[478] Even though his force was protecting the important river crossing at the town of Caia, they had gone without resupply for three months toward the end of 1989. Many of the men were on the verge of starvation and became increasingly desperate.

> There was a very large warehouse in town that was filled with dried and treated animal skins. Since all the roads in and out of town had been blocked by the enemy for many years, the owner simply left them there. The soldiers were so desperate for food that they began to break into the warehouse and steal the skins. The dried skins were 'cooked' for hours over fires and then eaten. The huge warehouse was emptied in just 15 days.[479]

Thanks to years of extensive Soviet-bloc military assistance, Frelimo's high command became very adept at planning large-scale (and often elaborate) military campaigns. Complete with timetables, lines of departure, and daily objectives, these ambitious operations usually called for sophisticated and complex maneuvers by multiple brigade-size units with extensive artillery and air support. After 1985 many of these were conducted as joint operations with Frelimo's Zimbabwean or Tanzanian allies.

The reality on the battlefield, however, was far different. Poor operational command, lack of coordination among units in the field, and unremitting communication problems too often were the norm. In the end massive amounts of ordnance were expended to overrun enemy bases, while the insurgents usually escaped largely unscathed. And even when successful in battle, field grade officers often felt neglected and under appreciated by the higher command authority. Said one officer, "There was a lack of incentives and we were rarely rewarded in terms of career advancement and increased responsibilities."[480] Amid growing frustration with the FAM's ineffectiveness, and worried about having its plans compromised by Renamo sympathizers or spies within the FAM, the Zimbabweans frequently opted, later in the war, to conduct unilateral operations. While this produced some tactical successes it further strained military-to-military relations between the two allies. As one Zimbabwean solider put it, "First we were told to guard the pipeline. Now we seem to be fighting the whole war."[481]

Thus, by 1990 Frelimo not only ceded the strategic, but the operational initiative as well, to Renamo. With few exceptions in the south or in Zambezia, the FAM was now squarely on the defensive. Moreover, in this new defensive role Frelimo's once overwhelming firepower and air superiority became increasingly irrelevant. Although air strikes and artillery bombardment proved useful in the past in attacking fixed insurgent positions, many FAM commanders now found it dangerous in a defensive close-air-support role. Serious problems with ground-to-air communications, and poor map reading skills by ground troops, often led to instances of Frelimo soldiers being killed by friendly fire.[482] Also, Renamo's extensive use of 14.5mm heavy machine guns in an air defense role when besieging towns and FAM garrisons made many air force pilots reluctant to drive home their attacks or brave anti-aircraft fire to deliver supplies to embattled troops.

All of the above had a profoundly destructive impact on FAM morale and this fear of having its army collapse would be a critical factor in driving Frelimo to finally sit down at the peace talk with Renamo. Dhlakama long considered weak morale to be Frelimo's Achilles' heel. "Not training, not equipment, because for me [Dhlakama] the battle was a political and moral one" and "our enemies did not have [strong] morale."[483] It was only a question of which side would outlast the other.

And while both sides were trying desperately to cope with the despondency and fatigue of war, Frelimo's military was near the end of its rope at the beginning of the 1990s. Some of its soldiers had been fighting constantly since 1977. "When will the war end?" mused one battle-hardened veteran. "I was 40 years old and the war was still going on, I had lost my youth." "We had no time to build our future—we were just fighting."[484] Some units along the Zambezi were losing 30 percent of their men to desertion in 1989–1990 with the deserters fleeing to Malawi or Zambia to escape the war.[485] Other soldiers would simply go absent without leave and be reported as killed in action by their comrades. Officers were not immune either. One company commander in Maputo Province deserted this way, reported as being killed during a firefight. Years later, after the end of the war, his commanding officer ran into him in Johannesburg, much to the surprise of both men.[486]

As peace negotiations in Rome gained momentum after mid-1990 and the prospect of peace became a mixed blessing, no one wanted to be too optimistic nor, more important, to be the last person to die in the war. "All we could do was hold on" and "hope the war would someday end," remembers one FAM soldier.[487]

The same feeling was apparent among Renamo troops as well. So much so, that by 1991 "you could see in certain areas that Frelimo and Renamo soldiers were exchanging letters [of truce] without their commanders knowing," said a senior Renamo commander.[488]

The road to Rome

Most realistic observers of the Frelimo–Renamo conflict long recognized that a negotiated settlement was the only way to achieve lasting peace in Mozambique. Both armies had weathered serious setbacks and survived. Each had pummeled the other on the battlefield, yet military victory remained as elusive as ever. The solution had to be a political one, a solution albeit only reluctantly accepted by Chissano and Dhlakama.

Talks about talks[489]

The push for a negotiated peace settlement to the war went back to at least the mid-1980s. Efforts in late 1984 to broker peace with South African-engineered talks in the aftermath of the Nkomati Accord were stillborn. Then Protestant and Catholic religious groups in the country throughout the second half of the decade repeatedly called for a peace dialogue. Neither Frelimo nor Renamo, however, were ready to talk seriously. However, with Chissano's behind-the-scene approval in late 1987, these church groups assumed a more active role in brokering direct talks.[490] A key player in this process was the Bishop of Beira, Jaime Gonçalves, who would personally meet with Dhlakama in Sofala Province in June 1988. This meeting almost certainly established a level of trust between the Renamo leader and the Mozambican religious mediators that would pay dividends in the years ahead.[491]

More progress came in early August 1989 when Dhlakama flew to Nairobi to discuss Frelimo's 'Twelve Principles' with a high-level Mozambican church delegation that included Gonçalves. (As previously noted, an attack on Renamo's Massala headquarters nearly derailed the meeting, but ultimately Dhlakama and his team arrived on 3 August). Renamo passed along to the church delegation its own 'Sixteen Points' declaration that, among other things, called for Renamo's political recognition. Frelimo summarily rejected the Renamo proposal. The talks then stalled despite the intervention of Kenyan and Zimbabwean intermediaries, and would eventually collapse by October. Although ultimately unsuccessful, the talks in Nairobi "created a whole new dynamic for peace by creating a forum in which both sides could formulate their demands."[492]

The direct involvement now of regional players, such as Kenyan President Moi and Zimbabwe's Mugabe (soon to be joined by President Banda of Malawi), along with American encouragement to both Frelimo and Renamo added new momentum in 1990. Important public pronouncements by Chissano in January 1990, over Frelimo's constitutional reforms and plans for free elections in 1991, fueled speculation of a pending Chissano–Dhlakama meeting. President Banda's attempt to broker such a face-to-face meeting, in Malawi in mid-year, failed when Dhlakama appears to have developed cold feet and scuttled the meeting by issuing new preconditions, including the unacceptability of a Zimbabwean mediator role while it still had troops fighting in Mozambique.[493]

Despite this apparent setback, the momentum for peace would be too much to stop now that Chissano and Dhlakama had publicly committed themselves to finding a solution. The only question was what path this process would take. Enter the Italian-based Catholic lay movement, *Sant'Egidio*, and its prestigious alumnus Archbishop Gonçalves to provide this path. The talks would begin in July 1990.

The Rome peace talks

In hindsight very few people would have predicted that the persistent efforts of a little known Catholic lay community would result in Frelimo and Renamo finally agreeing to end the war. At the start of talks on 8 July 1990 at the *Sant'Egidio* compound, enormous and persistent obstacles needed to be overcome. Issues ranging from constitutional reforms, elections and political party laws, to ceasefire arrangements, disengagement, demobilization, and the creation of a new national military, needed to be resolved. Many times the negotiations nearly collapsed or threatened to be derailed by seemingly intractable demands. But ultimately, after twelve rounds and more than two years, the effort would prove successful.[494]

Renamo's lack of political acumen and its highly centralized decision-making process created difficulties for the negotiations. Despite the best efforts of the Italian mediators to bolster the Renamo delegation's confidence, "they were fish out of water" and clearly a young and inexperienced Raúl Domingos, as the head of the negotiating team, was overwhelmed, according to one U.S. observer.[495] Dhlakama's request for assistance and advice on political issues was favorably received by the U.S. representative to the talks, as was Dhlakama's request for technical assistance in establishing a secure communication link from Renamo headquarters in Mozambique to Rome.[496] After some initial trepidation, the Frelimo delegation recognized that this type of active Western engagement would be necessary to facilitate the negotiations. Even with this added help in handling complex political issues, Renamo's sense of isolationism, and the requirement that Dhlakama sign off on all key decisions, would constantly hinder the pace of the talks.

Nonetheless, the first phase of direct talks was a milestone in ending the war. From early July to December 1990, slow but steady progress was made on developing an agenda, resolving the issue of mediation, and building some level of trust. Frelimo's surprising agreement to open discussions on Renamo's demand for the complete withdrawal of all Zimbabwean troops from

Mozambique as a pre-condition to any future ceasefire, however, produced the talk's first major breakthrough. After considerable back and forth, both sides with the help of mediators, formally agreed on 1 December to have all ZNA forces pull back to the Beira and Limpopo corridors. These corridors were defined as being a three kilometer strip on either side of the road, rail, and pipelines. Renamo agreed to refrain from attacking the corridors. The Frelimo delegation leader, Armando Guebuza, provided separate written assurance that "the government did not intend to use the corridors either to support a military escalation or to conduct offensive operations."[497] A newly-created Joint Verification Commission (JVC) with members appointed by Frelimo and Renamo, as well as a military representative, from the government and insurgents themselves, would monitor the compliance of the agreement.

Although problems over implementation and charges of technical violations of the agreement would arise in the ensuing months,[498] by 28 December all the estimated 5,000–6,000 Zimbabwean troops in Mozambique would complete their redeployment to the corridors. The task was simplified by Mugabe's later acknowledgement that only one battalion out of eight ZNA battalions was actually operating out of the corridors by late 1990.[499] Harare forces had thus already assumed a passive defensive posture, facilitating a winding down of the war. According to Domingos, the Zimbabwean pullback and partial ceasefire was the first really positive sign that things were moving forward and that there "was light [at the end of the tunnel]."[500]

The December partial ceasefire, however, did not put an end to all fighting. Frelimo and Renamo worked to shore up their existing military positions and consolidate their hold on territory. For the insurgents this meant dealing with the Naprama threat in Zambezia and Nampula provinces as we have previously noted. Renamo forces also flexed their muscles in the early months of 1991 by attacking vehicles along the Tete road east of the city. These attacks left dozens dead and temporarily halted emergency food shipments to Malawi. Likewise, small groups of guerrillas in the south under General Gomes continued to down power lines and periodically ambush rail and road traffic around Maputo throughout the year as a constant reminder that the war was far from over.

Nonetheless, change was in the air as a result of the Rome talks. In parts of the country Frelimo and Renamo soldiers were quietly exchanging letters of truce. These localized ceasefires started to become more generalized "and we saw that it was impossible to stop that," recalls a former senior Renamo commander.[501] Losing the ability to apply military pressure would seriously erode Renamo's greatest source of leverage in the negotiations: "it motivated us to speed up negotiations in Rome."[502] Many FAM soldiers too were encouraged by the prospect of the peace. "No one wanted to be the last to die in the war," remembers one soldier.[503].

However, the troops in the field would have to wait a little longer as the talks ground on through the remainder of 1991 and into January 1992. Negotiations over thorny political issues such as protocols on new elections laws, the establishment of political parties, post-ceasefire modalities (including the role of the United Nations and the composition of international observers), and implementation timetables, still needed to be finalized. Over the course of seven rounds of meetings, Frelimo and Renamo teams, with extensive behind-the-scenes help of the official mediators and support from Western governments, hammered out agreements. Much of the time was spent dealing with Renamo's ongoing unhappiness with the JVC's monitoring of December 1990 partial ceasefire violations.

Many of these problems and technical violations were the result of the vagueness of the original agreement, and the small size of the JVC team given the enormity of the task required. Despite their frequent threats to void the agreement and walk away, Renamo leaders apparently saw the greater value of neutralizing their gravest military threat—the Zimbabweans—and the agreement continued to hold.

As the Mozambican war entered its sixteenth year the task of bringing it to an end still continued to elude Frelimo and Renamo negotiators, but clearly the movement for peace was gaining speed by early 1992, and there was no turning back now—it was only a matter of time.

Outside the formal talks in Rome, private individuals and foreign governments were also working hard to bring about peace. One notable effort involved President Banda's facilitating of the first face-to-face meeting between Dhlakama and Mugabe in Malawi on 10 January 1992. According to accounts of the meeting, the two men, with very similar backgrounds (guerrilla fighters, Shona-speakers, and Catholic educated), established a rapport and a grudging respect for each other.[504] "You have your dignity and you know what you are fighting for," Mugabe reportedly told Dhlakama at the conclusion of their meeting.[505] Both men left the meeting convinced that peace could be achieved. Mugabe, in fact, would be instrumental in brokering the historic August 1992 meeting between Chissano and Dhlakama in Rome.

The final phase of the Rome talks began in June 1992. Both sides finalized the path to post-war elections, ceasefire arrangements, Renamo demobilization, and the formation of a new integrated national army. The capstone of this effort was the Mugabe-mediated meetings in Rome between Chissano and Dhlakama from 5–7 August that ultimately led to the signing of a declaration of intent to sign a ceasefire agreement by early October and formally end the war.[506] "I knew then [in early August] that peace would really happen," recalls Domingos.[507] On the Sunday morning of 4 October 1992, Chissano and Dhlakama signed the General Peace Agreement (GPA) in Rome. Archbishop Gonçalves was jubilant. The two leaders spoke briefly, thanking those who had supported the peace process and expressing hope for the future. "There is no hatred …," said Dhlakama, as "the armed struggle will be replaced by a political and democratic one."[508]

The war was finally over.

War's postscript

The signing of the GPA signaled the official end of the war, but much still needed to be done to ensure the peace. Renamo faced the challenge of moving its troops to designated assembly points. Large-scale desertions plagued many FAM units. Armed banditry by rogue soldiers and opportunistic Frelimo militiamen was rampant.

The devastation of war and drought had left large numbers of Mozambicans in desperate need of emergency food and medical assistance. And the UN peacekeeping force had yet to take up positions. Nevertheless, the desire for peace was so strong that none of this mattered much to the physically and mentally exhausted Frelimo and Renamo soldiers. When the ceasefire came it was easily complied with, said a senior Renamo commander, "because both sides were fed up with the conflict; we're tired of fighting."[509]

4 October is a date etched forever in these soldiers' memory. The news from Rome [announcing the GPA] "was a big joy to hear," recalls one Renamo veteran.[510] "It was finally over, now I could go home," remembers another Frelimo soldier.[511] Most were simply happy to be alive and never wanted to go back to military life: "things I saw, I should never have seen at my age," said one former child soldier.[512] (In fact, Renamo would have problems in finding enough suitable volunteers to fill its quota of the newly integrated army.) Many soldiers returned home in the years ahead to joyous reunions with family members who thought them dead. Others, however, would struggle to reunite with their families and fragmented communities and start anew.

In the years following the end the war, the former enemies would overcome enormous obstacles to peace. Renamo forces were demobilized. A new national military—the Armed Forces for the Defence of Mozambique (FADM)—formed. Political parties were created. Foreign investment returned, and the country began to rebuild. With the country's first ever multi-party legislative and presidential elections on 27–29 October 1994, Mozambique entered a new era. Chissano defeated Dhlakama to capture the presidency, but Renamo was able to win 112 seats to Frelimo's 129 in the new post-war parliament. An estimated 5.4 million people voted in the elections as the ultimate endorsement by the Mozambican people. And the peace held.

Now more than 20 years since the end of the conflict the war is barely a memory for most of the country's young population, many of whom were not yet born at the time of the GPA signing. It is important nonetheless that they never forget this history that shaped modern-day Mozambique into what it is today. Moreover, the war's legacy will continue to shape their lives and influence the country's political, economic and social direction for some time.

Many of the war's underlying problems have yet to be resolved, but there should be little doubt as to the central lesson of the war: Any peaceful resolution of differences—no matter how imperfect—is always preferable to the cost of violence.

NOTES

1. This section draws largely from Newitt's *A History of Mozambique* and Isaacman and Isaacman's *From Colonialism to Revolution.*
2. See Isaacman and Isaacman, *From Colonialism to Revolution* for a detailed look at Mozambican resistance to colonial rule, pp. 61-78.
3. Isaacman and Isaacman, p. 83.
4. Newitt, p. 522.
5. See MacQueen, *Decolonization of Portuguese Africa*, for a detailed discussion of the fall of the Caetano government, pp. 64-93.
6. Venter, *The Zambesi Salient*, p. 270.
7. Henriksen, *Mozambique: A History*, p. 220.
8. ZANLA was the armed wing of the Zimbabwe African National Union (ZANU) headed by Robert Mugabe. ZANLA's top military commander from 1973 to his death in late December 1979 in a road accident was Josiah Tongogara. Rex Nhongo (now known as Solomon Mujuru), the ZANLA chief of operations, succeeded Tongogara and went on to head the post-independence Zimbabwean army.
9. Petter-Bowyer, *Winds of Destruction*, p. 222.
10. Ibid, pp. 247-252; Geldenhuys, *Rhodesian Air Force Operations*, p. 208.
11. Gilles and Segal, *China and the Arms Trade*, p. 45.
12. *Time*, "The World: Poised Between Peace and War," October 11, 1976.
13. The aftermath of the Nyadzonya raid was shrouded in controversy. ZANLA and the UNHCR called it a "massacre;" an unprovoked attack on a refugee camp that killed or wounded 1,350 people. The Rhodesian military, however, claimed it was a ZANLA training camp housing mainly male recruits and thus a legitimate military target. Lieutenant-Colonel Ron Reid Daly, commanding officer of the Selous Scouts, cites later captured internal ZANLA documents to show that over 90 percent of those killed at Nyadzonya were military age men. See Reid-Daly, *Selous Scouts - Top Secret War*, pp. 217-222.
14. "Military and Police Implications of the Quarterly Threat: 1st July to 30th September 1977," OCC/81, Secret, July 20, 1977 as found in Flower, *Serving Secretly*, p. 308.
15. Moorcraft and McLaughlin, *The Rhodesian War*, p. 67.
16. The total cost of Rhodesian attacks and South Africa economic measures against Mozambique in the four years preceding Zimbabwe independence was put at $556 million by the Mozambican government, but many believe the cost was significantly higher. Martin and Johnson, "Mozambique: To Nkomati and Beyond," p. 17.
17. Cowderoy and Nesbit, *War in the Air*, p. 173.
18. This in no way downplays the hard work and cutting edge scholarship on the war or Renamo that was undertaken in the past. Many of these groundbreaking accounts contain highly usefully and relevant information and, accordingly, are cited extensively within this book where appropriate. Nonetheless, many popular

and "factual accounts" of the war are fraught with major inaccuracies, contain unsupported allegations or biased reporting, and rely heavily on the selective use of information. Unfortunately, over time these flawed works have come to be widely accepted as a true reflection of the historical record without critical examination.

19. Isaacman and Isaacman, *Mozambique: From Colonialism to Revolution, 1900–1982*, p. 177; Minter, *Apartheid's Contras*, p. 33; Hall and Young, *Confronting Leviathan*, 117; Nilsson, *Unmasking the Bandits*, p.21; Legum, *CSIS Africa Notes*, July 1983.
20. Major Alvaro Manuel Alves Cardoso has often been confused with DGS Inspector Oscar Cardoso in the literature concerning Renamo's founding. In addition to sharing the same surname, both men were deeply involved in developing the flecha concept in Angola for the Portuguese. It was Major Alvaro Cardoso, however, who was charged with transforming the flechas in Angola into a commando unit. He was sent to Mozambique in 1973 to activate a flecha unit there and it was Alvaro and 40 of his men that crossed into Rhodesia following the Lisbon coup in 1974.
21. One of those involved in studying the *flecha*s and their training was a young Ron Reid-Daly, who would lead the Selous Scouts—the Rhodesian pseudo-terrorist and tracking unit—when they were formed in late 1973.
22. Flower, *Serving Secretly*, p. 140.
23. Ibid, p. 301.
24. Ibid, p. 302.
25. Reid-Daly, *Top Secret War*, p. 69.
26. Fauvet, "Roots of counter-revolution: The Mozambique National Resistance," p. 115-116.
27. Ibid, p. 116.
28. Author's correspondence with a former CIO officer and Renamo training instructor, January 2011.
29. Author's correspondence with a former CIO officer and Renamo training instructor, January 2011.
30. Martin & Johnson, p. 4.
31. Author's correspondence with a former CIO officer and Renamo training instructor, January 2011.
32. See Vines, *Renamo: From Terrorism to Democracy in Mozambique?* p. 15 for a more detailed look at these groups.
33. For a detailed look at *Voz da África Livre* operations see Cabrita, pp. 139-143.
34. Cabrita, p. 134.
35. Jorge Jardim was a politically well-connected Portuguese businessman with extensive economic interests in Mozambique and Malawi, who was involved in all sorts of political intrigue throughout the colonial period and in the immediate aftermath of independence. He bankrolled numerous political parties and paramilitary organizations from the 1960s up to 1975. His falling out with the Smith government in 1966 over his role in circumventing a UN ban on oil imports to Rhodesia, however, bared any involvement in the creation of Renamo and tainted Cristina's early involvement. Jardim died in Libreville, Gabon in 1982.

36. Cabrita, pp. 134-135.
37. Ibid, pp. 135-136.
38. Ibid, p. 145.
39. Martin and Johnson, p. 7.
40. Also alternatively spelled as Matsangaice, Matsangaise or Matzangaisa in some accounts, André Mathadi Matsangaissa was born in Chirara, Manica Province in 1950 and died on October 17, 1979 in battle. He became the face of Renamo, so much so that for many years after his death Renamo soldiers would still be known as "Matsangas" by the local population.
41. Cabrita claims the name has been incorrectly cited by the media from the beginning, as the actual name of the camp was taken from the *Serra Cudzo* (Cudzo Mountain). On older maps this was listed as "*Sa Cudzo*" with the Sa being a Portuguese abbreviation for mountain. Somehow the two words became amalgamated into "Sacuzdo" and then further shortened to "Sacuze," now the most common usage in the literature. Author's email correspondence with João Cabrita, April 2010.
42. Cabrita, p. 145.
43. Ibid, p. 144.
44. Ibid, p. 147.
45. Martin and Johnson, "Mozambique: To Nkomati and Beyond," p. 17.
46. Ibid, p. 6.
47. Some early accounts, such as Colin Legum's *CSIS Africa Notes*, 1983 and Joseph Hanlon's *The Revolution Under Fire*, 1984 inaccurately identified Retreat Farm (located near the town of Bindura about 45km) northeast of Salisbury as Renamo's first base. While this camp may have been used to train Mozambican dissidents like former Portuguese colonial soldiers and the flechas it was never used by the CIO to house or train Renamo cadres.
48. Author email correspondence with a former Rhodesian instructor, January 2010.
49. Martin and Johnson, p. 6.
50. See Cabrita, *The Torturous Road to Democracy*, pp. 150-153 for a detailed account of Orlando Cristina's early fund raising efforts.
51. Coventry's team at Odzi consisted solely of professional CIO officers with military backgrounds and a few territorial soldiers on rotation. Some accounts incorrectly state that Captain Robert McKenzie (aka Bob McKenna) and his SAS 'A' squadron were involved in training Renamo soldiers at Odzi (Jack Wheeler, "Chapter 3: Mozambique" in Michael Radu's *The New Insurgencies: Anticommunist Guerrillas in the Third World*, 1990), but this was not the case. The SAS would later be involved in training recruits inside Mozambique following Renamo's establishment of bases there after August 1979.
52. Author email correspondence with a former Rhodesian instructor, January 2010.
53. *Resistência Nacional Moçambicana*, "A Guerrilha," 1980, although earlier versions of this manual were in use from early 1977.
54. Author email correspondence with a former Rhodesian instructor, January 2010.

Similar observations were made by former Renamo combatants who were trained at Odzi.

55. Author's correspondence with a former CIO officer and Renamo training instructor, January 2011.
56. Cabrita, p. 154 citing figures provided by Orlando Cristina.
57. Operation Bumper lasted from mid-September to the end of December 1979, although at least one 'emergency supply drop' in southern Sofala Province took place on January 10, 1980. Estimated total tonnage based on Rhodesian military communications traffic and analysis by the author.
58. Rhodesian Air Force, Air HQ Ops cable, Top Secret, Air Task orders September 28 to October 5, 1979.
59. Cowderoy and Nesbit, p. 188 citing John Fairey's flight journal.
60. John Fairey's journal entries courtesy of John Reid-Rowland, December 2009.
61. Ibid.
62. Author email correspondence with former Rhodesian Air Force officer, April 2010.
63. Rhodesian military communications cable, Top Secret, Fire Force Bravo (Air) Grand Reef to ComOps, 19 October 1979.
64. Rhodesian military communications cable, G/1/7, Top Secret, ComOps (Wing Commander Jones) to Air Det Thrasher, 25 October 1979.
65. As cited in Johnson and Martin, p. 6.
66. Ibid
67. Author interview with former Renamo combatant, Maputo, Mozambique, November 2009. I agreed to maintain confidentiality for former soldiers interviewed. Some didn't have problems with their names being used, but I decided on a blanket confidentiality approach for consistency. Where I have permission from very senior leaders, I have cited their names. I did nearly all rank and file interviews in November 2009 and October 2010 with the help of the Mozambican veterans association. There were over two dozen in all.
68. Petter-Bowyer, p. 487.
69. Author email correspondence with a former Rhodesian instructor, January 2010.
70. Cabrita, p. 152
71. Ibid, p. 148.
72. See for example, Vines, *Terrorism in Mozambique*, p. 16.
73. This account of events comes from a former Renamo soldier involved in the failed mission. Author interview with former Renamo combatant, Maputo, Mozambique, November 2009.
74. Stockholm International Peace Research Institute (SIPRI), SIPRI Arms Transfers Database.
75. Newitt, *A History of Mozambique*, p. 565.
76. Cristina put the number at 917 at the end of 1978. Cabrita, p. 154.
77. Combined Operations Headquarters, G/4/1, Top Secret, "Short-Term Strategy for Mozambique, 23 March to 23 July 1979," 3 April 1979.
78. Author correspondence with a former SAS officer, February 2011.

79. See Cole, *The Elite*, for detailed accounts of both these operations (Mavuze, p. 246; Beira, pp. 260-264). It has subsequently come to light since the end of the war that the Beira sabotage was actually conducted by a 24-man SAS team in a seaborne assault with the assistance of South African recce commandos. Renamo was used as cover for the operation and allowed to claim credit. See Moorcraft and McLaughlin, *The Rhodesian War*, p. 158; Stiff, *Silent War*, p. 260.
80. Rhodesian military communications cable, 1 SAS, Top Secret, *IntSum for Period 17–24 July 1979*, 24 July 1979.
81. Rhodesian military communications cable, 'A' Squadron to 1 SAS, Top Secret, *Op Blanket Period 261400B to 271400B*, 27 July 1979.
82. Operation Manacle called for the destruction of all key road and rail bridges across the Zambezi River and throughout Tete Province, but lack of resources prevented its full implementation before the Lancaster House ceasefire came into effect. Nesbit and Cowderoy, *Britain's Rebel Air Force*, pp. 107-108.
83. See Cabrita, pp. 155-157 for a detailed account of these deployments.
84. Author interview with former Renamo combatant, Maputo, Mozambique, November 2009.
85. Author interview with former Renamo combatant, Maputo, Mozambique, November 2009
86. *Voice of Free Africa*, "Mozambique Dissident Group's 'Military' Claims," 20 April 1979.
87. Author correspondence with former Renamo combatant, October 2010.
88. Cole, p. 339. For a detailed—although misleading—account of this mission, Operation Norah, see Cole, pp. 339-346.
89. Stiff, pp. 272-273 provides a corrected account of this mission, dispelling Cole's 'SAS–Renamo version' of the story, pp. 346-352.
90. Cowderoy and Nesbit, *War in the Air*, p. 180.
91. See Cowderoy and Nesbit, pp. 179-183; Petter-Bowyer, pp. 537-543; Reid-Daly, pp. 392-404; and Binda, *The Saints*, pp. 400-406 for detailed accounts of Operation Miracle from differing perspectives.
92. Petter-Bowyer, p. 543.
93. The CIO's final numbers on December 20, 1979 reported ZANLA as having 10,275 fighters deployed inside Zimbabwe-Rhodesia; 3,500 trained guerrillas, but held in external bases; and 14,000 recruits undergoing training, for a total of 27,775. The combined ZANLA and ZIPRA force was estimated at more than 50,000. Flower, p. 248.
94. Some of the more notable include Cole, p. 248; Martin and Johnson, p. 11; Hanlon, p. 221; Vines, p. 16; Minter, *Apartheid's Contras*, p. 33; and Hoile, *Mozambique—A Nation in Crisis*, p. 74.
95. Author interview with former Renamo combatant, Maputo, Mozambique, November 2009.
96. Author interview with former Renamo combatant, Maputo, Mozambique, November 2009.

97. Martin and Johnson, p. 11.
98. Ibid.
99. Author correspondence with a former CIO officer and Renamo training instructor, January 2011.
100. Dhlakama later acknowledged that 'some of the older Renamo commanders objected to my being in the leadership.' Cabrita, p. 161.
101. Rhodesian military communications cable, 'A' Squadron to 1 SAS, Top Secret, Op Bumper Period 301600B to 011600B, 2 December 1979.
102. Hanlon (p. 221) in fact claims "the base fell on 22 October," which was impossible given the constant flow of Operation Bumper aircraft into Gorongosa until the middle of December.
103. Dudley Coventry as cited in Martin and Johnson, p. 10.
104. These figures do not include an estimated 600-1,000 men either undergoing training or recuperating between missions at Odzi nor an additional 300-400 local recruits being trained at bases inside Mozambique. This would bring Renamo's total strength to between 2,200 and 2,800 by the end of 1979.
105. Rhodesian military communications cable, Top Secret, 1 SAS to ComOps, 14 November 1979.
106. Rhodesian military communications cable, Top Secret, 'A' Squadron to 1 SAS, 2 December 1979.
107. Rhodesian military communications cable, Top Secret, 'A' Squadron to 1 SAS, 4 December 1979.
108. Rhodesian military communications cable, Top Secret, 'A' Squadron to 1 SAS, 7 and 8 December 1979.
109. Rhodesian military communications cable, 'A' Squadron to 1 SAS, 15 December 1979.
110. Rhodesian military communications cable, Top Secret, 'C' Squadron to 1 SAS, 31 December 1979.
111. Rhodesian military communications cable, Top Secret, MID Intelligence Report – Mozambique, 17 and 27 December 1979.
112. Rhodesian military communications cable, Top Secret, Fire Force Bravo (Air) FAF 8 to Air HQ Ops, 21 December 1979.
113. Rhodesian military communications cable, Top Secret, ComOps to 1 Brigade, 2 Brigade, Selous Scouts, and Rhodesian Light Infantry, 21 December 1979.
114. Rhodesian military communications cable, Top Secret, *Terms of Reference Operation Bumper*, 22 December 1979.
115. Flower, *Serving Secretly*, p. 262.
116. See Moorcraft and McLaughlin, *The Rhodesian War*, pp. 166-167 for details and the reasons behind this move.
117. Rhodesian military communications cable, Top Secret, 'A' Squadron SAS to 1 SAS, "Reference Air Support for Op Bumper and Op Miracle," 9 December 1979.
118. The details of the South African connection are discussed in-depth in Chapter 5 of this book.

119. Rhodesian military communications cable, Top Secret, Air Headquarters Ops to Air Detachment Thrasher, 14 December 1979.
120. Martin and Johnson, "To Nkomati and Beyond," p. 13.
121. Author interview with former Frelimo combatant, Maputo, Mozambique, November 2009.
122. Martin and Johnson, p. 13.
123. Moorcraft, *African Nemessis*, p. 261.
124. Captured Renamo documents and van Niekerk's nearly ten-year association with Dhlakama clearly paint a close personal relationship, but Dhlakama still remains guarded and circumspect in discussing van Niekerk. The author was unable to draw him out on the subject during the May 2012 interview.
125. Author interview with former Renamo combatant, Maputo, Mozambique, November 2009.
126. Author's interview with João Cabrita, Maputo, Mozambique, May 2012.
127. Author's interview with Afonso Dhlakama, Nampula, Mozambique, May 2012.
128. Author interview with Raúl Domingos, Maputo, Mozambique, November 2009.
129. Recruited in May 1980, Domingos would become Dhlakama's chief secretary and later rise within the organization to become the Southern Front military commander, Renamo Chief of Staff, and ultimately the lead negotiator at the Rome peace talks.
130. Author interview with Raúl Domingos, Maputo, Mozambique, November 2009.
131. Quote as cited in Martin and Johnson, p. 12.
132. See Martin and Johnson, pp. 13-16 for the most widely cited account of the transfer.
133. See Cabrita, *The Tortuous Road to Democracy*, for a very detailed look at the ends and outs of this political maneuvering, pp.182-184.
134. Cabrita, p. 172. This also conveniently covered the SADF faction pushing a 'southern strategy' where Renamo would be positioned nearer the South African–Mozambican border, thus making it easier to re-supply, enabling it to directly threaten the capital, and providing a buffer against potential ANC incursions via Mozambican territory.
135. Ibid, p. 163.
136. Handwritten letter date April 14, 1980 from Luke Mhlanga to Dudley Coventry written from "Citagonga Mt., Mozambique." Copy in author's possession, courtesy of Danny Hartman.
137. The original source of the shoot-out legend appears to have come from an *Africa Confidential* article in the early 1980s and has been blindly repeated since as fact by multiple authors, including Anders Nilsson, *Unmasking the Bandits: The True Face of the M.N.R* (1990), p. 26; Alex Vines, *RENAMO: Terrorism in Mozambique* (1991), p. 17; and Margaret Hall and Tom Young, *Confronting Leviathan: Mozambique Since Independence* (1997), p.120, as well as in innumerable journal articles. Not to be outdone, the CIA even cited the 'shoot out' story as background in its early intelligence analysis of Renamo throughout much of the 1980s.

138. Author interview with former Renamo combatant, Maputo, Mozambique, November 2009; see also Cabrita, p. 163.
139. Moorcraft, p. 260.
140. Author's interview with former Renamo combatant, Maputo, Mozambique, November 2009.
141. See Cabrita for additional details on Operation Leopard, pp. 173-174.
142. Ibid, p. 175.
143. Ibid, p. 175.
144. Martin and Johnson, p. 19.
145. See Robert Davies, "The SADF's Covert War against Mozambique" for an analysis of the political factors behind this strategy, pp. 104-115.
146. Martin and Johnson, p. 19.
147. Author interview with former Frelimo combatant, Maputo, Mozambique, November 2009; Hanlon, p. 224.
148. Cabrita, p. 193.
149. Author interview with former Frelimo combatant, Maputo, Mozambique, November 2009.
150. These accounts reference Martin and Johnson's work citing the so-called 'Eastwood report,' but without the caveats. Martin and Johnson's original citation of Eastwood's claim that Renamo had "by December 1980 between 6,000 and 7,000 fully armed men" (pp. 18-19) came with an extensive endnote (p. 346). This endnote calls into question Eastwood's ulterior motive and suspect troop numbers. Most accounts referencing Johnson and Martin, however, fail to add this important qualifier. Cabrita independently comes up with an estimated strength at 6,000, but it also appears too high given all Renamo's setbacks, p. 176.
151. Thomashausen, *Africa Insight*, Vol.13, No. 2, 1983, p. 126; Jack Wheeler, "Mozambique" in Michael Radu, *The New Insurgencies: Anti-Communist Guerrillas in the Third World* (New Brunswick, NJ: Transaction Publishers, 1990), p. 173, which are pro-Renamo accounts.
152. Martin and Johnson citing accounts by local villagers in the area of Gogoi, p. 20.
153. Hall and Young, *Confronting Leviathan*, citing press sources, p. 126. Cabrita, however, claims that the refugees were in fact fleeing "as a result of FAM [sic FPLM] operations in the Espungabera region," p. 194.
154. See Martin and Johnson for a detailed account of the Gingles incident, p. 22. These covert operations built on a pattern of direct military involvement that began with the January 1981 SADF cross-border raid on ANC houses in the Maputo suburb of Matola that left thirteen dead.
155. Remarks by Afonso Dhlakama and other senior commanders, as cited by Cabrita, p. 200.
156. Not unlike many aspects of the war, authors would use various elements of Burlison's observations to support their often conflicting views of Renamo. See Hall and Young, p.126; Hanlon, *Revolution Under Fire*, p. 223 and 228; Turner, *Continent Ablaze*, p. 137; Vines, p. 95 for example.

157. Cabrita, p. 194.
158. Ibid, p. 196.
159. Ibid, p. 196. Renamo's Female Detachment (DF) was formed in 1980 and its personnel primarily served as nurses, radio operators, logisticians, intelligence officers, and instructors. Others served with the Department of Internal Administration or on the General Staff. Cabrita interview with former Renamo Female Detachment captain, September 1996.
160. This account is taken from Cabrita (pp. 200-201) and from information obtained in the account of a Frelimo officer present at the battle. Author interview with former Frelimo combatant, Maputo, Mozambique, November 2009.
161. Author interview with former Frelimo combatant, Maputo, Mozambique, November 2009.
162. See Martin and Johnson, pp. 19-21; Nilsson, pp. 24-37; and Hanlon, pp. 222-223 for a discussion of the Garagua Documents.
163. Renamo also claimed to have recruited another 800 men in Gaza and Inhambane provinces by December 1981, which would more than double the insurgent's strength south of the Save River. "General Headquarters Minutes," undated (circa late 1981), *Garagua Documents.*
164. Author interview with former Frelimo combatant, Maputo, Mozambique, November 2009.
165. Cabrita, p. 197.
166. Author interview with former Frelimo combatant, Maputo, Mozambique, November 2009.
167. Cabrita, pp. 197-198.
168. Ibid, p. 210.
169. Author's interview with former Frelimo combatant, Maputo, Mozambique, October 2010.
170. Operation Lifeline would eventually expand to include ZNA joint responsibility with Mozambique to protect the entire 250 kilometer length of the corridor. It would also set the pattern for the June 1984 dispatch of elements of the ZNA's 1 Mechanized Battalion to protect the Tete Corridor, the main road running from Zobue on the Malawi border through Tete city to Nyamapanda on the Zimbabwe border, through the use of armed convoy escorts as part of Operation Cob Web.
171. See Cabrita for background on the PRM and long running merger talks with Renamo, pp. 202-203.
172. Borges Coelho and Macaringue, "The Role of Mozambique's Armed Forces in a Changing Security Context," p. 43.
173. Ibid
174. Hanlon, p. 232.
175. See Cabrita for a detailed look at this operation, pp. 206-210.
176. *Voz da África Livre*, February 2, 1983.
177. Cabrita, p. 207.
178. Ibid, p. 210.

179. Hanlon, p. 230.
180. One of the more notable Renamo bases to fall was the Tome provincial base in Inhambane on August 23, 1983 that yielded over 9 tons of supplies and munitions. Much of the capture material was airdropped by the SAAF only days prior to the base's capture. Subsequent interrogations of Renamo prisoners and captives also revealed the extensive nature of South African military assistance to the insurgents in the province. Turner, p. 139.
181. Hanlon, p. 255.
182. Minter, "The Mozambican National Resistance (Renamo) as Described by Ex-participants," p. 14.
183. *The Star,* Johannesburg "Renamo's Dhlakama holds high hopes for 1999 election," March 13, 1996.
184. Moorcraft, *African Nemesis*, p. 130.
185. In a September 30, 1985 press conference the Mozambican government released a 32-page booklet, *The Gorongosa Documents*, drawn from documents discovered during the capture of Renamo's headquarters at Casa Banana. The publication highlighted the extent of South African–Renamo cooperation, which extended well beyond the March 1984 signing of the Nkomati agreement.
186. *The Star,* Johannesburg, "Renamo's Dhlakama holds high hopes for 1999 election," March 13, 1996.
187. In 1979, No. 3 Squadron had 11 RhAF Dakotas plus two additional SAAF Dakotas operational. Nine of the eleven were configured to carry cargo and parachutists. Cowderoy and Nesbit, *War in the Air*, p. 133.
188. Rhodesian military communications cable, Operation Bumper air tasking order, Top Secret, Com Ops to Army HQ, 2 November 1979.
189. Author correspondence with former Rhodesian Air Force pilot, December 2009.
190. Rhodesian military communications cable, Top Secret, Air HQ Ops to Air Det Thrasher, 10 January 1980.
191. Author correspondence with Paul Moorcraft, May 2010.
192. Martin and Johnson, "To Nkomati and Beyond," p. 13.
193. Colin Legum, *The Battlefronts of Southern Africa*, pp. 248-249. Legum also claims that van Niekerk was present and serving at Renamo's Garagua (Chicarre) base in 1979 after "Gorongosa was destroyed by the Mozambican army in November"[sic], which is impossible given that Garagua/Chicarre was not established until after the loss of the Sitatonga base in July 1980, well after Zimbabwean independence.
194. Operation Altar was the code name for South African assistance to Renamo from March 1980 until January 1983. After that time it was renamed Operation Mila. A national serviceman, Roland Hunter, serving under Colonel van Niekerk was later charged with high treason for passing information to the ANC, but, to avoid exposing Operation Mila, Hunter was allowed to plead guilty to illegal possession of classified documents and was sentenced to five years. His planned defense testimony detailing Operation Mila only became public in late 2000. *Independent on Line*, "New details show SADF supported Renamo," December 2, 2000.

195. Author's calculation based on sampling of Operation Mila documents. Minter initially came up with a figure of 148 tons/year for the early 1980s, but later revised this to 180 tons. Minter, *Apartheid's Contras*, Endnote 39, p. 201.
196. Although 28 Squadron also flew C-160 aircraft, none were ever used in Mozambican resupply operations. Author interview with former South African Air Force officer, November 2009, Johannesburg, South Africa.
197. Author interview with former South African Air Force officer, November 2009, Johannesburg, South Africa.
198. Court documents, *The State vs. Roland Mark Hunter, Derek André Hanekom and Patricia Elizabeth Hanekom*, Schedule B, Section 3.6.
199. Ibid. Section 2.9.
200. Ibid.
201. Author correspondence with former South African Air Force C-130 navigator, December 2009.
202. Ibid.
203. Ibid.
204. Martin and Johnson, "To Nkomati and Beyond," p. 20
205. Stiff, *Silent War*, p. 372.
206. Gorongosa Documents, December 30, 1983 entry.
207. Ibid. February 8, 1984 entry.
208. One Renamo recruit, who was part of a small group of 18 selected for advanced medical training, remembers being picked up by submarine off the Inhambane coast and taken to South Africa in January 1982. Author interview with former Renamo combatant, Maputo, Mozambique, October 2010.
209. Author correspondence with former South African Navy sailor, November 2010.
210. Author correspondence with former Zimbabwean army officer, April 2010.
211. As cited in Minter, *Apartheid's Contras*, p. 187.
212. Hanlon, *Revolution under Fire*, p. 263.
213. Gorongosa Documents, February 11, 1984 entry.
214. Ibid.
215. Cabrita, *The Tortuous Road to Democracy*, p. 181.
216. Author phone interview with David Scott-Donelan, May 20, 2010.
217. Court documents, *The State vs. Roland Mark Hunter, Derek André Hanekom and Patricia Elizabeth Hanekom*, Schedule B, Section 2.3.3.
218. Author phone interview with David Scott-Donelan, May 20, 2010.
219. Ibid.
220. Capt. Jake Jacobs account as cited in Stiff, p. 372.
221. Author phone interview with David Scott-Donelan, May 20, 2010.
222. Davies, "The SADF's Covert War against Mozambique," p. 104.
223. Hall and Young, for example claim that Pretoria "allowed 1,500 guerrillas to cross over into Mozambique with their weapons, before closing their camps in the Transvaal" following the signing of the Nkomati Accord (*Confronting Leviathan* , p. 147). Another early reference by Martin and Johnson about the possibility of

employing 8,000 former Renamo soldiers as mineworkers in South Africa as part of a 1984 peace settlement (p. 32), has often been misread and reported as "the dilemma of what to do with maybe 8,000 Renamo recruits thought to be still in South Africa," Stiff, p. 378. All these pale, however, in comparison to Maputo's wildly exaggerated claim in August 1984 that "there were still 18,000 MNR [Renamo] cadre in SA [South African] military camps" (cited in Legum, p. 355).

224. Chicarre (or Garagua) became Renamo's new headquarters in August 1980 following Frelimo's capture of Sitatonga base the previous month.
225. Author phone interview with David Scott-Donelan, May 20, 2010.
226. Captain Jake Jacobs account as told by Stiff, p. 371.
227. Weinstein, *Inside Rebellion*, pp. 146-147.
228. Gorongosa Documents, January 16, 1984 entry.
229. Ibid, December 26, 1983 entry; February 20, 1984 entry.
230. Ibid, December 26, 1983 entry; February 20, 1984 entry.
231. Colonel Bert Sachse account as cited in Stiff, p. 374. Captain Scott-Donelan believes, however, that "about 40 men" may have remained with the recces after Nkomati. Author phone interview with David Scott-Donelan, May 20, 2010.
232. The Renamo unit was accompanied by five specialists from SADF's 32 Battalion for this operation, according to a former Renamo commander. Author interview with former Renamo combatant, Maputo, Mozambique, November 2009.
233. See Stiff, pp. 392-405 for a review of recce operations in Mozambique from 1981 to 1983.
234. As cited in Stiff, pp. 381-382. Stiff also says that he was "repeatedly assured by numerous senior officers in Special Forces" that they did indeed disengage and "anything that occurred afterwards, if anything happened at all, occurred under the auspices of ... Lieutenant-General Pieter van Westhuizen [Chief of Staff – Intelligence] and not Special Forces." Stiff, p. 377.
235. Court documents, *The State vs. Roland Mark Hunter, Derek André Hanekom and Patricia Elizabeth Hanekom*, Schedule B, Section 1.7.
236. Ibid, Section 2.2.5.
237. Ibid, Section 2.7.1.
238. Ibid, Section 2.4.
239. Ibid, Section 2.9.4.
240. The assassination of Cristina remains shrouded in controversy and even continues to surface in South African legal cases decades later. See Cabrita for a detailed discussion of the assassination and several competing theories, pp. 189-192, or van Niekerk's 22 November 2000 court testimony in Dr. Wouter Basson's murder trial.
241. Van Niekerk 22 November 2000 testimony, *Dr. Wouter Basson Trial Report 36, Friday November 17–Thursday 23 November 2000*.
242. *Sunday Independent*, "New Details Show SADF Supported Renamo," December 12, 2002.
243. Author interview with Professor André Thomashausen, Pretoria, South Africa, November 2009.

244. The Accord of Nkomati, Article Three, Paragraph 1.
245. Author phone interview with David Scott-Donelan, May 20, 2010.
246. Gorongosa Documents, March 5, 1984 entry.
247. Ibid, February 24, 1984 entry.
248. Ibid, September 4, 1984 entry.
249. Ibid, June 21, 1984 entry.
250. Ibid, August 16, 1984 entry.
251. Ibid, letter From Commandant Charles to President of Renamo, June 21, 1985.
252. Ibid, letter "From the President of Renamo to Friend Commandant Charles," June 16, 1984.
253. It is unclear from the Gorongosa Documents themselves if all these "humanitarian flights" actually took place as scheduled, but several notations appear to indicate that at least some of the supplies may have been delivered.
254. Gorongosa Documents, June 21, 1984 entry.
255. Ibid, February 24, 1984 entry.
256. Ibid, "Conversation between H.E. and Colonel Vanikerke on 5.6.85."
257. Court documents, *The State vs. Roland Mark Hunter, Derek André Hanekom and Patricia Elizabeth Hanekom*, Schedule B, Section 2.7.
258. Author interview with former Renamo combatant, Maputo, Mozambique, November 2009.
259. Author interview with former Renamo combatant, Maputo, Mozambique, November 2009.
260. Minter cites several accounts for 1988. Minter, "The Mozambican National Resistance (Renamo) as Described by Ex-participants," p. 11.
261. For the U.S. connection, see Kathi Austin, *Invisible Crimes.*
262. Minter, "The Mozambican National Resistance (Renamo) as Described by Ex-participants," p. 12. However, Mr. De Oliveira said that on June 24, 1987 van Niekerk visited the Renamo office in Lisbon. Accompanied by two South African electronics specialists, they installed a telefax and a cipher machine to allow Mr. De Oliveira to send coded messages to a South African Army camp at Phalaborwa, in the Transvaal. From there, the messages were relayed to Renamo rebel units inside Mozambique. *The New York Times*, "South Africa Apparently Shifting Loyalty to Support Mozambique," May 3, 1988.
263. See for example, *Weekly Mail* (South Africa), "Renamo's secret SA bases," March 16-22, 1990; *The Independent*, "SA 'Still Supplies' Renamo Rebels," March 11, 1989; AIM, "Jovens denunciam continuo apoio sul-africano," August 8, 1989; and *Mail & Guardian*, "Opperman reveals Renamo links," March 22-28, 1996.
264. *Weekly Mail* (South Africa), "While Renamo talks go on, more talk of SA connection," August 18-24, 1989.
265. *Ibid* "Renamo's secret SA bases," March 16-22, 1990.
266. Central Intelligence Agency/Directorate of Intelligence, "Mozambique: RENAMO at a Crossroads," March 1991, pp. iv and 13.
267. Ibid, p 13.

268. Ibid, p 14.
269. Stiff, p. 375 quoting Craig Williamson.
270. Often overlooked in any assessment as to the wisdom of Machel signing the Nkomati Accord is the long-term strategic benefit "that it removed the threat of conventional attack by South Africa" and "this meant the army could focus almost entirely on fighting Renamo." Borges and Macaringue, "The Role of Mozambique's Armed Forces in a Changing Security Context," p. 44.
271. *The Herald* (Harare), June 24, 1982 as cited in Martin and Johnson, "To Nkomati and Beyond," p. 70.
272. Ibid, p. 69.
273. Ibid, p. 68.
274. Mlambo, "Raids on Gorongossa," Table 2. Comparison of Transportation Costs: Durban/Beira to Zimbabwe.
275. Martin and Johnson, "To Nkomati and Beyond," p. 71.
276. Hanlon, *Beggar Your Neighbours*, p. 28.
277. Vines, *Renamo: Terrorism in Mozambique*, p. 61 citing interview with Commander Michael Evans.
278. Author interview with former ZNA officer; Johannesburg, South Africa, October 2010.
279. Mlambo, "Raids on Gorongossa."
280. Ibid
281. Author interview with former ZNA officer, Johannesburg, South Africa, October 2010.
282. Author interview with former Renamo commander, Maputo, Mozambique, November 2009.
283. Author interview with former Renamo commander, Maputo, Mozambique, November 2009 .
284. Vines, "The Business of Peace," pp. 66-68.
285. Ibid p. 67.
286. Thomashausen, "The Mozambique National Resistance," p. 32.
287. Author interview with Raúl Domingos, Maputo, Mozambique, October 2010.
288. Thomashausen, pp. 34-36.
289. Sam Barnes, "The Socio-Economic Reintegration of Demobilised Soldiers in Mozambique." See Jessica Schafer, *Soldiers at Peace*, pp. 53-76 for a more balanced, yet complex, view of Renamo's child soldiers.
290. *Ministério das Finanças* – Gabinete de *Reintegração* – (Maputo, 1992) as cited in João Cabrita, *The Tortuous Road to Democracy*, p. 258.
291. Author interview with former Renamo combatant, Maputo, Mozambique, November 2009.
292. Ciment, *Angola and Mozambique*, p. 149.
293. Martin and Johnson, p. 35.
294. Hall and Young, *Confronting Leviathan*, p. 160.
295. G/2/3, *Report on Operation Grapefruit*, Army Headquarters (Harare) August 1985 as

cited in Mlambo, "Raids on Gorongossa."

296. The official Zimbabwean record of the attack is sparse and has never been publicly released. Widely published popular accounts are filled with numerous errors and unsubstantiated facts thanks to the propaganda war between Frelimo and Renamo. The official Renamo communiqué, for example, claimed that 12,000 ZNA and 8,000 FAM participated in the assault and killed two Soviet officers coordinating the attack. Likewise, Frelimo said it killed 500 or so insurgents in the battle. The account related here is drawn from what I consider to be the most reliable information and based on interviews and recollections of people with first-hand knowledge of the event. Nonetheless, it is far from perfect, but in my view more accurately reflects the events as they occurred.
297. Author's phone conversation with former ZNA soldier, March 2010. It is important to note that Renamo's "Gorongosa" base at Casa Banana in 1985 was located some 30km from the original "Gorongosa" base on the mountain itself that was established during the Rhodesian period.
298. Author interviews with former Renamo combatants, Maputo, Mozambique, November 2009 and October 2010.
299. One myth refers to the role of Dudley Coventry or other "former CIO officers" in locating the base given their past association with Renamo during the Rhodesian period. Martin and Johnson claim that "The senior instructor [Coventry]... commanded a ZNA unit which did the reconnaissance and participated in the assault to retake it on 28 August 1985" and that Machel later presented Coventry "with a Swiss-army penknife with a Frelimo crest on it" (Note 20, p. 345). This account has been consistently repeated over the years as fact, most recently by Stiff, *The Silent War*, p. 380. The story is completely false. First, as noted above, the Casa Banana base was established after the Rhodesian period and at a different location. Second, Coventry's role in the operation was to help coordinate logistics support for the Para Group from Chimoio where he remained throughout the operational phase, according to Lieutenant-Colonel Lionel Dyck, the officer in command. And third, the knife was given to Dyck and he still has it in his possession to this day.
300. Author interview with former ZNA officer, Johannesburg, South Africa, October 2010.
301. Former U.S. intelligence officer, Washington, DC, September 1998.
302. Author interview with former ZNA officer, Johannesburg, South Africa, October 2010.
303. Author interview with Lionel Dyck, Cape Town, South Africa, October 2010.
304. Ibid.
305. Ibid, and follow up email exchange November 2010.
306. Author interview with former Renamo combatant, Maputo, Mozambique, October 2010.
307. Author interview with former ZNA officer, Johannesburg, South Africa, October 2010.
308. Mlambo, "Raids on Gorongossa."

309. *Mozambique Notes,* "The Gorongosa Story," p. 4.
310. Author interview with Lionel Dyck, Cape Town, South Africa, October 2010. Dyck also recalls seeing "large piles of ivory" that subsequent were sent to Chimoio and then disappeared.
311. *Associated Press*, "Claims Troops Crush Mozambican Guerrillas' Base," September 7, 1985.
312. Author interview with Lionel Dyck, Cape Town, South Africa, October 2010. As noted previously, Martin and Johnson mistakenly identity Dudley Coventry as the recipient of Machel 's gift.
313. This battle has been depicted by Mlambo as a planned diversionary attack by the Zimbabweans to draw attention away from their pending assault on Casa Banana. According to Lieutenant-Colonel Lionel Dyck, however, an Islander surveillance aircraft spotted unusual activity in the area and then upon closer investigation was fired on by the insurgents. Dyck hastily assembled a small attack force at Chimoio in response, and only afterward found out the target was Renamo's provincial base for Manica. Author interview with Lionel Dyck, Cape Town, South Africa, October 2010.
314. Turner, *Continent Ablaze*, p. 142.
315. Martin and Johnson, p. 36.
316. Cabrita, *The Tortuous Road to Democracy*, p. 248.
317. Mlambo, "Raids on Gorongossa."
318. For a detailed account of Operation Octopus see, Mlambo, "Raids on Gorongossa."
319. Moorcraft, *Mugabe's War Machine*, p. 124.
320. Author interview with former ZNA officer, Johannesburg, South Africa, October 2010.
321. Author interview with former ZNA officer, Johannesburg, South Africa, October 2010.
322. "Report on the Attack on Marromeu," (Harare) February 4, 1986 as cited in Mlambo, "Raids on Gorongossa."
323. Author's interview with Lionel Dyck, October 2010, Cape Town, South Africa.
324. HQ/C2/6/AIR, Air Force of Zimbabwe file (Harare, 1986) as cited in Norman Mlambo, "Raids on Gorongossa."
325. Author email correspondence with former ZNA officer, April 2010.
326. "Report on the Attack on Marromeu," (Harare) February 4, 1986 as cited in Mlambo, "Raids on Gorongossa."
327. Turner, p. 143.
328. This account of Operation Zero is drawn primarily from Mlambo, "Raids on Gorongossa."
329. Some accounts, such as Turner's, put the size of attacking ZNA force at 3,000 and claim it was supported by 24 helicopters and 17 Mozambican and Zimbabwean aircraft (p. 143), but these numbers seem unrealistically high given all the problems Harare had in assembling and deploying the force. Mlambo does not cite a number in his account of the operation.

330. Mlambo, "Raids on Gorongossa."
331. Ibid.
332. Turner, p. 143.
333. Mlambo, "Raids on Gorongossa."
334. Author interview with former Renamo combatant, Maputo, Mozambique, October 2010.
335. Author interview with senior Renamo commander, Maputo, Mozambique, November 2009. It is interesting to note that several other senior Renamo commanders viewed Zimbabwean tactics with disdain—"they did not like to fight face-to-face" and would "only fight on their own terms" and with air power.
336. See Vines, *Renamo: Terrorism in Mozambique*, pp. 92-94 for a discussion of the various types of bases and administrative zones.
337. See Moorcraft, *African Nemesis*, p. 279-281 for a journalist's account of visiting several Renamo camps in 1986.
338. Renamo document in author's possession, *Situaçãao Operacional do Batl. Dragão*, July 11, 1988.
339. João Cabrita, p. 253.
340. Renamo document in author's possession, *Situação Operacional do Batl. Dragão*, July 11, 1988.
341. General Herminio Morais as cited in Cabrita, p. 253.
342. General Adriano Faustino as cited in Cabrita, *The Tortuous Road to Democracy*, p. 253.
343. Author interview with former Renamo commander, Maputo, Mozambique, May 2012.
344. Vines, p. 62.
345. Central Intelligence Agency, "Mozambique: Coping with the Insurgency," *National Intelligence Daily*, November 19, 1986, p. 12.
346. Moorcraft, p. 281.
347. Cabrita, p. 238.
348. Ibid.
349. Radio RSA, October 14, 1986 as cited in Cabrita, p. 238.
350. See Cabrita, pp. 239-242 for a discussion of the alleged Malawian connection.
351. See for example, *Washington Times*, "Rebels in Mozambique Aim to Split Country," November 11, 1986.
352. Author inteview with Afonso Dhlakama, Nampula, Mozambique, May 2012.
353. Author interview with former Renamo combatant, Maputo, Mozambique, October 2010.
354. To this day there is controversy surrounding the crash, and events immediately preceding and following it. The Mozambican government claimed the 'accident' was part of an elaborate plot by South Africa to remove Machel. An international crash investigation team, however, blamed the Soviet crew and its failure to follow proper procedures for an instrument landing. See Cabrita, *A Morte de Samora Machel*, for a recent look at the controversy.

355. No one, not even the government of Zimbabwe, knows the actual financial cost of Zimbabwe's involvement in Mozambique. A figure commonly bandied about was $1 million per day in 1988 (*New York Times*, February 12, 1988), but this seems inordinately high. Mlambo, with access to documents listing army and air force expenditures in Mozambique from 1985 to 1990, puts the cost at just under $150 million for this time period. He cautions, however, that these are incomplete *estimates* and fail to account for many items, including the cost of damaged or destroyed aircraft and equipment or the cost of transportation and rations to troops in the field. He concludes that "there is no doubt that there was gross negligence in accounting for Zimbabwe's war effort in Mozambique." Mlambo, "Raids on Gorongossa," Table 4. ZNA and AFZ Expenditures in Mozambique 1985 to 1990.
356. Moorcraft, *Mugabe's War Machine*, p. 126. Mlambo, using official army and air force documents, lists 320 killed and 635 injured from 1984 to 1990. Mlambo, "Raids on Gorongossa," Table 5. ZDF casualties in Mozambique, 1984–1990.
357. The AFZ lost seven aircraft between 1983 and 1990; four Allouette III, one Agusta Bell 412, one Dakota transport, and one Casa 212 transport. There were also 100 accidents and special occurrences that resulted in serious damage to aircraft over the same period. Mlambo, "Raids on Gorongossa."
358. Central Intelligence Agency, "Mozambique: Coping with the Insurgency," p. 13.
359. Troops from the Tanzania People's Defence Force (TPDF) would eventually join this offensive and play an important role in recapturing several towns, but the first 1,000 combat troops would not arrive until March 1987. Cabrita, *The Tortuous Road to Democracy*, p. 248.
360. Central Intelligence Organization, "ZNA Operations in Mozambique," Top Secret CIO memorandum (undated) of field assessment following 31 May to 11 June 1987 visit, p. 6. Copy in author's possession.
361. Renamo press release, "Communique from Renamo Headquarters," 27 January 1987.
362. This new training began at Cuamba in Niassa Province in 1983 under the auspices of the British firm, Defence Systems Limited, in a contract underwritten by the UK government. In 1986 all UK-funded military training would be transferred to Nyanga, Zimbabwe. Cabrita, p. 249.
363. Author interview with former Frelimo combatant, Maputo, Mozambique, October 2010.
364. Author interview with former Frelimo combatant, Maputo, Mozambique, October 2010
365. Author interview with former Frelimo combatant, Maputo, Mozambique, October 2010
366. Resistência Nacional Moçambicana, "Balanço do Dia," 4 September 1987. Renamo document in author's possession.
367. Turner, *Continent Ablaze*, p. 146.
368. Resistência Nacional Moçambicana, "*Balanço* do Dia," 9 September 1987. Renamo document in author's possession.

369. Author interview with senior Renamo commander, Maputo, Mozambique, November 2011.
370. The first two battalions created were named the 1st and the 2nd, but latter battalions would be named after animals, such as the Lion, Buffalo or Dragon. Author interview with Afonso Dhlakama, Nampula, Mozambique, May 2012.
371. Renamo press releases, "Communique from the Department of Defense of Renamo," 6 October 1987; "Military Communique," 9 November 1987; "Communique," 31 December 1987.
372. Author interview with former Frelimo combatant, Maputo, Mozambique, November 2009.
373. Author interview with former Frelimo combatant, Maputo, Mozambique, October 2010.
374. Author interview with former Frelimo combatant, Maputo, Mozambique, November 2009.
375. Author interview with former Frelimo combatant, Maputo, Mozambique, November 2009
376. The *Washington Times*, "RENAMO rebels choke off Mozambique capital," January 7, 1988.
377. Ibid.
378. Renamo press release, "Renamo Call for Negotiations and End of Civil War," 30 March 1988.
379. Author interview with former Frelimo combatant, Maputo, Mozambique, October 2010.
380. Author interview with former Frelimo combatant, Maputo, Mozambique, October 2010.
381. Author interview with former Frelimo combatant, Maputo, Mozambique, November 2009.
382. *The Washington Times*, "Mozambique claims refuted by RENAMO," May 12, 1987.
383. Resistência Nacional Moçambicana, "Balanço do Dia," September 3, 1987. Renamo document in author's possession.
384. Lemia, "Pós-independência, guerra e reassentamento da população no Distrito de Namacurra," p. 31. Maier, *Conspicuous Destruction*, p. 40.
385. Darch, "Are there Warlords in Provincial Mozambique?" p. 38. There are several conflicting versions concerning the date and nature of Meque's death, but Darch's account seems the most reliable. His time frame is also supported by Renamo documents in the author's possession, including exchanges of messages from Dhlakama to Meque from May 1988.
386. Lemia, "Pós-independência, guerra e reassentamento da população no Distrito de Namacurra," p. 31.
387. Moorcraft, *African Nemesis*, p. 288.
388. General Herminio Morais as cited in Cabrita, p. 256. Renamo also claimed that the Zimbabweans had been using chemical defoliants extensively since late 1986 along both the Beira and Tete corridors.

389. Vines, *Renamo: From Terrorism to Democracy*, p. 1; Christian Michelsen Institute, "Norwegian Assistance to Countries in Conflict," p. 37 citing UN figures; and Leitenberg, "Deaths in Wars and Conflicts in the 20th Century," p. 15.
390. A U.S. State Department-funded consultant, Robert Gersony interviewed some 200 Mozambican refugees in early 1988; after hearing repeated accounts of beatings, rape, abductions, looting and mutilations he concluded that Renamo was at the center of a campaign of systematic and coordinated violence. His findings were released in April 1988 in his report, "Mozambique Refugee Accounts of Principally Conflict Related Experiences in Mozambique," commonly referred to as the Gersony Report.
391. Weinstein, *Inside Rebellion* , p.230.
392. Ibid.
393. Author interview with former senior Renamo commander, Maputo, Mozambique, November 2009.
394. For example, Central Intelligence Agency's *Mozambique: RENAMO at a Crossroads*, pp. 2-3.
395. Weinstein, p. 230 and p. 232.
396. Ibid, p. 232.
397. Vines, p. 85; Schafer, p. 64.
398. Author interview with Afonso Dhlakama, Nampula, Mozambique, May 2012.
399. Vines, p. 85.
400. Author interview with Afonso Dhlakama, Nampula, Mozambique, May 2012.
401. This was particularly true during Operation Leopard in 1980 and Operation Cabana in 1982. Cabrita, p. 173 and p. 208.
402. Author interview with José Luis Cabaço, Maputo, Mozambique, November 2009.
403. Ibid.
404. Cabrita, p. 249.
405. Ibid, p. 208.
406. Central Intelligence Organization, "ZNA Operations in Mozambique," p. 2.
407. Ibid p. 3.
408. Lemia, "Pós-independência, guerra e reassentamento da população no Distrito de Namacurra", p. 32.
409. *The Washington Post*, "Mozambique Says Photos Document Rebel Massacre," July 23, 1987; *Los Angeles Times*, "Toll Over 380; Guerrillas Blamed; Massacre in Mozambique," July 24, 1987; *The New York Times*, "American Tells of Mozambique Raid," July 25, 1987.
410. Author interview with former Frelimo combatant, Maputo, Mozambique, October 2010.
411. Author interview with former Frelimo combatant, Maputo, Mozambique, October 2010.
412. Cabrita citing his interviews with a former Renamo provincial intelligence chief and a Frelimo intelligence operative's account, p. 267.
413. Wheeler, "Mozambique," p. 186. *The Washington Times*, "Commentary: Massacre or

manipulation?" July 30, 1987.
414. Author interview with Prof. André Thomashausen, Pretoria, South Africa, November 2009.
415. Author interviews with former Frelimo combatants, Maputo, Mozambique, November 2009 and October 2010.
416. Comments of Deputy Assistant Secretary for Africa Affairs Roy Stacey, April 28, 1988 as cited in Human Rights Watch, *Conspicuous Destruction*, p. 192.
417. Vines, p. 1.
418. See Vines, pp. 53-58 for background on the Malawi-Mozambique bilateral relationship.
419. See Cabrita, pp. 240-241 and Vines, p. 56 for details on the planned 'invasion' of Malawi just prior to Machel's death.
420. Vines, endnote 120, p. 141.
421. Author interview with former Renamo combatant, Maputo, Mozambique, October 2010.
422. Vines, p. 58.
423. Cabrita, p. 248. Vines however put this force at 4,000 and estimates that the TDPF may have committed 5,000–7,000 personnel to effort at its peak, p. 66.
424. Author interview with former Frelimo combatant, Maputo, Mozambique, November 2009.
425. Central Intelligence Organization, "ZNA Operations in Mozambique," p. 2.
426. Cabrita, p. 249.
427. Vines, p. 67.
428. Ibid.
429. *Christian Science Monitor*, "Rebuilding a vital rail in Mozambique," October 13, 1988.
430. *Landmine Monitor* (1999) cited the regular use of landmines along both the Limpopo and Beira corridor by Zimbabwean troops during the war. Subsequent post-war demining operations would yield 8,379 anti-personal mines, 1,332 fragmentation mines and 109 anti-tank mines by October 1995. Synge, *Mozambique: UN Peacekeeping in Action*, p. 80.
431. Author correspondence with a foreign military observer, April 2010.
432. Author interview and correspondence with Lionel Dyck, Cape Town, South Africa, October 2010.
433. Vines, p. 51. Thatcher also reportedly was very influential in convincing President Reagan to avoid assisting Renamo militarily in any way during the 1980s.
434. The British firm, Defence Systems Limited, conducted FAM training from 1983 to 1985 in Mozambique under a 1.6 million GBP contract from the British government before the training mission was transferred to the British training team in Zimbabwe. Cabrita, p. 249; Moorcraft, *African Nemesis*, p. 285.
435. Author correspondence with former British military adviser, May 2010.
436. Author correspondence with former British military adviser, May 2010.
437. Author email correspondence with Major-General T.P. Toyne Sewell, February

2010.

438. Author correspondence with former British military adviser, May 2010.
439. Author correspondence with a foreign military observer, April 2010.
440. See Vines, pp. 34-38 for a discussion of Renamo's internal political fractionalization, and speculation regarding who was responsible for the Fernandes assassination and other deaths. For an alternative view see, Cabrita, p. 246, or *InformAfrica*, "Evo Fernandes death: trail points to Maputo," Vol 1, No 8, April, 1988.
441. Finnegan, pp. 91-92.
442. *Chicago Tribune*, "Mozambique War Claims Economy among Its Victims," April 29, 1987.
443. See Harper-Roland, *Sunday Bloody Sunday*, pp. 310-338 for a firsthand account of the experiences of a DSL contractor providing security services to Lonhro farms and facilities in southern Gaza Province from late 1989 to early 1991.
444. Author interview with former Frelimo combatant, Maputo, Mozambique, November 2009.
445. Author interview with former Frelimo combatant, Maputo, Mozambique, November 2009.
446. Author interview with former Frelimo combatant, Maputo, Mozambique, November 2009.
447. Author interview with former Frelimo combatant, Maputo, Mozambique, November 2009.
448. Author interview with former Renamo combatant, Maputo, Mozambique, November 2009.
449. Author interview with former Renamo combatant, Maputo, Mozambique, November 2009.
450. Often misreported as an attack on "Renamo's Gorongosa base" (Tuner, p. 147) or in the "Gorongosa district" (Vines, p. 123) this operation actually took place some 80 km to the north in the Maringue District, where Dhlakama relocated his headquarters following the fall of Casa Banana in August 1985. Despite this attack, the Renamo headquarters would remain at Massala until the end of the war. Cabrita (p. p. 269) contains references to this location from a Renamo general actually present during the attack.
451. *Mozambique Information Agency*, Mozambiquefile, No. 157, August 1989, p. 5, as cited in Vines, p. 123.
452. The terms "Naprama" or "Naparama" are most commonly used in the literature and I adhere to that usage here. However, Nordstrom, who spent time living among the movement's followers and interviewing them, points out that "Naprama/Naparama" is actually the formal term that refers to use of special medicinal plants to protect warriors in battle and members of the movement actually referred to themselves simply as "Parama." Nordstrom, *A Different Kind of War Story*, p. 72 note 15.
453. See for example, Nordstrom, *A Different Kind of War Story*, pp. 57-62; Wilson,

"Cults of Violence and Counter-Violence in Mozambique;" Weinstein, *Inside Rebellion*, pp. 272-274; Human Rights Watch, *Conspicuous Destruction,* pp. 39-40; Finnegan, *A Complicated War*, pp. 254-255.

454. Wilson, p. 527.
455. Nordstrom, p. 58; *Washington Post*, "Healer in Mozambique Leads Attacks on Rebels," August 4, 1990.
456. *Chicago Tribune,* "Mystic Warriors Gaining Ground in Mozambique War," December 9, 1990.
457. *Los Angeles Time,* "Mystery Man Takes Up Mozambique Battle," December 31, 1990.
458. Nordstrom, p. 60.
459. Comments of a Zambezi villager in 1990 as cited in Nordstrom, p. 60-61.
460. Human Rights Watch, *Conspicuous Destruction*, p. 40.
461. Ibid, p. 39. Dhlakama did confirm that he personally directed the initial operations against Naprama. Author interview with Afonso Dhlakama, Nampula, Mozambique, May 2012.
462. Ibid.
463. Ibid, p. 39-40; Weinstein, p. 274.
464. Ibid, p. 40.
465. Nordstrom, p. 60.
466. In 1989 the UN Economic Commission for Africa estimated that the war's destruction and related losses at $15 billion. Christian Michelsen Institute, "Norwegian Assistance to Countries in Conflict," p. 37.
467. Author interview with former Renamo combatants, Maputo, Mozambique, October 2010.
468. Author interview with former Renamo combatant, Maputo, Mozambique, November 2009.
469. Author interview with Raúl Domingos, Maputo, Mozambique, November 2009.
470. Author interview with Prof. André Thomashausen, Pretoria, South Africa, November 2009.
471. Comments of former U.S. intelligence officer, Washington, DC, September 1998.
472. Author interview with former Renamo combatant, Maputo, Mozambique, November 2009.
473. See for example, reporting from the Dragon Battalion that was deployed in northern Sofala Province in late 1988. "Situação Logistica do Batl. Dragão, Julho 1988." Renamo document in author's possession.
474. Author interview with former Renamo combatant, Maputo, Mozambique, October 2010.
475. Author interview with former Renamo combatant, Maputo, Mozambique, November 2009.
476. See for example, reporting from the 7 Battalion's political officer on problems concerning unit members assaulting and robbing civilians in the Mutarara District of Tete in mid-1989. "Comunicamos ao Gabinete Presidencial que no Dia 17/4/89,"

Msg. N-2/5/89. Renamo document in author's possession.

477. Author interview with former Frelimo combatant, Maputo, Mozambique, November 2009.
478. Author interview with former Frelimo combatant, Maputo, Mozambique, November 2009.
479. Author interview with former Frelimo combatant, Maputo, Mozambique, November 2009.
480. Author interview with former Frelimo combatant, Maputo, Mozambique, November 2009.
481. *The Sunday Times* (London), "Renamo's hard men rule over the bush," April 5, 1987.
482. Author interview with former Frelimo combatant, Maputo, Mozambique, November 2009.
483. Author interview with Afonso Dhlakama, Nampula, Mozambique, May 2012.
484. Author interview with former Frelimo combatant, Maputo, Mozambique, November 2009.
485. Author interview with former Frelimo combatant, Maputo, Mozambique, November 2009.
486. Author interview with former Frelimo combatant, Maputo, Mozambique, November 2009.
487. Author interview with former Frelimo combatant, Maputo, Mozambique, November 2009.
488. Author interview with former Renamo combatant, Maputo, Mozambique, November 2009.
489. See Vines (1996), pp. 120-128 and Hume, *Ending Mozambique's War*, pp. 26-32 for a detailed discussion of the various complex efforts at brokering peace talks.
490. Ibid, p. 121.
491. For a look at the critical role of Catholic and Protestant church groups in pushing peace talks see Alex Vines and Ken Wilson, "Chapter 9: Churches and the Peace Process in Mozambique," in Paul Gifford (ed.) *The Christian Churches and the Democratisation of Africa* (New York: Brill, 19995) pp. 130-147.
492. Wilson, p. 140.
493. Vines (1996), p. 128.
494. Hume's account contains the best insider account of the Rome talks, as well as an in-depth look at actual mechanics of the peace process.
495. Comments of former U.S. observer to the Rome talks, October 1998.
496. Hume, pp. 40-42 and p. 47.
497. Ibid, p. 46.
498. The very narrow definition of the corridors created problems for Frelimo and the Zimbabweans given the existing location of water and power lines, as well as the ZNA logistics base at Chimoio airfield, that were technically 'outside' the Beira corridor. This resulted in a constant stream of charges by Renamo to the JVC that the government was in violation of the agreement. See Hume, pp. 47-48 for the

challenges facing the JVC early on.

499. Chityo and Rupiya, "The Zimbabwe Defence Force from 1980-2005," p. 356.
500. Author interview with Raúl Domingos, Maputo, Mozambique, October 2010.
501. Author interview with former Renamo commander, Maputo, Mozambique, October 2010.
502. Author interview with former Renamo commander, Maputo, Mozambique, October 2010.
503. Author interview with former Frelimo combatant, Maputo, Mozambique, October 2010.
504. Moorcraft (2012), p. 127 and Chan, *Robert Mugabe*, pp. 85-86.
505. Author interview with Afonso Dhlakama, Nampula, Mozambique, May 2012.
506. See Hume, pp. 111-114 and Vines (1996), p. 138 for a detailed look at these meetings.
507. Author interview with Raúl Domingos, Maputo, Mozambique, October 2010.
508. Radio Mozambique, October 4, 1992 broadcast as cited in Hume, p. 138.
509. Author interview with former Renamo combatant, Maputo, Mozambique, November 2009.
510. Author interview with former Renamo combatant, Maputo, Mozambique, October 2010.
511. Author interview with former Frelimo combatant, Maputo, Mozambique, November 2009.
512. Author interview with former Renamo combatant, Maputo, Mozambique, November 2009.

SELECTED BIBLIOGRAPHY

Austin, Kathi. *Invisible Crimes: U.S. Private Intervention in the War in Mozambique.* Washington, DC: Africa Policy Information Center, 1994.

Barnes, Sam. "The Socio-Economic Reintegration of Demobilised Soldiers in Mozambique. The Soldier's View." Maputo: United Nations Development Programme, 1997.

Borges Coelho, João-Paulo and Paulino Macaringue. "The Role of Mozambique's Armed Forces in a Changing Security Context" in Peter Batchelor, Kees Kingma and Guy Lamb (eds.) *Demilitarisation and Peace-building in Southern Africa: The Role of the Military in State Formation and Nation-Building, Volume III.* Aldershot, UK: Ashgate Publishing, Ltd., 2004.

Binda, Alexandre and Chris Cocks. *The Saints: The Rhodesian Light Infantry.* Johannesburg: 30 Degrees South, 2007.

Cabrita, João. *Mozambique: The Tortuous Road to Democracy.* New York: Palgrave, 2000.

_____________. *A Morte de Samora Machel.* Maputo: Edições Novafrica, 2005.

Central Intelligence Agency. "Mozambique: Coping with the Insurgency," *National Intelligence Daily.* Washington, November 19, 1986.

_____________. *Mozambique: RENAMO at a Crossroads*, Directorate of Intelligence Research Paper. Washington, March 1991.

Central Intelligence Organization. "ZNA Operations in Mozambique." Harare, Undated (circa June 1987).

Chan, Stephen. *Robert Mugabe: A Life of Power and Violence.* London: I.B. Tauris & Co., 2003.

Chitiyo, Knox and Martin Rupiya. "Chapter 13: Tracking Zimbabwe's Political History: The Zimbabwe Defence Force from 1980-2005" in Martin Rupiya (ed.) *Evolutions and Revolutions: A Contemporary History of Militaries in Southern Africa.* Pretoria: Institute for Security Studies, 2005).

Ciment, James. *Angola and Mozambique: Postcolonial War in Southern Africa.* New York: Facts on File, 1997.

Cole, Barbara. *The Elite: The Story of the Rhodesian Special Air Service.* Amanzimtoti, Transkei: Three Knights Publishing, 1985.

Cowderoy, Dudley and Roy Nesbit. *War in the Air: Rhodesian Air Force 1935-1980.* Alberton, South Africa: Galago Publishing, 1987.

Darch, Colin. "Are there Warlords in Provincial Mozambique?" *Review of African Political Economy*, No. 45/46 (1989): 34-49.

Davies, Robert. "The SADF's Covert War against Mozambique," in Jacklyn Cock and Laurie Nathan (ed.) *War and Society: The Militarisation of South Africa*. Cape Town: David Phillip Publisher, 1989.

Fauvet, Paul. "Roots of counter-revolution: The Mozambique National Resistance." *Review of African Political Economy*, 11:29, Summer 1984.

Finnegan, William. *A Complicated War: The Harrowing of Mozambique*. Berkeley, CA: University of California Press, 1992.

Flower, Ken. *Serving Secretly: Rhodesia's CIO Chief on the Record*. Alberton, South Africa: Galago Publishing, 1987.

Geldenhuys, Prop. *Rhodesian Air Force Operations with Air Strike Log*. Durban: Just Done Productions Publishing, 2007.

Gilks, Anne and Gerald Segal. *China and the Arms Trade*. Beckenham, UK: Croom Helm, 1985.

Hall, Margaret and Tom Young. *Confronting Leviathan: Mozambique since Independence*. Athens, OH: Ohio University Press, 1997.

Hanlon, Joseph. *Beggar Your Neighbours: Apartheid Power in Southern Africa*. London: Catholic Institute for International Relations, 1986.

____________. *Mozambique: The Revolution under Fire*. London: Zed Books, 1984.

Harper-Roland, Jake. *Sunday, Bloody Sunday*. Alberton, South Africa: Galago Publishing, 2009.

Henriksen, Thomas. *Mozambique: A History*. London: Rex Collings, 1978.

Hoile, David. *Mozambique—A Nation in Crisis*. London: Claridge Press, 1989.

Human Rights Watch. *Conspicuous Destruction: War, Famine and the Reform Process in Mozambique*. New York: Human Rights Watch, July 1992.

Hume, Cameron. *Ending Mozambique's War*. Washington, DC: U.S. Institute for Peace, 1994.

Isaacman, Allen and Barbara Isaacman. *Mozambique: From Colonialism to Revolution, 1900-1982*. Boulder, CO: Westview Press, 1983.

Legum, Colin. *The Battlefronts of Southern Africa*. New York: Africana Publishing, 1988.

____________. *CSIS Africa Notes*. Washington: Center for Strategic and International Studies. No. 16, July 15, 1983.

Lemia, Rosário. "Pós-Independência, Guerra e Reassentamento da População no Distrito de Namacurra, 1975-1998-9." Unpublished dissertation Departamento de História. Maputo: Universidade Eduardo Mondlane, 2001.

MacQueen, Norrie. *The Decolonization of Portuguese Africa*. London: Longman, 1997.

Martin, David and Phyllis Johnson. "Mozambique: To Nkomati and Beyond," Johnson, Phyllis and David Martin (eds.), *Destructive Engagement: Southern Africa at*

War. Harare: Zimbabwe Publishing House, 1986.

Mlambo, Norman. "Raids on Gorongossa: Zimbabwe's Military Involvement in Mozambique 1982-1992," SACDI Defence Digest, Working Paper No. 3. Found at http://ccrweb.ccr.uct.ac.za/archive/defencedigest/defdigest03.html

Minter, William. "The Mozambican National Resistance (Renamo) as Described by Ex-participants." Research Report Submitted to the Ford Foundation and the Swedish International Development Agency, Washington, DC, March 1989.

____________. *Apartheid's Contras: An Inquiry into the Roots of the War in Angola and Mozambique.* London: Zed Books, 1994.

Moorcraft, Paul. *African Nemesis: War and Revolution in Southern Africa 1945-2010.* London: Brassey's, 1994.

____________. *Mugabe's War Machine.* Jeppestown, South Africa: Jonathan Ball Publishers, 2012.

Moorcraft, Paul and Peter McLaughlin. *The Rhodesian War: A Military History.* Barnsley, UK: Pen & Sword Books, Ltd., 2008.

Mozambique Notes. "The Gorongosa Story." New York: The Mozambique Resource Center, April 1986.

Nesbit, Roy and Dudley Cowderoy. *Britain's Rebel Air Force: The War from the Air in Rhodesia, 1965-1980.* London: Grub Street Press, 1998.

Newitt, Malyn. *A History of Mozambique.* London: Hurst, 1995.

Nilsson, Anders. *Unmasking the Bandits: The True Face of the M.N.R.* London: ECASAAMA/UK Publication, 1990.

Nordstrom, Carolyn. *A Different Kind of War Story.* Philadelphia: University of Pennsylvania Press, 1997.

Petter-Bowyer, PJH. *Winds of Destruction: The Autobiography of a Rhodesian Born Pilot Covering the Rhodesian Bush Was of 1967-1980.* Victoria, Canada: Trafford Publishing, 2007.

Reid Daly, Ron. *Selous Scouts - Top Secret War.* Alberton, South Africa: Galago Publishing, 1982.

Schafer, Jessica. *Soldiers at Peace: Veterans and Society after the Civil War in Mozambique.* New York: Palgrave Macmillian, 2007.

Stiff, Peter. *Silent War: South African Recce Operations, 1969-1994.* Alberton, South Africa: Galago Publishing, 2000.

Synge, Richard. *Mozambique: UN Peacekeeping in Action 1992-94.* Washington: U.S. Institute of Peace, 1997.

Thomashausen, André. *Africa Insight*, Vol.13, No. 2, February 1983.

____________. "The Mozambique National Resistance" in C.J. Maritz (ed.),

Weerstandsbeweging in Suider-Afrika. Potchefstroom, South Africa: Potchefstroomse Universiteit, 1987.

Turner, John. *Continent Ablaze: The Insurgency Wars in Africa, 1960 to the Present*. London: Arms and Armour, 1998.

Venter, Al. *The Zambesi Salient: Conflict in Southern Africa*. Cape Town: H. Timmins, 1974.

Vines, Alex. "The Business of Peace: 'Tiny' Rowland, financial incentives and the Mozambican settlement," in *The Mozambican Peace Process in Perspective*. Accord Issue 3, January 1998.

____________. *Renamo: Terrorism in Mozambique*. London: James Currey, 1991.

____________. *Renamo: From Terrorism to Democracy in Mozambique?* London: James Currey, 1996.

Weinstein, Jeremy. *Inside Rebellion: The Politics of Insurgent Violence*. New York: Cambridge University Press, 2007.

Wheeler, Jack. "Mozambique" in Michael Radu, *The New Insurgencies: Anti-Communist Guerrillas in the Third World*. New Brunswick, NJ: Transaction Publishers, 1990.

Wilson, Kenneth. "Cults of Violence and Counter-Violence in Mozambique." *Journal of Southern African Studies*, Vol. 18, No. 3, September 1992: 527-582.

INDEX

1 Para Group, ZNA 136-139, 145, 176
1st Mechanized Battalion, ZNA 131
2nd Brigade, FPLM 83, 84
3 Brigade, ZNA 89-90, 130, 144
3rd Brigade, FPLM 70, 71, 78
4 Brigade, ZNA 91,176
4th Brigade, FPLM 70, 71, 78
5 Recce 107-108, 110
5th Brigade, FPLM/FAM 70, 71, 137
8th Brigade, FAM 161-162
28 Squadron, SAAF 103-105
44 Squadron, SAAF 103, 105

África Livre 35
African National Congress *see* ANC
African nationalism 20, 27-28, 97
Afro-Portuguese community 19
AFZ *see* Air Force of Zimbabwe
Agusta Bell-205 helicopters 44-46
airdrops 44-46, 100-101
Air Force of Zimbabwe (AFZ) 131, 137-140, 142, 144, 147, 176
Alouette III helicopters 44-46, 57
America *see* United States
ammunition *see* weapons and ammunition
ANC 27-28, 75, 80, 97, 110, 114, 125
Angola 19-20, 22-23, 27, 35, 97
anti-apartheid struggle 18, 24, 32, 65, 96, 128, 178
Antonio, Manuel 190-193
apartheid *see* anti-apartheid struggle
Armed Forces for the Defence of Mozambique (FADM) 205
Armed Forces Movement (MFA) 21-22
Armed Forces of Mozambique *see* FAM
atrocities *see* violence

Banda, Hasting 37, 149, 151, 172, 200, 203-204
banditry 76, 186, 192, 197, 204 *see also* violence
Barrett, Lieutenant-Colonel Garth 52
Beira corridor 89, 128-129, 163-164, 181, 189
Beira harbor 56, 101, 111
BMATT *see* British Military Advisery Training Team
Botha, P. W. 53-54, 67, 71-72, 97-98, 120
Britain 69, 175-176, 178-180
British Military Advisery Training Team (BMATT) 175, 179-180
brutality *see* violence
Buchan, Lieutenant Charlie 54
Burlison, John 83
Burt, Peter 37, 39
bush war 97-102, 152

C-47 transport aircraft *see* Dakotas
C-130 transport aircraft 69, 77, 100-101, 103-105, 117
Cabaço, José Luis 168
Cabrita, João 36, 38, 39, 59, 73, 76, 79
Caetano, Marcelo 21
Cahora Bassa Dam project 28-29, 80, 120, 181
Campos, Colonel Costa 37
Cardoso, Alvaro Manuel Alves 33, 34
Carrington, Lord 69
Casa Banana base 82-83, 86, 88, 115, 136-140, 143-145, 151, 189
Central Intelligence Agency, USA *see* CIA
Central Intelligence Organization
  see Rhodesian Central Intelligence Organization
Chicarre base 77, 81, 84, 86, 109
Chicualacuala rail line 88, 128-129, 134, 160
child soldiers 9, 134-135, 188, 205
Chimoio airfield 131
Chimoio Circle (New Chimoio) base 56-57
Chissano, Joaquim
  elections on 27-29 Oct. 1994 205
  as leader of Frelimo 151, 153, 161, 171-173, 177-178, 180, 182
  peace talks 120, 200, 204
church groups, role in peace talks 200
CIA 35, 121, 149, 153
'Cinco, Commander' 191
CIO 30, 34-39, 42-45, 48-53, 59, 72-74, 99, 101-102
civilians
  freed 160, 188, 191
  refugees 22, 24, 32, 82, 163-164, 169, 172, 182
  suffering of 55, 149, 163, 196, 204
  violence against 147, 155, 158-160, 164-171, 182, 186, 191-192
Cold War 18, 20, 23-24, 65, 96-97, 120-122, 124, 171, 177-178
colonial rule 19-22
Combined Operations Headquarters (ComOps), Rhodesia 46-48, 51, 54, 56, 60, 64
Comoro Islands 119
Coventry, Major Dudley 43, 47, 59, 73-74, 99,

101
Cristina, Orlando 36-39, 43, 48, 73-75, 112-113

D-3 and D-4 civilian aircraft 116
da Gama, Vasco 18
Dai, General 137
Dakotas (Daks) 44-46, 63, 100, 139, 142-144
DC-3 and DC-4 aircraft 103
decolonization 20-22
Delta Base 189 *see also* Casa Banana base
DGS (Portuguese secret police) 33
Dhlakama, Afonso
  background of 48-49
  Casa Banana attack 138-139
  elections on 27-29 Oct. 1994 205
  on Frelimo's morale 150, 198
  Gorongosa camp 63
  on *Grupo Limpa* 167
  Lancaster House talks 69
  Mlanga and 76-77
  Operation Cabana 92
  overseas support 79-80, 113, 178
  peace talks 121, 160-161, 189, 200-201, 204
  as political leader 94, 113-114
  rise of 58-60
  Rowland and 132
  South Africa and 72-73, 82-84, 99, 110, 112, 117, 121
  in Tete Province 90
  Zimbabwe and 147
Direcção Geral de Segurança (DGS) 33
Directorate of Special Tasks (DST), SA 102-103, 112-119, 123-124
Domingos, Raúl 73, 115, 133-134, 194, 201-202, 204
Dragon Battalion, Renamo 146
droughts 92, 95, 133, 182, 195-196, 204
DST *see* Directorate of Special Tasks
Dyck, Lieutenant-Colonel Lionel 136, 138-140, 142-143, 176

Eastern Bloc 41, 49, 63, 91
economy of Mozambique, impact of war on 31, 53-54, 95, 157-158, 182
Eduardo, Major General Tome 84
elections in Mozambique, 27-29 Oct. 1994 24, 205
elections in Zimbabwe, 4 Mar. 1980 67
ethno-regional conflict 165-166

FADM (Armed Forces for the Defence of Mozambique) 205
Fairey, John 45-46
FAM
  Casa Banana attack 136, 140
  civilians, violence against 167-170
  Nkomati Accord 94-95, 133
  in north of Mozambique 162-164
  officers 180, 197-198
  Operation Cabana 91-93
  Operation Octopus 140-143
  peace talks 199, 203
  "Red Beret" commandos 156-157, 161
  supply shortages 185, 197-198
  training 174-175, 179-180
  Zimbabwe and 155
Fauvet, Paul 34
female soldiers 9, 83, 108, 162
Fernandes, Evo 113, 119, 180
flechas 33-35
Flower, Ken 33-34, 39, 42, 47, 51-52, 61, 72, 102
Forças Armadas de Defensa Moçambique see FADM
Forças Armadas de Moçambique see FAM
FPLM (*Forças Populares De Libertação De Moçambique*) 47-48, 53, 55-66, 70-71, 77-78, 81, 83-84, 87-89, 101, 168
Frama Inter Trading Company 103
Franque, Mário (Mario Frank) 78, 83
Frelimo
  civilians, violence against 167-168
  diplomacy 171-182
  historical context 18-22
  independence of Mozambique 23, 25-27
  Matsangaissa's death 58
  Nkomati Accord 94-95, 114, 125
  in north of Mozambique 162-164, 187-190
  operational effectiveness 193, 196-199
  Operation Cabana 91-93
  Operation Leopard 77-78
  Operation Punishment 84
  peace talks 135, 201-205
  Renamo and 23-24, 50-56, 60-64, 70-71, 85-89, 153-158, 181-190
  South Africa and 96, 120
  in south of Mozambique 158-162, 186-187
  Third Party Congress in Feb. 1977 49-50
  training 174-175, 179-180
  Western assistance 177-182
  ZANLA and 27-31
  Zimbabwe and 67-70, 77-78, 125-135, 152
Frente de Libertação de Moçambique see Frelimo
Front for the Liberation of Mozambique *see* Frelimo

Front for the National Liberation of Angola 35

Garagua Documents 84, 105
GE *see Grupos Especiais*
GEP *see Grupos Especiais Pára-quedista*
Gersony, Robert 164
Gersony Report 164, 166, 169, 171
Gingles, Lieutenant Alan 82
Gomes, General Costa 21
Gomes, General Francisco Paulo 161, 186, 202
Gonçalves, Archbishop Jaime 200-201, 204
Gorongosa camp 44-45, 54-58, 63, 70
Gorongosa Documents 118, 139-140
Grupo Limpa, Renamo 167
Grupos Especiais (GEs) 33, 37
Grupos Especiais Pára-quedista (GEPs) 33, 37
Guebuza, Armando 202

Hama Thai, Lieutenant-General António 155, 156
Hartman, Danny 59
Hercules aircraft *see* C-130 transport aircraft
Hickman, Major Jesse 131
Homoíne massacre 169-171 *see also* violence
Hunter strike aircraft 46, 55, 57, 62, 139

independence of Mozambique 21-25
independent militia forces 185-186
Italy 181, 201

Jambe base 82, 92
Jardim, Jorge 33, 37
Joint Verification Commission (JVC) 202, 203

Kenya 119, 200
Kruger National Park 120

Lancaster House peace talks 51, 54, 55-56, 60, 64, 67, 69, 178
leaflets *see* propaganda material
Legum, Colin 101-102
Letaba Ranch camp 108, 115, 133
Lidimo, Lagos 168
Limpopo corridor 175-177, 180, 182, 202
Lonhro 132-133
Lusaka Accord 22
Lynx aircraft 55, 62

Mabote, Colonel-General Sebastião 156
Machel, Samora
  Casa Banana attack 140
  death of 150-151, 153
  FPLM 60-61, 84-85
  Malawi and 172
  Mugabe and 31, 50, 65, 125-128, 135-136, 152
  Nkomati Accord 114, 125
  Operation Cabana 91-93
  Rhodesia and 29-31, 41, 63
  South Africa and 96
  Soviet Union and 49-50
  Western assistance 177-178
Macomo, Orlando 47, 49
Magama, Colonel Flint 141-143
Malan, General Magnus 97
Malawi 117, 119-120, 131, 149-150, 163, 169, 172-173, 200
Manje, General Languane Vareia 78, 83, 158
maps of Mozambique
  Central region 25, 40, 125
  Gorongosa area 126
  North region 183
  Provincial 17
  South region 67, 153
massacres *see* Homoíne massacre
Massala base 146, 189, 200
Matsangaissa, André Matade (Commander André) 38-39, 42-43, 47-49, 51, 54-55, 58-60, 74
Mavuze hydro-electric power station 52-53
May, Eric "Ricky" 43, 72, 99
Meque, Calisto 90, 163
MFA (Armed Forces Movement) 21-22
Mhlanga, Lucas "Luke" 61, 69, 76-77
militia forces, independent 185-186
MNR (Mozambique National Resistance) *see* Renamo
Moi, Daniel arap 200
Mondlane, Eduardo 21, 65, 96
Monte Cassino 57
Movimento das Forças Armadas see MFA
Mozambique National Resistance (MNR) *see* Renamo
Mt. Xilvuo communications center 56
Mugabe, Robert
  Chissano and 174-177
  elections 4 Mar. 1980 67
  Machel and 31, 50, 65, 125-128, 135-136, 152
  peace talks 200, 202, 204
  ZANLA 57-58
Mulhanga, Lucas *see* Mhlanga, Lucas "Luke"
Muzorewa, Abel 51

Namibia *see* South West Africa
Naprama 186, 190-193, 202
National Highway 1 79, 80, 87, 134
National Railways of Zimbabwe (NRZ) 128-129, 175-176
National Union of Mozambique (UNAMO) 163
Ncala corridor 135, 172, 180, 187
New Chimoio (Chimoio Circle) base 56-57
New Farm 56
Newitt, Malyn 50
Nkomati Accord 73, 93-95, 99, 102-103, 106-107, 114-122, 125, 133, 135
Nkomo, Joshua 28, 51
non-government self-defense forces 185-186
NRZ *see* National Railways of Zimbabwe
Nyadzonya base 30, 41-42
Nyerere, Julius 136, 173

Ofensiva Relâmpago 158
Offensiva Vento 162
Operations
  Altar/Mila 102-112, 115-117
  Arrow 62
  Blanket 53
  Bumper 44-46, 55, 64, 69, 100-101
  Cabana 91-93
  Cob Web 131
  Dingo 56
  Eland 30
  Grapefruit (Casa Banana attack) 136-140
  Leopard 77-78
  Lifeline 90, 130-131
  Manacle 54, 60
  Mila (was Altar) 102-112, 115-117
  Miracle 56-57
  Ndonga Chirenje (Remove Ndonga) 148
  Octopus 141-143
  Open Way 176-177
  Polo 98
  Punishment 84
  Repulse 30
  Thrasher 30
  Uric 31
  Zero 144-145

pamphlets *see* propaganda material
Partido Revolucionário de Forças Moçambique (PRM) 90-91
peace talks 24, 135, 182, 183, 189, 195, 199-204
peasantry *see* civilians
Phiri, Gimo (Jimo) 35, 90-91, 163
Popular Forces for the Liberation of Mozambique *see* FPLM
Portugal 18-22, 25-29, 180-181
Portuguese secret police 33
posters *see* propaganda material
Presidential Guard Brigade, ZNA 137-139
private security firms 179, 186
PRM (*Partido Revolucionário de Forças Moçambique*) 90-91
propaganda material 56, 104, 112-113
Protea (ship) 106

radio communications 47, 52, 56, 62, 111-112, 117, 119, 194-195
RBC (Rhodesian Broadcasting Corporation) 35, 37
Reagan, Ronald 177
recce commando operations 56, 82, 101, 105, 107-111, 115
"Red Beret" commandos, FAM 156-157, 161
re-education camps 38-39, 48, 55
refugees 22, 24, 32, 82, 163-164, 169, 172, 182 *see also* civilians
Reid-Daly, Lieutenant-Colonel Ron 34
Reims-Cessna F-337 aircraft *see* Lynx aircraft
Renamo
  African support 119, 124, 172-174
  Casa Banana base 82-83, 136-141
  civilians, violence against 164-170
  divisions within 113, 119, 123-124
  Dragon Battalion 146
  Frelimo and 23-24, 46-54, 60-66, 70-71, 85-91, 153-158, 181-190
  Gorongosa camp 44-45, 54-58
  Grupo Limpa 167
  Lancaster House talks 64, 67-70
  Matsangaissa's death 58-60
  Naprama and 192
  Nkomati Accord 93-95, 125, 133-135
  in north of Mozambique 162-164, 187-190
  Operation Cabana 91-93
  Operation Leopard 77-78
  origins of 31-38
  overseas support 113, 118-119, 124, 171-172, 178, 180-182
  peace talks 135, 199, 201-205
  as political organisation 119, 123-124
  PRM and 90-91
  recruitment 48, 55, 134-135
  Rhodesia and 42-45, 99-102
  South Africa and 71-75, 79-85, 93-96, 98-99, 102-115, 117, 120, 122-124, 129

in south of Mozambique 158-162, 186-187
supply shortages 193-196, 199
training 43-44
Zimbabwe and 67-70, 73-79, 131-132, 145-152, 160
resettlement programs in Mozambique 85
Resistência Nacional Moçambicana see Renamo
resupply missions
airdrops 44-46, 100-101
seaborne 105-106, 118
RhAF (Rhodesian Air Force) 29, 44-46, 55, 57, 59, 61-62, 100-101
Rhodesia (later Zimbabwe) *see also* Zimbabwe
anti-Frelimo groups 32-36
independence of Mozambique 27-30, 41
Lancaster House talks 51-52
operations in Mozambique 30-31, 41-42, 50
Renamo and 65
South Africa and 69-70, 97-98
Rhodesian Air Force (RhAF) 29, 44-46, 55, 57, 59, 61-62, 100-101
Rhodesian Broadcasting Corporation (RBC) 35, 37
Rhodesian bush war 97-102, 152
Rhodesian Central Intelligence Organization (CIO) 30, 34-39, 42-45, 48-53, 59, 72-74, 99, 101-102
Rhodesian Combined Operations Headquarters *see* Combined Operations Headquarters
Rhodesian Light Infantry (RLI) 29, 57
Rhodesian Special Air Service *see* Special Air Service
RLI *see* Rhodesian Light Infantry
Roberto, Holden 35
Rowland, Tiny 132-133
Russia *see* Soviet Union

SAAF 75-77, 86, 88, 100-101, 103-105, 117
Sacuze re-education camp 38-39, 55
SADF
operations in Mozambique 82, 110-111
Renamo and 75, 79-80, 84, 98-99, 101-102, 107-112, 114-116, 118, 120, 122-124
SAN (South African Navy) 105
Sant'Egidio Catholic lay community 181, 200-201
SAS (Special Air Service) 29-30, 34, 43-44, 47, 52-57, 59-64, 69, 101-102
SAS Protea 106
SAS Tafelberg 106, 110-111
Save River 83
Sawong (Savong) base 111-112
Scott-Donelan, Captain David 108-109
seaborne resupply 105-106, 118
Selous Scouts 30, 34, 47, 70
Serving Secretly: Rhodesia's CIO Chief on the Record 33-34
Shangaan people 165-166
Shona-speaking people 165-166
Short-Term Strategy for Mozambique, 23 March to 23 July 1979 52
Silva, A.C. 181
Sitatonga base 61, 77-78, 101
Sithole, Ndabaningi 148
Smith, Ian 28, 29, 31, 51, 98
Smith, Lieutenant-Colonel Rupert 179
Soames, Lord 67, 69, 73
South Africa
communications support to Renamo 111-112, 117
Frelimo and 158
independence of Mozambique 22, 27-28, 41
intelligence support to Renamo 111-112, 117
logistics support to Renamo 102-107
Nkomati Accord 95, 125
peace talks 135
under P. W. Botha 53-54, 67-70
Renamo and 51, 71-75, 79-82, 93, 96-99, 112-114, 122-124
Rhodesian bush war 97-102
training support to Renamo 107-111, 115
Zimbabwe and 128-130
South African Air Force *see* SAAF
South African Defence Force *see* SADF
South African Navy (SAN) 105
South West Africa (now Namibia) 22, 27, 80
South West Africa People's Organization (SWAPO) 27
Soviet Union 49-50, 57, 63, 91, 120, 171, 197 *see also* Cold War
Soweto riots in 1976 22, 97
Special Air Service (SAS) 29-30, 34, 43-44, 47, 52-57, 59-64, 69, 101-102
Special Group Paratroops *see Grupos Especiais Pára-quedista*
Special Groups *see Grupos Especiais*
Special Task Force, Zimbabwe 130-131, 138, 144
Spinola, General 21-22
STF *see* Special Task Force, Zimbabwe
St. Mielie base 112, 115
submarines 106
SWAPO 27

Tafelberg (ship) 106, 110-111
Tanzania 84-85, 91, 135-136, 152, 168, 172-173, 182
Tanzania People's Defence Force (TPDF) 140-141, 173
Tete corridor 131, 132, 163, 187
Thatcher, Margaret 171, 178, 180
Toronga training camp 62-63
'Total Strategy' concept 97
Toyne Sewell, Brigadier General Tim 179
TPDF *see* Tanzania People's Defence Force
Tsequete, Abel 90

UN *see* United Nations
UNAMO *see* National Union of Mozambique
United Kingdom *see* Britain
United Nations 163, 203
United States 119, 120-122, 171, 177-178, 200-201 *see also* Cold War

Van der Westhuizen, Lieutenant-General Pieter 116
Van Niekerk, Colonel Cornelius "Charles" ("Commander Charlie") 72-73, 75, 80, 84, 99-102, 105-107, 113-114, 116-118, 123
Vines, Alex 133, 171, 173, 178
violence 62, 87, 158, 164-169 *see also* banditry
Vofal base 112, 115
Voice of Free Africa (*Voz da África Livre*) 36-39, 42, 48, 73, 81, 101, 112, 115

Waterkloof airbase 73, 103-105
weapons and ammunition 52, 100-101, 104, 107, 147, 160
Weekly Mail 121
Weinstein, Jeremy 165, 166
women *see* female soldiers
Wonder Air 103
Wonderboom airport 103

Young Pioneers 37
young soldiers *see* child soldiers

Zambezia Province 90
Zambia 60, 172, 173-174
ZANLA 27-31, 41-42, 47-48, 53-58, 60-63
ZANU 29, 51, 67, 152
ZANU-Ndonga party 148
ZAPU 28, 51
Zimbabwe (was Rhodesia) *see also* Rhodesia
  Beira corridor 131-133
  Casa Banana attack 137-140
  Frelimo and 89-90, 125-130, 151-155, 174-177, 182, 198
  liberation of 50-52, 65-66, 67
  Operation Cob Web 131
  Operation Grapefruit 136-140
  Operation Lifeline 130-131
  Operation Octopus 140-144
  Operation Open Way 176, 177
  Operation Zero 144-145
  peace talks 200-202
  post-Nkomati period 133-136
  Renamo and 132, 145-148
  South Africa and 128-130
Zimbabwe African National Liberation Army *see* ZANLA
Zimbabwe African National Union *see* ZANU
Zimbabwe African People's Union *see* ZAPU
Zimbabwe National Army *see* ZNA
Zimbabwe People's Revolution Army *see* ZIPRA
Zinave National Park 83
ZIPRA 41, 60
ZNA 89-90, 130-132, 136-145, 148, 155, 163, 167-168, 174-176, 187-190, 202
Zobo City *see* Letaba Ranch camp
Zvinavashe, Major General Vitalis 130, 137, 144